Life in the
LIGHT

A STUDY COMPANION TO 1 JOHN

Michael L. Pagano

True Christian Ministry

Life in the Light

Copyright © 2026 by Michael Pagano

All rights reserved.

No part of this book may be reproduced, stored in a retrieval system, or transmitted in any form or by any means, electronic, mechanical, photocopying, recording, or otherwise, without prior written permission of the author, except in the case of brief quotations embodied in critical articles and reviews. For all inquiries, email contact@truechristianministry.com

Scripture quotations are from the Holy Bible, English Standard Version® (ESV®), copyright © 2001 by Crossway, a publishing ministry of Good News Publishers. Used by permission. All rights reserved.

Scripture quotations from the Legacy Standard Bible® (LSB®), copyright © 2021 by The Lockman Foundation. Used by permission. All rights reserved.

ISBNs

Paperback: 979-8-9942829-0-8

Hardcover: 979-8-9942829-1-5

Ebook: 979-8-9942829-2-2

Published by True Christian Ministry

www.TrueChristianMinistry.com

Dedication

I thank my Lord and Savior Jesus Christ for granting me the opportunity to write this book. I should have died many years ago, yet He was pleased to spare my life and save me. I could not begin this work without first giving all glory to God our Father through our Lord Jesus Christ. Over the past four years, I have been entrusted with a following online that I could never have amassed apart from His Spirit. He is the beginning and the end of all things; therefore, I will always begin by acknowledging Him and end by giving Him glory. May this book honor Him, and may the words that follow help those who love Him draw nearer to Him.

To my wife, Tenasia, without you this would not have been possible. You are my wife, my best friend, and the mother of our children, and I cannot imagine life without you. You have always supported me while also challenging me to grow. You do not offer blind affirmation, nor are you merely agreeable; you genuinely desire what is best for me and for our family. You are the most beautiful woman I will ever know, and I do not mean this merely in a physical sense, though you are undeniably beautiful. Your heart and mind possess a beauty that eclipses the outward. You are a woman who seeks no recognition, yet has a heart eager to serve. I believe you are a gift from God, an answer to many prayers, and the very person He ordained to complete me. I thank God for you daily. Every page of this carries your quiet support, and that is no exaggeration. Many will never fully understand the sacrifice required of a wife when her husband is in the public eye, pulled in countless directions. Sharing your husband is not easy. Thank you for your selflessness and your understanding.

To my children, Michael, Tiana, and Korbin, how deeply I love you. Your mother is not the only one who must sacrifice; you also share me with the world, and that is not easy. Even when it may not always appear so, everything I do is done with you in mind.

To my sons, Michael and Korbin, I hope to be an example for you, yet I do not want you to aspire merely to be like me. I want you to be better than me. I will set the bar, and it will be your responsibility to surpass it. Love God, love the brotherhood, and serve God with hearts devoted to truth.

To my daughter, Tiana, you are precious and deserving of a love entirely contrary to this world. Do not believe its lies. You deserve to be loved as Christ loved His church. I pray that I would model for you the kind of man who is worthy of your heart. Do not settle for less, because anything less is unworthy of you. Give your heart first to your Father in heaven, and let any man who desires it be required to go to Him in order to receive it.

To my parents, I thank you for never seeing me as defined by my sin, but for always extending the grace of God toward me. I gave you many reasons and opportunities to turn away, yet the love of Christ always shone through both of you. After years of struggle and failure, it became my joy to welcome you into my home, to have you with me and my family after moving away from our home state. My father, John Pagano, passed away in December 2020, but the impact of his life is one I will never forget. He demonstrated the love of God through his actions and taught me the Scriptures not by words alone, but in the example of his life. His dedication to the Lord and love for his neighbors laid a foundation in me for which I will forever thank God. My mother, Victoria Pagano, you saw past my identity in sin and never stopped believing that I could have a heart for Christ. They say the prayers of a mother are powerful, and I believe your

DEDICATION

prayers were always before the Lord, even while I was living in rebellion. I love you both and thank God for you every day.

To my brother in Christ, Jeandre, a true brother in the faith. When I stumbled across this random South African online and invited him to join me on my brand-new podcast, I never would have guessed he would become the start of my most important friendship outside my household. From the moment you joined me on that first episode, I knew I wanted to serve alongside you. Now, not only have you co-hosted our online Bible studies for over three years, but you have become family. Many of my supporters and listeners are aware of your contributions to the podcast, but few know how you have been there to uplift me when the pressures of being a public figure hit. Our families now know each other, our wives have become friends, and I have traveled across the world to sit and break bread with you. Thank you for your commitment to the Lord and the friendship you have extended toward me. May God bless you and Diane, and your beautiful children, Jaime, Jordyn, Erin, and Dominic. "Two are better than one because they have a good return for their labor. For if either of them falls, the one will lift up his companion. But woe to the one who falls when there is not another to lift him up." (Ecclesiastes 4:9-10 esv)

To the True Christian Ministry (TCM) community, I wish I could name each of you individually, but I know I would inevitably leave someone out. Please know that I love you all and am deeply grateful for the support you have shown me over the years. I may be the visible face of TCM, the one most people see and hear, but this ministry has never been the effort of one individual. It is the work of the body of Christ. Thank you for your steadfast support, and for the labor you pour into building and fostering an online community that has grown far beyond what I ever imagined.

LIFE IN THE LIGHT

To my pastor, Jason Collins, and my home church, Crossroads, thank you for cultivating a church community that has shown me what true Christian fellowship looks like. I pour myself out daily for those in need, and had I not had a place where I could be poured back into, I would have failed long ago. I am deeply thankful to have been blessed with a church home like Crossroads, a place where I am able to grow, be strengthened, and remain anchored.

Jason, your pastoral care, faithfulness, and dedication have been a continual source of encouragement and inspiration to me. I am honored to call you my pastor and to serve under your spiritual oversight. Thank you.

Contents

Introduction	1
1. 1 John 1 Walking in the Light	21
2. 1 John 2 Abiding in the Light	36
3. 1 John 3 Children of God	113
4. 1 John 4 Love Perfected	192
5. 1 John 5 That You May Know	241
Epilogue	297
6. Appendix: The Comma Johanneum	300
7. Bibliography	313

Introduction

I write these things to you who believe in the name of the Son of God, that you may know that you have eternal life.
(*1 John 5:13, ESV*)

PURPOSE

These words were chosen by the Apostle John as he closes his epistle. This is not the first time John expresses such intentions. At the end of his Gospel, he likewise shares his purpose for writing. John's passion for his readers is evident throughout his writings, and it is a beautiful thing. It is these words that have drawn me to write this book. The purpose behind John's epistle is to give believers confidence in their faith—not to incite fear or worry. They remind us where our focus should lie, and this is exactly my aim in writing.

I pray that the Lord guides my words with every line of this book. My hope is not that my words replace Scripture, but that they confess my love for it and help you see why I treasure it so deeply. I want to stir a love for God's Word in you. It breaks my heart when I meet young Christians who have access to Scripture yet still walk in fear or doubt. I ask myself: Are they reading the same thing I am reading? Do they not see the promises of our Lord? Oh, what I would give to see someone read this book and fall deeply in love with the Scriptures. That is my sole goal—the reason I am writing this book, even before writing about myself.

I would love to pour out my life story and testimony onto the pages, sharing what God has guided me through, and the hope that is in me. I would also love to engage in doctrines and theological discussions about the nuances of our faith. However, before guiding believers deeper into these areas, I feel obligated to ensure they truly know Jesus—the One who gives strength—and that they can be confident in their standing in Christ. What better way to begin this journey than by exploring the work of the Apostle John in his first epistle?

John concludes his Gospel with the words: *"Now Jesus did many other signs in the presence of the disciples, which are not written in this book; but these are written so that you may believe that Jesus is the Christ, the Son of God, and that by believing you may have life in his name."* (John 20:30-31, ESV). Then, in his epistle, he says he writes so that those who believe in the name of the Son of God may know that they have eternal life.

Here we have the last living Apostle, the disciple whom Jesus loved. The young boy who heard of Jesus one day and gave his life to Him. The boy entrusted with the care of His mother. The boy who grew into a man living in the ways of Jesus. Now, at the end of his life, he could teach endlessly about Christ, yet time is limited. He gives us the Gospel *"so that you may believe,"* and the Epistle *"so that you may know."*

> *Note:* John refers to himself in his Gospel as *"the disciple whom Jesus loved."* Is this pride or ego? In the Greek, the word used is *ephilei* (ἐφίλει), rooted in *phileo* (φιλέω), meaning active, ongoing love.[1] In modern English, this could be understood as *"the disciple whom Jesus keeps loving."* This is not prideful, nor is John claiming a unique favor from Jesus. He is not naming himself but identifying himself through Christ's eternal love. His identity rests not in his name, but in being loved by Jesus.

For this reason, I believe 1 John should be close to the heart of every believer. Every word of this letter is full of love, grace, and peace, while also issuing a stern warning to those who may claim faith falsely. Though John writes to believers, there is a clear call to reflection. I love all of God's Word, but I confess a special connection to 1 John. I pray others find the same comfort in it that I do.

I do not believe I can add anything to God's Word, nor make the words of 1 John more powerful than they already are. My hope is simply to ignite a love for the words already on the page and a passion to understand them more clearly. May you be blessed by God our Father through His Son Jesus Christ, in the power of the Holy Spirit, as you study His Word.

---

1. The Greek term ἐφίλει (ephilei), used by John in John 21:7, 20, 24, is rooted in φιλέω (phileo), meaning active, ongoing love. For lexical reference, see BDAG: A Greek-English Lexicon of the New Testament and Other Early Christian Literature, 3rd ed., ed. Frederick W. Danker, s.v. φιλέω.

The Urgency to Test Yourself

I am writing this book not only to give my brothers and sisters assurance of their salvation, but also to confront those whose faith is empty. My prayer is that the Lord would place these words into the hands of those who call themselves Christians yet have built their confidence on shallow foundations, those who have built their house on sand rather than on the rock (Matthew 7:24–27).

In places like the United States, Christianity has often been reduced to a cultural label. Countless people claim to follow Christ, yet neither read Scripture, gather with the church, nor order their lives according to His words. Many parents bear the name of Christ while failing to raise their children with a biblical worldview or meaningful instruction in the faith. This neglect has not only become common, it has become normal.

We live in what could rightly be called the "you shall not judge" era of American Christianity. In this version of the faith, the only test of salvation is whether someone once prayed a prayer or invited Jesus into their heart. Beyond that moment, nothing further is expected. Any call to examine fruit, obedience, or love for Christ is quickly dismissed. The only rebuke permitted is directed toward the one calling others to godliness.

This book is written to press the professing believer to ask a sobering question: Do I believe, or do I only say that I believe? Belief always produces action. If I believe airplanes are safe, I will fly. If I believe a food is harmful, I will avoid it. If I believe something is trustworthy, I will place my confidence in it.

In the same way, if someone says he believes in the Lord Jesus Christ, that He died for our sins, was crushed for our iniquities, was buried, and rose again for our salvation (Isaiah 53:5; 1 Corinthians 15:3-4), how can his life remain indistinguishable from those who do not believe? Too often, accountability is dismissed as works based salvation. But this is not about works. It is about evidence.

If I truly believe that God hates sin, hates it so deeply that Christ endured the cross because of it (Romans 5:8), how can I make peace with what He despises? Scripture does not leave this unclear: "There are six things that the Lord hates, seven that are an abomination to him" (Proverbs 6:16-19). If I regularly consume or celebrate what God hates, what does that reveal about my faith? What does it reveal about my heart?

Paul exhorts us plainly: "Let love be genuine. Abhor what is evil; hold fast to what is good" (Romans 12:9). The mark of a true Christian is not only love for God, but a growing hatred for what He hates. Scripture goes further still: "The fear of the Lord is hatred of evil" (Proverbs 8:13). When God grants true repentance, our affections change. What once enticed us begins to grieve us.

Am I saying that you must be sinless to be saved? No. Scripture is clear: all have sinned and fall short of the glory of God (Romans 3:23). The Christian life is marked by grace, repentance, and growth. But there is a real difference between stumbling in weakness and making peace with sin.

John speaks plainly: "The one who says, 'I have come to know Him,' and does not keep His commandments, is a liar" (1 John 2:4). This is not written to crush the tender conscience, but to expose empty profession and false assurance. Scripture calls us to honest self examination, not to drive us into despair, but to bring us to clarity.

So I leave you with a final question for reflection. Does your life bear the marks of someone genuinely following Christ, or merely someone who claims His name? Is there evidence of repentance, love for righteousness, and a growing hatred for sin? These questions are not meant to drive you away from

Christ, but to drive you toward Him, where true assurance is found.

I am not concerned with measuring the degree of change or listing specific evidences, but I am deeply concerned that there is some change. As preacher Paul Washer once illustrated:[2]

"Imagine that I show up late for a preaching engagement, and I run up onto the platform, and all the leaders are angry with me and say, 'Don't you appreciate the fact that you are given an opportunity to speak here? And yet you come late!' I might reply, 'Brothers, you have to forgive me.' 'Why?' they ask. 'Well, I was out here driving on the highway, and I had a flat tire. When I was changing the tire, the lug nut fell off. I wasn't paying attention that I was on the highway, and I ran out and grabbed the lug nut. I picked it up in the middle of the highway, but when I stood up there was a thirty-ton logging truck going one hundred miles an hour about ten yards in front of me. That truck ran me over, and that's why I'm late.' I know few people study logic anymore, but there would be only two logical conclusions you could draw. First, I am a liar; or second, I am a madman. You would probably say to me, 'That is absolutely absurd. It is impossible to have an encounter with something as large as a logging truck and not be changed.' And so my question to you would be, 'Which is larger? A logging truck or God?' How is it, then, that so many people today profess to have had an encounter with Jesus Christ, but they are not permanently changed?"

The point is undeniable: true faith in Christ leaves a mark. An encounter with the living God cannot result in an unchanged life.

---

2. Paul Washer, *Narrow Gate Narrow Way* (Greenville, SC: HeartCry Missionary Society, 2010), 28–29.

Confession of Faith

Before engaging with this book, it is important to understand the foundation upon which it is written. My confession of faith is grounded in Scripture and outlines the beliefs that guide the reflections, explanations, and exhortations contained herein. Even for readers familiar with my teaching, I recommend reading it carefully, as it provides essential context for interpreting the insights and applications that follow.

God

I believe in the eternal and everlasting God, who has revealed Himself to the Patriarchs and Prophets as the Most High, YHWH ("I Am That I Am") (*Exodus 3:14*). YHWH is the Creator of all, the one true God (*Genesis 1:1; Isaiah 45:18*). I believe that this one true God, YHWH, has revealed Himself in *three persons*: **The Father, The Son,** and **The Holy Spirit** (*Matthew 28:19; 2 Corinthians 13:14*). These three persons are not merely limited to the finite word "persons"; God is one Being while simultaneously being three (*Deuteronomy 6:4; John 10:30*). The members of the Godhead are co-eternal and co-equal (*John 1:1; John 14:9; John 16:13*). There has never been a time when the Father was not the Father, the Son not the Son, or the Spirit not the Spirit (*John 1:1-3; Hebrews 13:8*). The Father is the source of all (*1 Corinthians 8:6*), the Son is sent by the Father as the image and revelation of the invisible God (*John 1:18; Colossians 1:15*), and the Spirit proceeds from the Father as the Comforter and Helper (*John 14:16-17; John 15:26*).

The Trinity

I confess and believe in the Trinity. I do not have the time to unpack this fully for those who are unfamiliar with the doctrine, but for those who want a deeper dive, I recommend the book *The Forgotten Trinity* by Dr. James R. White. Dr. White's work on the doctrine of the Trinity is an incredible piece of literature and any Christian would benefit from reading it. From this book I will draw one of the clearest and simplest definitions of the Trinity: *"Within the one Being that is God, there exists eternally three coequal and coeternal persons, namely, the Father, the Son, and the Holy Spirit."*[3]

To clarify for some who struggle with this concept, this book is not an exhaustive teaching on the Trinity, but it is important to address what we confess as Christians. A common struggle comes from misunderstanding the word "God." God is not merely a name; God is **what** He is. The English word "God" is derived from the Hebrew *El* or *Elohim*, and in the New Testament, the Greek *Theos*. These words describe **what** God is, not **who** He is. They convey His **Being** itself, much like "human" describes what you are, but not who you are by name. Just as you refer to me as "Michael" rather than "human," we must understand that God is not simply "God," but YHWH, and YHWH is Father, Son, and Holy Spirit.

I acknowledge that the Trinity is a profound mystery, beyond full human comprehension, yet Scripture consistently affirms it. As Paul concludes in 2 Corinthians:

---

3. James R. White, *The Forgotten Trinity* (Minneapolis: Bethany House, 1998), 23.

"The grace of the Lord Jesus Christ and the love of God and the fellowship of the Holy Spirit be with you all" (2 Corinthians 13:14).

This doxology encapsulates the eternal unity and distinct roles of the Triune God—Father, Son, and Spirit—inviting believers into fellowship with Him.

Need for Salvation

In the presence of a holy God, humanity is utterly lost. Our best efforts, apart from His grace, are insufficient and impure—Scripture calls them "filthy rags" (Isaiah 64:6). All have sinned and fall short of the glory of God (Romans 3:23), and from the very beginning, humanity has depended entirely on God's provision. Even before the fall, Adam's life and obedience were sustained by God's word and promise alone (Genesis 2:16-17).

When sin entered the world through Adam, death spread to all, confirming humanity's universal need for rescue (Romans 5:12). Left to ourselves, we are incapable of restoring our relationship with God, incapable of achieving righteousness, and incapable of escaping the consequences of sin. Apart from divine intervention, our condition is hopeless, our hearts are bound to rebellion, and no human effort can reconcile us to the Creator.

The Gospel

The Gospel, or Good News, is the message of God's Kingdom—His eternal plan for His reign (Mark 1:15). It was first revealed to Adam and Eve (Genesis 3:15), promising a coming Seed who would undo the effects of sin. Throughout the Old Testament, the prophets pointed to this Seed as King and Savior (2 Samuel 7:12-13; Isaiah 9:6-7). At the appointed time, the Eternal Son of God came in the flesh (Isaiah 9:6; John 1:14), humbling Himself to live among humanity (Philippians 2:6-8; Luke 2:7). Though fully God, He did not cling to His divine prerogative but submitted to the Father's will, bearing witness to righteousness (Romans 3:21-22; 1 Peter 2:22).

Jesus was captured, betrayed, unjustly tried, beaten, and ultimately crucified (Isaiah 53:3-5; Luke 23:34). In His suffering, He bore the full weight of our sins, satisfying the righteous wrath of God and condemning sin in His own flesh (Romans 8:3). On the cross, He fulfilled the legal demands of God's law, nailing the record of our transgressions to Himself (Colossians 2:14) and declaring in triumph, "It is finished" (John 19:30). His death was the fulfillment of prophecy, carefully foretold in Scripture (Matthew 27:57-60; Isaiah 53:9).

Three days later, Christ rose from the dead, triumphing over sin, death, and the grave (Matthew 28:6; 1 Corinthians 15:4). Through His resurrection, He guarantees eternal life for all who believe in Him (Romans 6:9-10; 1 Peter 1:3). The finished work of Christ provides full forgiveness, reconciliation with God, and justification to all who believe (Romans 5:18-19; Hebrews 3:15). In Him, the righteous demands of God are satisfied, and sinners are brought near to the Father **by grace alone, through faith alone, in Christ alone** (Ephesians 2:8-9; 2 Corinthians 5:18-21).

Salvation

All people are appointed to die and then face judgment (Hebrews 9:27). Salvation, therefore, is not a superficial belief or religious affiliation, but a decisive act of God whereby the sinner is reconciled to Him through Jesus Christ. Salvation is not merely forgiveness of sins, but Christ Himself representing the believer before the Father. Scripture teaches that Jesus intercedes for us as our advocate, having canceled the record of debt that stood against us (Romans 8:34; 1 John 2:1; Colossians 2:14).

Salvation comes through trusting in the person and work of Jesus Christ alone. He is the only way to the Father, the exclusive means of reconciliation between God and man (John 14:6; Acts 4:12). This salvation did not originate at the cross but was promised long before it. Abraham rejoiced to see Christ's day, Noah found grace in the eyes of the Lord, David spoke of resurrection, and the prophets longed for the fulfillment now revealed in Christ (John 8:56; Genesis 6:8; Psalm 16:10; Luke 10:24). What was anticipated in promise is now fulfilled in the Son, and we are justified by faith in Him (Romans 5:1).

Scripture never presents salvation as an object that can be worn, carried, or set aside. Salvation is a person. Simeon declared of Jesus, "my eyes have seen your salvation" (Luke 2:30). To have salvation is to have Christ, and to be united to Him. The believer is described as being in Christ, and Christ as dwelling in the believer, the hope of glory (Romans 8:1; Colossians 1:27). This union is not maintained by human effort but is brought about by God Himself. Those who receive Christ are born again, not by human will, but by the will of God (John 1:12-13). If anyone is in Christ, he is a new creation (2 Corinthians 5:17).

Salvation is the reception of a new heart and a new spirit. God promises to remove the heart of stone and give a heart of flesh, placing His Spirit within His people and causing them to walk in His ways (Ezekiel 36:26-27). Paul describes this transformation as a circumcision made without hands (Colossians 2:11). The Holy Spirit is given as a seal and guarantee of the believer's inheritance until the final redemption (Ephesians 1:13-14; 2 Corinthians 1:21-22). Salvation, therefore, is not fragile or temporary. It is an eternal union with Christ, grounded in the finished work of God and secured by His Spirit.

A common question arises: how were people saved before the coming of Christ? The answer lies in understanding that the basis of salvation has always been the work of Jesus Christ, even before He came in the flesh. In every age, God has provided a way for sinners to be reconciled to Himself through faith. The difference is not the requirement—faith has always been necessary—but the content of that faith, which unfolds according to God's progressive revelation.

Consider Abraham, who "believed God, and it was counted to him as righteousness" (Genesis 15:6). Abraham trusted in the promise of a coming Savior, even though he did not see the fulfillment. David trusted in God's promises of resurrection and deliverance, declaring hope in the One who would come to save His people (Psalm 16:10). The prophets anticipated the coming Messiah, proclaiming God's future redemption and calling people to trust in God's faithfulness. In every instance, salvation was by God's grace, appropriated through faith, and grounded in His promises.

The key distinction before Christ was the content of faith. Believers then trusted in the promise of the coming Messiah; now, we trust in the Messiah who has come. The object of faith has always been God, but what is fully revealed in His Son and His work is now known. Salvation, in every age, is by grace through faith, always pointing to Christ—before, in the promise; now, in the fulfillment.

Regeneration and Sanctification

Justification by faith is made effective in the believer through the work of the Holy Spirit. Scripture teaches that anyone who belongs to Christ has the Spirit of God dwelling within them (Romans 8:9). The Spirit convicts the world of sin, reveals truth, and applies redemption to the heart of the believer (John 16:8; John 14:16-17; Acts 1:8).

Regeneration is the Spirit's act of imparting new life. It is the moment in which the believer is made alive, born again, and transformed inwardly. This new birth is not a moral adjustment but a spiritual resurrection. Sanctification then follows as the ongoing work of the Spirit, setting the believer apart for God and progressively conforming them to the image of Christ (1 Thessalonians 4:3; 1 Peter 1:2). Though distinct, regeneration and sanctification are inseparable aspects of the Spirit's work. The same Spirit who gives life also sustains, disciplines, and matures the believer.

This work is not uncertain or dependent on human perseverance alone. God seals His people with the Holy Spirit as a pledge of what is to come, assuring them that what He has begun, He will complete (Ephesians 1:13-14; Philippians 1:6). The Spirit actively preserves the believer, shaping their desires, convicting their conscience, and producing fruit that reflects genuine faith. Sanctification is evidence of regeneration, not its cause, and it flows from God's faithful commitment to finish His work.

Glorification

Glorification is the final stage of redemption, when Christ returns and completes what He began. At His coming, the dead in Christ will be raised, and those who belong to Him will be transformed, receiving glorified bodies fit for eternal life (1 Thessalonians 4:16-17; 1 Corinthians 15:51-53). This transformation is not symbolic but bodily and real, marking the full restoration of God's people.

Because believers are united with Christ in His death and resurrection, they are assured participation in His glory (Romans 6:5). Glorification guarantees freedom from sin, suffering, and death forever. God Himself will dwell with His people, wiping away every tear, and death shall be no more (Revelation 21:4).

Glorification is not a possibility but a certainty. It rests not on human faithfulness, but on God's promise. The same Father who planned salvation, the same Son who accomplished redemption, and the same Spirit who applies and preserves it will bring believers safely into eternal glory. Salvation begins in grace, is sustained by grace, and ends in glory.

Authority of Scripture

Scripture alone bears divine authority as "God-breathed" (2 Timothy 3:16), equipping believers for every good work (2 Timothy 3:16-17). The Word is described as a sword (Ephesians 6:17; Hebrews 4:12) and a lamp to guide our path (Psalm 119:105). Jesus treated Scripture with utmost authority (Matthew 4:1-11; Matthew 5:18; Luke 24:27). God holds all accountable to His Word (Deuteronomy 6:6-9; Isaiah 5:24; Hosea 4:6), which remains sufficient for faith and practice (2 Timothy 3:16-17; Isaiah 8:20; James 1:22). From the earliest believers to the Christians who came before us, Scripture has stood as the ultimate standard in which all truth is measured. They looked to the Word to keep every teaching, every tradition, and every practice aligned with God's will, affirming that nothing else holds the same weight or authority.

Bible Translations Used in This Book

Throughout this book, I quote from two translations: the English Standard Version (ESV) and the Legacy Standard Bible (LSB). In the spirit of transparency, let me explain why I have chosen to use both.

When I first began writing, my goal was to use a single translation throughout—specifically, the ESV. If you are familiar with my weekly Bible studies on YouTube, you know this is my preferred translation. In my personal study, I consult several versions, but when teaching, consistency aids understanding. For that reason, I primarily teach from the ESV to maintain uniformity across my lessons and discussions.

I do not hold the view that a person must read a specific translation to be a Christian. Such thinking is both dangerous and misguided. As Dr. Michael Heiser notes, "I always point out that there is no one Bible translation that is consistently superior to all others. All translations have problems; they all take liberties; they all have strengths."[4] These statements remind us that no translation is perfect, and all are attempts to convey the words and thoughts of the original Greek and Hebrew.

Through my study and research, I have found the ESV to be exceptionally well-crafted and faithful, fully sufficient for both study and teaching. The LSB, a newer translation, is likewise precise and trustworthy in its rendering of the biblical text.

The only reason I have chosen to use two translations in this work, rather than one, is legal. Copyright laws allow the free quotation of hundreds of verses from a translation, but not

---

4. Michael S. Heiser, "Which Bible Translation? A Few Thoughts," DrMSh.com, https://drmsh.com/which-bible-translation-a-few-thoughts/ — accessed December 9, 2025.

an entire biblical book without written permission from the publisher. Since this commentary covers the entirety of 1 John, I have divided my quotations accordingly: the first two chapters will be quoted from the ESV, and the final three chapters from the LSB.

I do not consider one translation superior to the other, and I do not believe this division will cause any issue. Many readers will likely follow along in their preferred translation. In fact, I encourage it. Whether you use the Christian Standard Bible (CSB), King James Version (KJV), or New International Version (NIV), to name a few, I invite you to read along in your translation of choice. Doing so will allow you to observe slight differences in wording while seeing the unified message of truth.

In 1 John 5, I also address certain textual differences that appear in modern translations but are not found in the KJV. The use of multiple translations is not an attempt to avoid these discussions but to engage them honestly. These are important matters that deserve careful attention.

The Nature of the Word

The Bible is a unique collection of 66 books, written and preserved over centuries. These are witness accounts of God's revelation. Men inspired by God wrote what they saw and heard, each within their historical and cultural context. Though written in human circumstances, Scripture carries the voice of the eternal God. God's wisdom weaves through time—speaking to people in every generation while addressing their specific situations.

God gave Moses knowledge of the beginning, giving us Genesis. From Moses to Malachi, the prophets recorded God's words. Then came the intertestamental period—centuries of silence—until Jesus fulfilled the Law, the Prophets, and the Psalms (Luke 24). He then sent His apostles, who bore witness to the Messiah and recorded what they saw. These writings, inspired by the Holy Spirit, became the rest of Scripture. Today, we have 66 books: 39 Old Testament books pointing to the coming Messiah, and 27 New Testament books proclaiming that He has come and will return.

But what is the Bible for? What is the nature of these writings? In short, as 2 Timothy 3:16-17 (ESV) states: "All Scripture is breathed out by God and profitable for teaching, for reproof, for correction, and for training in righteousness, that the man of God may be complete, equipped for every good work."

If this is true—that these words are God-breathed—then Scripture should be the most important thing in a Christian's life. It should be the lamp to our feet and the word we turn to for guidance, encouragement, strength, and hope. Sadly, we live in a culture that labels itself as Christian, yet few truly understand what that means. Many who claim the name of Christ rarely touch the Scriptures; instead, Bibles collect dust on shelves, treated more like artifacts than the bread of life. Many mimic the traditions and rituals, only to return to living like Romans.

Don't believe me? Take today's Christian culture and place it in the early church period. Put it in the Roman Empire—and remove the persecution. They would eat, drink, and sleep Roman propaganda, education, and entertainment. Christian parents are more concerned with how their children perform in the coliseum than how they grow in knowledge of God's Word. We sacrifice money, time, and energy to ensure our children are educated in the ways of the world, yet we struggle to give more than an hour a week to Christian learning.

If I were to hand the average person a book and say, "This book will help you earn one million dollars," or, "This book will guide you to lose weight and get the body you want," and that person truly believed me, they would dive into it and read it carefully. Yet many people say they believe the Bible is the Word of God, capable of making one complete, and yet it sits unopened. We must ask: Do we actually believe what we say about the words within it?

Perhaps this isn't you. You may have been raised by Bible-believing Christians who lived what they taught—who didn't live a double life or glorify the world. I am actually one of those children, blessed to be raised in that kind of home. We exist. The sad part is, I don't see many of us continuing that legacy with our own children. This cultural disconnect fundamentally shows itself in how we read Scripture—how we view, approach, and interpret it.

How to Read Scripture

Reading the Bible faithfully requires care and intentionality. Too often, believers treat individual verses as isolated commands or nuggets of wisdom, divorced from their surrounding context. I am reminded of my time in Marine Corps Boot Camp, where the highlight of the day was receiving mail. I would get letters from my parents, my siblings, and my friends. Each letter was a lifeline, but I couldn't just grab a random envelope, turn to page three, and read a few lines.

Each letter was from a different person with a different intent, and that alone was enough to change the context of the language used. That context was built on our specific relationship and the experiences we had shared together. To understand what was being said, I had to understand who was saying it and what they meant to me. The same is true for the Word of God: context matters.

When reading the Bible, we must remember it was written for a particular audience, in a particular time and place. Who is writing? To whom are they writing? Why? What specific circumstances are they addressing? Ignoring these questions risks misunderstanding the text. Scripture is not a generic collection of wisdom; it is a living communication from God, flowing through human authors, and intended to shape our hearts and minds. Because of this, we should approach Scripture as a coherent letter from God to His people.

Understanding the author, the audience, and the historical and cultural background is vital. It is also helpful to remember that verse numbers were added in the 16th century for navigation, not interpretation. Treating isolated sentences as universal commands can easily lead to legalism or misapplication. I encourage you to invest time in basic hermeneutics—the study of how to interpret Scripture—so you can better discern the intended meaning of the text.

One key principle to grasp early on is the relationship between Indicative and Imperative statements.

Indicative statements declare truth—they describe reality or identity. For example: "You are the light of the world" (Matthew 5:14).

Imperative statements instruct action—they tell us how to live because of that truth. For example: "Let your light shine before others" (Matthew 5:16).

The indicative always precedes the imperative. God first reveals who we are in Christ, then calls us to live accordingly. Misunderstanding this sequence can lead to applying commands without grasping the foundational truth, which often produces confusion, fear, or legalism. As you read John's letters, you will see this principle repeatedly: Scripture first describes our identity in Christ, then calls us to live in that reality.

Chapter One

1 John 1

Walking in the Light

Overview

Chapter 1 of John's epistle is rich with truth that can easily be overlooked. Many readers sometimes skim the introductions of New Testament letters, assuming the language is repetitive or merely formal. Yet these openings often provide a glimpse into the heart of the author. The way they speak of our Lord and address their audience reveals their intentions and priorities. While much of the New Testament contains warnings and strong rebukes, the introductions to the letters demonstrate that such firmness is never for condemnation but for guidance and care. John's letter exemplifies this principle, setting a tone of pastoral wisdom and theological precision that carries throughout the epistle.

From the very first lines, John emphasizes the central truths of the gospel: the incarnation of Christ, the life and light He brings, and the fellowship believers enjoy with God and one another. His deliberate language—how he refers to Jesus and addresses his readers—underscores both the reality of Christ and the relational nature of salvation. To appreciate the depth of his insight, it helps to understand John himself. He was the youngest of the Apostles when he first began following Jesus. By the time he wrote his letters, he was the last living apostle, a seasoned elder who had walked with Christ for decades, witnessing both His earthly ministry and His glory revealed in vision. Over the course of his life, John authored the Gospel bearing his name, the three epistles, and the Revelation of Jesus Christ. It is believed that 1 John was written after his exile on Patmos, where he received profound visions of Christ and the end times. This is not the young disciple who followed Jesus along the shores of Galilee, but a seasoned Apostle whose years of fellowship, ministry, and revelation inform every word he writes.

Although the letter's ultimate purpose is stated most clearly in chapter 5, when John writes, "that you may know that you have eternal life" (1 John 5:13), the themes of assurance, love, and fellowship are established immediately in chapter 1. As you read, you may encounter passages that cause you to pause or raise questions. I encourage you to press forward, as many answers unfold in the context of the whole letter. These words are meant not to produce fear or guilt, but to guide you into truth, strengthen your faith, and draw you into the life-giving fellowship of God.

In chapter 1, I explore entire sections, highlighting key themes. Beginning in chapter 2, I will take a line-by-line approach, unpacking the deep theological statements John addresses. This is not like most commentaries, which focus solely on the text itself. I also step aside from John's letter to discuss foundational truths of the faith, ensuring no prior knowledge is assumed. We will touch on many scriptures beyond 1 John in this book. My goal is to answer any questions you may have and guide you toward a full understanding of the letter's message.

Throughout the epistle, John emphasizes the inseparable connection between believing in Christ, walking in His light, and loving others. Chapter 1 introduces these themes by contrasting the life-giving light of Christ with the darkness of sin, highlighting the confession and fellowship that define the Christian life. Understanding these foundational truths from the outset equips the reader to follow the letter's argument and receive the full richness of its pastoral guidance.

1 John 1:1–4 (ESV)
That which was from the beginning, which we have heard, which we have seen with our eyes, which we looked upon and have touched with our hands, concerning the word of life—the life was made manifest, and we have seen it, and testify to it and proclaim to you the eternal life, which was with the Father and was made manifest to us—that which we have seen and heard we proclaim also to you, so that you too may have fellowship with us, and indeed our fellowship is with the Father and with his Son Jesus Christ. And we are writing these things so that our joy may be complete.

John's opening lines immediately establish his credibility as a trustworthy witness. He is not passing along secondhand reports or speculative ideas, but speaking with authority as one who personally encountered the living Christ. By using repeated sensory language—"we have heard," "we have seen," "we looked upon," "have touched"—John emphasizes the physical and tangible reality of the incarnation.[1] The Word of Life was not an

---

1. **Incarnation.** Literally "in flesh"; the doctrine that in Jesus of Nazareth God took on human flesh and became the divine God-man. Grant R. Osborne, *Baker Encyclopedia of the Bible*, 1025.

abstract concept or philosophical notion, but a real person, with whom the Apostles had direct lived interaction. Their testimony carries weight because it is grounded in firsthand experience. They are not preserving stories for tradition's sake, but proclaiming historical truth, rooted in events they personally witnessed.

John concludes this introduction with a profound pastoral hope: "so that you too may have fellowship with us." His desire is not merely to recount events, but to draw readers into a shared experience of the life of Christ. This fellowship extends beyond human companions to include both the Father and His Son, Jesus Christ, establishing from the start that Christian life is rooted in relationship with God. John emphasizes the personal and relational nature of faith without delving yet into the deeper dynamics between Father and Son, reserving that fuller treatment for later in the letter.

The Father and the Son

The Lord Jesus Christ declares in His high priestly prayer, *"And this is eternal life, that they know you, the only true God, and Jesus Christ whom you have sent"* (John 17:3). From the very beginning of the New Testament, believers are called into fellowship with the Father through His Son. This is not incidental language, nor is it a theological afterthought. It is the consistent pattern of apostolic proclamation. Salvation, life, and fellowship are always presented as coming from the Father, through the Son, by the Spirit.

John will later expound on this reality in greater depth, especially when he makes clear that one cannot have the Father without the Son, nor the Son without the Father. That more detailed discussion belongs where John himself places it, later in the letter, and I will address it there. For now, the purpose is not to explore the depth of Trinitarian relationships, but to establish something foundational that must be held from the beginning.

Throughout the New Testament, and especially in the introductions of its letters, the Father and the Son are always distinctly and deliberately identified. They are never merged, confused, or treated as interchangeable persons. The Apostles do not speak of a vague divine figure who appears now as Father and now as Son, nor do they allow the reader to collapse the Son into the Father or the Father into the Son. While God is one in essence, He is never presented as one in person. The unity of God does not erase distinction, and distinction does not threaten unity.

This pattern is not accidental. It guards the believer from false conceptions of God and anchors the faith in the God who has revealed Himself as He truly is. From the opening lines of Scripture to the final blessings of the epistles, the Father and the Son stand together, distinct yet inseparable, each acting in perfect harmony in the work of redemption. John begins his letter within this same apostolic framework, grounding the reader immediately in the truth that Christian fellowship is always with both the Father and His Son, Jesus Christ, never one to the exclusion of the other.

Historical Background: Docetism

John's primary aim in this letter is to provide assurance of salvation. Alongside this pastoral concern, however, is a secondary purpose, to confront a growing heresy within the early church. This broader heretical movement is commonly referred to as Gnosticism,[2] a category that included several related errors.

More specifically, John is addressing the teaching of Docetism, derived from the Greek word *dokein*, meaning "to seem" or "to appear." Rooted in Gnostic thought, Docetism taught that all flesh is inherently evil while spirit alone is good. If this premise were true, then Christ could not have truly come in the flesh. Jesus, according to this teaching, only appeared to be human, but was not genuinely incarnate. Such a belief denies the incarnation itself, the truth that "the Word became flesh," and rejects what would later be defined in church history as the hypostatic union[3], the doctrine that Jesus Christ is fully God and fully man. This heresy was actively spreading during the time of John's writing, and it explains why John places such heavy emphasis on the physical reality of Christ's humanity, both in his Gospel and in this epistle.

With this in mind, John's opening words take on sharper focus. He is not merely offering poetic testimony or establishing apostolic authority, but deliberately confronting claims that threatened the heart of the gospel. By emphasizing that Christ was heard, seen, looked upon, and physically touched, John

---

2. **Gnosticism** refers to a broad set of early religious movements that emphasized secret or special knowledge (*gnōsis*) as the means of salvation. Gnostic systems typically viewed the material world as evil or inferior and elevated the spiritual realm as good, often leading to the denial of the true incarnation of Christ.

3. **Hypostatic Union.** The union of the divine and human natures in the one person of Christ, without change, mixture, or confusion, each nature retaining its own properties. Richard Watson, *A Biblical and Theological Dictionary*, s.v. "Hypostatical Union."

draws an unmistakable line in the sand. The Jesus proclaimed by the Apostles was no phantom, no divine appearance cloaked in illusion, but one who truly took on flesh.

John's insistence is purposeful, not incidental. It is both pastoral and corrective. He frames his language to leave no room for a Christ who only seemed human, or whose physical life could be dismissed as unnecessary or corrupt. Every sensory detail reinforces the reality of the incarnation and directly counters the core claims of Docetism. While these truths remain essential for the church in every age, understanding the heresy John addresses helps us see why he speaks with such precision and repetition at the start of this letter.

While John ensures the reader that Jesus truly came in the flesh and walked among us, he consistently uses his language to present both the tangible Christ and the infinite Lord. He affirms not only that Jesus was physically present, but that the One who was seen, heard, and touched is also eternal. John's reference to "the beginning" is therefore a deliberate affirmation of the eternal nature of Christ. This language echoes the opening of John's Gospel (John 1:1-14), where the Word is described as preexistent, with God, and as God. Jesus, the Word of Life, did not come into existence at some point in history. He existed eternally with the Father. This establishes that the eternal Word, who later became incarnate, was active at creation according to God's eternal plan.

The phrase "eternal life" is central to John's theology. It is not merely a future hope or an abstract concept, but a present reality that was "made manifest" in Jesus Christ. Eternal life is not simply about what happens after death, but about knowing God now through His Son. For this reason, John writes not only to defend the truth of the gospel, but to invite others into the same fellowship with God that the Apostles themselves enjoy.

John's proclamation, then, is neither self-centered nor academic. His desire is that his readers would enter into fellowship with him and with the other apostles. This fellowship is not merely agreement in doctrine, but a living relationship with the Father and His Son, Jesus Christ. Fellowship with God stands at the very heart of the Christian faith. The Apostle writes so that others may share in this fellowship and, as a result, share in the fullness of joy that flows from it.

He closes this opening section by revealing the ultimate aim of his writing: that his readers may experience the joy that flows from knowing God and sharing in His life. The gospel is not presented as a burden or merely a moral system, but as the source of deep and abiding joy. This joy is rooted in reconciliation with God and fellowship with Him. The apostles' joy is made complete when others come to share in the life they themselves have received in Christ. In other words, the introduction points toward the same ultimate goal that John makes explicit later: that believers may know they have eternal life through fellowship with God and His Son.

The Word of Life

John opens this epistle similarly to how he opens his Gospel, anchoring his message in the preeminence and eternality of Christ. In the Gospel, he declares, "In the beginning was the Word" (John 1:1). In both writings, Jesus is identified as the *Logos* (λόγος)—not merely a spoken word, but the eternal, self-expressing Word. This distinction is significant. In Matthew 4:4, when Jesus speaks of living by "every word that comes from the mouth of God," the Greek term used is *rhema* (ῥῆμα), referring to a spoken utterance. By contrast, John employs *Logos* to convey the dynamic, creative, and divine self-expression of God made manifest in Christ.

To the Greek world, *Logos* signified the rational principle that orders the cosmos, providing unity, coherence, and meaning to all that exists. It was understood as the underlying reason that gives structure to the universe, a concept developed in Stoic philosophy as *logos spermatikos*, the seminal Word that shapes and informs all matter. To the Jewish mind, by contrast, the Word of God was inherently creative and powerful, the divine instrument through which God brought all things into being.[4] John draws upon both of these frameworks to communicate a profound truth: this eternal, divine *Logos* did not remain abstract but became incarnate, dwelling among humanity in the person of Jesus Christ.

Even John's grammar reflects careful theological intent. He begins with the phrase "that which," employing neuter language before transitioning to masculine terms. This stylistic movement mirrors a deliberate theological progression, from the abstract proclamation of the *Logos* to the full personal revelation of Jesus Christ. The language echoes Genesis 1:1, and in John 1:1, the verb choice is especially significant. John uses *ēn* ("was") rather than *egeneto* ("came into being"), emphasizing that Christ eternally existed, while all created things came into existence through Him (John 1:3).[5]

John is insistent that this message is not mythological or symbolic. He and the other Apostles heard Christ, saw Him, and touched Him. His appeal is grounded in eyewitness testimony. He is stating plainly that this message is rooted in lived, historical reality.

---

4. Logos: J. N. Birdsall, "Logos," *New Bible Dictionary*, ed. D. R. W. Wood et al., 693.

5. James R. White, The Forgotten Trinity: Recovering the Heart of Christian Belief, chap. 4, "A Masterpiece: The Prologue of John."

Why is this so important? John is not claiming merely to believe in a man named Jesus who claimed to be divine. He is confessing that he personally **saw and touched the risen Christ** and bore witness to His resurrected life. This is not second-hand belief or theological speculation, but eyewitness testimony. Critics of Christianity often assert that the Apostles fabricated their accounts, yet such claims are difficult to sustain. The Apostles were not confessing belief in a myth, but testifying to having seen Jesus alive after His crucifixion. It was this claim—that Christ had risen and that they had seen Him—that provoked opposition, persecution, and ultimately their deaths. *(Acts 4:19-20; 2 Peter 1:16)*

It is possible for people to die for beliefs they think are true. It is far less likely for many individuals to willingly endure suffering and death for what they know to be a lie. The Apostles were not persuaded merely by words or ideas. What provoked opposition was their insistence that Jesus had risen bodily from the grave. Early Roman writers, such as Pliny the Younger, writing around AD 112 to Emperor Trajan, noted that some Christians—men and women alike—refused to abandon what he called this "superstition," singing hymns to Christ as God even when arrested and threatened with punishment.[6] The resurrection was the truth authorities sought to suppress.

This single fact stands at the center of the Christian faith. The resurrection confirms everything Jesus said and did. It validates His identity and disarms death itself, the greatest weapon of the enemy. As Paul states, if Christ has not been raised, then our faith is in vain *(1 Corinthians 15:14)*. For this reason, the apostles' confession that they saw the risen Christ, bearing the marks of

---

6. Pliny the Younger, *Letters* 10.96-97, written c. AD 112 to Emperor Trajan, trans. Betty Radice, *Loeb Classical Library* (Cambridge, MA: Harvard University Press, 1969).

crucifixion, is of immense importance. They did not die for an idea they found convincing. They endured suffering and death because they encountered the risen Lord.

1 John 1:5-10 (ESV)
This is the message we have heard from Him and proclaim to you, that God is light, and in Him is no darkness at all. If we say we have fellowship with Him while we walk in darkness, we lie and do not practice the truth. But if we walk in the light, as He is in the light, we have fellowship with one another, and the blood of Jesus His Son cleanses us from all sin. If we say we have no sin, we deceive ourselves, and the truth is not in us. If we confess our sins, He is faithful and just to forgive us our sins and to cleanse us from all unrighteousness. If we say we have not sinned, we make Him a liar, and his word is not in us.

John moves from his introduction about the eternal nature of Christ to a practical application for the Christian life, grounding his message in the truth that God is light. The statement, "God is light," conveys more than God's moral purity; it communicates the very nature of His revelation. Light represents truth, holiness, and purity—all inherent in God's character. Darkness, in contrast, represents sin, deception, and the absence of God. Understanding this contrast is foundational for grasping what it means to live as a believer.

John calls out the inconsistency of claiming fellowship with God while living in darkness. True fellowship with God requires walking in His light—a life characterized by integrity, righteousness, and transparency. If we live in unrepentant sin yet claim to be in fellowship with God, we are deceiving ourselves. Fellowship is not merely intellectual assent to truth but a tangible, lived experience of God's light in our daily conduct.

John emphasizes the necessity of acknowledging sin. Denial of sin leads to self-deception and undermines the truth of God's Word. Confession is not merely the acknowledgment of individual wrongs but a recognition of our overall sinfulness and alignment with God's understanding of human nature. As he writes, "If we say we have no sin, we deceive ourselves" (1 John 1:8). Confession positions the believer to receive God's forgiveness and cleansing—a thorough and complete work that restores fellowship with Him.

The promise of forgiveness is central to this passage. If we confess our sins, God is faithful and just to forgive us and cleanse us from all unrighteousness (1 John 1:9). This forgiveness is not earned by merit but flows from God's character: His justice ensures that sin is addressed, and His faithfulness ensures that grace is applied. Through the blood of Jesus, believers are restored to fellowship with God, renewed in spirit, and empowered to walk in His light.

Finally, John addresses the absurdity of claiming never to have sinned. This not only insults the truth of God's Word but also contradicts the foundational message of the gospel: all have sinned and fall short of the glory of God (Romans 3:23). The Christian life requires ongoing repentance, confession, and transformation. To deny this is to place oneself in opposition to God's revealed truth.

The Comparison of Two Types of Men

Here in the first chapter of his letter, John sets up a comparison between two kinds of people within the visible church—the gathered community of professing believers, which includes both true believers and those who merely appear to believe. From the beginning, it is important to see that John is drawing categorical lines: the true believer and the liar. As the letter continues, he will develop this contrast repeatedly, and if we do not grasp the framework he establishes here, it becomes easy to treat isolated verses as if John is giving requirements for salvation rather than describing its fruits. Do not fall into the error of turning what John presents as the product of salvation in Christ into the requirement for salvation in Christ.

John contrasts the one who claims fellowship with God yet walks in darkness with the one who walks in the light. Similarly, he contrasts those who confess their sin with those who deny it. Many readers struggle with this distinction and ask questions such as, "Does this mean we must confess every sin to be forgiven? If someone dies without confessing a sin, are they condemned?" These questions often arise from isolating a single verse. To understand John's point, we must recognize the kind of contrast he is making. He is not setting a requirement to confess each individual sin; rather, he is highlighting the believer's recognition of dependence on God. As James 1:23-25 illustrates, looking into the perfect law of liberty is like gazing into a mirror: the one who truly sees himself acknowledges his condition and responds in obedience. John's purpose, then, is not to provide a checklist for salvation, but to distinguish those who humbly recognize their need for God from those who refuse to acknowledge their guilt at all.

The Contrast of Light and Darkness: The Pharisee and the Tax Collector

He also told this parable to some who trusted in themselves that they were righteous, and treated others with contempt: "Two men went up into the temple to pray, one a Pharisee and the other a tax collector. The Pharisee, standing by himself, prayed thus: 'God, I thank you that I am not like other men, extortioners, unjust, adulterers, or even like this tax collector. I fast twice a week; I give tithes of all that I get.' But the tax collector, standing far off, would not even lift up his eyes to heaven, but beat his breast, saying, 'God, be merciful to me, a sinner!' I tell you, this man went down to his house justified, rather than the other. For everyone who exalts himself will be humbled, but the one who humbles himself will be exalted."(Luke 18:9-14, ESV)

Jesus addresses those who trust in themselves, relying on their own works for righteousness. They fail to recognize their sin and, in doing so, look down on others as inferior. As Isaiah declares regarding our futile righteousness, all our deeds are like a polluted garment (Isaiah 64:6). The Pharisee exemplifies this attitude: he boldly stands in the presence of God, thanking Him for not being like "other men" and judging the tax collector. By contrast, the tax collector recognizes his sin and unworthiness, humbling himself before God with a plea for mercy. Jesus concludes that the humble are exalted, and the self-exalting are humbled.

The core flaw Jesus addresses is **self-deception and minimization of sin**, which leads to pride, judgment of others, and separation from God. Recognizing our sin and humbling ourselves before the Lord is essential for true fellowship with Him.

This comparison between the true believer and the false believer is not a new concept revealed in John's teaching. It is present throughout the teachings of our Lord. I referenced the Parable of the Pharisee and the Tax Collector because it is one of my favorites, but this principle appears from the opening of the Gospels to the very end. From the beginning, when John the Baptist is preparing the way for Christ, he declares that the winnowing fork is ready and that the wheat will be separated from the weeds (Matthew 3:12). Many of Jesus's parables distinguish those of true faith from those of false faith, and at the conclusion of His three-year ministry, in the Olivet Discourse, Jesus describes the final separation of the goats from the sheep (Matthew 25:31-46). John is not presenting a new revelation here; he is echoing this teaching at the close of 1 John 1. The believer who denies sin lifts themselves up and separates from the light, while the one who confesses and humbles themselves is forgiven and restored. This is not a prescription for salvation but a pastoral challenge: evaluate your own heart. Do you recognize your sin and need for a Savior, or do you claim the light while remaining in darkness, blind to your own spiritual condition? True fellowship with God begins with honest self-examination and the recognition of His holiness.

As we conclude chapter 1, there is one final point to notice. John's opening chapter highlights two essential realities for those who have fellowship with God: who you say Jesus is, and who you say you are. We acknowledge who He is—the eternal Son of God, who came in the flesh, our Savior, the Word of Life—and we acknowledge who we are—a sinner in need of His grace and mercy.

This is the message at the heart of the Gospel: the bad news is who we are and what we've done, but the good news is who He is and what He's done. No one can come to Christ without acknowledging both.

Chapter Two

1 John 2

Abiding in the Light

Overview

As we move into chapter 2, John begins to build upon the foundation laid in chapter 1. His purpose there was to establish the essential categories of Christian life: who Christ is, and who we are in light of Him. Because of that foundation, we were able to walk through the chapter in two main sections that introduced John's framework—light and darkness, truth and falsehood, confession and denial.

In chapter 2, John shifts from laying groundwork to unfolding the practical and pastoral implications of that foundation. The rest of this letter moves forward with a more elaborate and deliberate structure, so we will now take the text line upon line and verse by verse. John does not ramble; he weaves together themes of assurance, obedience, love, and perseverance in a way that demands close attention.

Chapter 2 opens with one of the most comforting truths in all Scripture: we have an Advocate with the Father, Jesus Christ the righteous. From there, John addresses how genuine believers walk in obedience, how love for our brothers and sisters testifies to the life of God within us, and how we must guard ourselves against the deceptions of the world and the antichrist spirit that denies the Son. This chapter deepens the contrast between true and false believers introduced in chapter 1 and shows how the life of Christ is manifested in those who truly belong to Him.

1 John 2:1 (ESV)
My little children, I am writing these things to you so that you may not sin. But if anyone does sin, we have an advocate with the Father, Jesus Christ the righteous.

John's pastoral heart shines through as he addresses his readers as *"little children."* As the last living Apostle, he writes not only as a fellow child of God but as a loving older brother in the family of God. His term of endearment is not condescending; rather, it communicates deep affection and concern for their spiritual well-being. His desire is that they would not sin, yet he does not ignore the reality of human weakness and failure. The Christian life is not about attaining sinless perfection, but about living in such a way that sin does not dominate or define us. John wants his readers to recognize the seriousness of sin while also offering hope and reassurance when they inevitably stumble, reminding them that God's love and mercy remain steadfast.

The key promise is this: When we sin, we have an advocate who pleads our case before the Father. Jesus Christ fills this role, and His advocacy is grounded not in our righteousness, but in His own—He is *the Righteous*, the One who perfectly fulfilled the law and lived a life without sin, making Him the perfect mediator. As our advocate, He not only intercedes on our behalf but also fully understands our struggles and our need for forgiveness.

You may wonder, *What exactly is an advocate, and why is it essential that the Lord Jesus Christ fills this role?* John chooses his word carefully. The Greek term **paraklētos** (παράκλητος) carries legal overtones and depicts someone who stands beside another in their defense— "referring to one who comes alongside to assist, speak, or act on behalf of another. Outside the New Testament, the word often describes someone serving as a legal representative in a court of law."[1] Scripture intentionally uses legal imagery. God is the Judge, we stand as the defendants, and the law rightly condemns us. There is a real, objective demand for sin to be answered. Not only do we need an advocate, we need one who is truly qualified to stand in our place.

This is where John's point confronts any teaching that distorts who Jesus is. If Jesus is not both fully God and fully man, He cannot serve as the Advocate John proclaims. In chapter 1, I showed how John was addressing docetism, a heresy that denied Jesus's true humanity. While docetism is not a widespread issue today, the principle remains vitally important because, throughout history, Satan has sought to distort the identity of Christ. As the Apostle Paul warns in his letter to the Corinthians, some will 'preach to you a different Jesus' (2 Corinthians 11:4), emphasizing the importance of guarding against false portrayals of our Savior. Various movements, both ancient and modern, have attempted to reshape who Jesus is—thereby undermining His ability to serve as our Advocate. Examples include Arianism, which denied His full divinity; Nestorianism, which compro-

---

1. G. D. Taylor, "Testimony," in *Lexham Theological Wordbook*, ed. Douglas Mangum et al.

mised the unity of His person; and in more recent times, groups like the Mormons and Jehovah's Witnesses.

They may use Christian language and affirm that Jesus died and rose again, yet the Jesus they describe is not the eternal Son incarnate revealed in Scripture. Some portray Him as a created being, the first and greatest of God's creatures. Others depict Him as a spirit-brother among other created beings or as one who progressed into divinity. Still others claim that Jesus is merely an exalted angel who temporarily took on human flesh. Each of these views acknowledges His significance, yet all of them deny His true deity and the reality of His incarnation.

What does this have to do with Jesus being our Advocate? Everything. A created being cannot mediate before the eternal God. A mere man cannot stand between sinners and the holy Judge. An angel cannot represent humanity. Only one who is both truly God and truly man can serve as our **paraklētos** — the One who stands between God and us. And this truth is not new. One of the oldest books of Scripture anticipates it. In Job chapter 9, Job recognizes that even if he were blameless in his own eyes, he could not stand before God to plead his case. No man can bridge that infinite divide. What Job longed for and knew he needed, Christ alone provides.

Job declares, "How can a man be in the right before God? If one wished to contend with him, one could not answer him even once in a thousand times" (Job 9:2-3). In these words, we see the profound awareness of God's majesty and the futility of human defense. Job reflects on the impossibility of standing in judgment before the Almighty, acknowledging that no amount of human righteousness or eloquence could meet God's perfect standard. He continues, "Though I am in the right, my own mouth would condemn me; though I am blameless, he would prove me perverse" (v.20). Here, Job recognizes that even his most blameless actions and intentions, when weighed against

God's holiness, fall short. Human comparison cannot account for divine perfection, and human effort cannot provide justification.

Finally, Job confesses the depth of his need: "For he is not a man, as I am, that I might answer him, that we should come to trial together. There is no arbiter between us, who might lay his hand on us both" (v.32-33). In these words, the gravity of his situation becomes clear. Job acknowledges that no other creature, angel or human, can stand between him and God to mediate, defend, or reconcile. He sees that he cannot justify himself, and without an advocate, he faces the full weight of God's judgment alone. This moment beautifully foreshadows the coming of Christ, the one true Arbiter, who alone can stand between God and humanity. Job, unknowingly, is crying out for the Savior we all need—our Lord Jesus, our perfect Advocate and Mediator. If the Son stands between the Father and Job—or between the Father and us—He can petition on our behalf. He has the right to do so because He is fully God. He is equal with the Father, yet He also took on flesh, making Him fully man, able to relate to our struggles. Hebrews 2:17-18 affirms that He knows our sufferings; though sinless, He was tempted in the flesh. The Lord Jesus is the perfect Advocate—both Son of God and Son of Man. No one else can occupy this position.

Fast forward to Job's ending. I have met so many Christians who love this moment when God finally speaks, and when He does, the power of His words leaps off the page. However, as amazing as this moment is, it is equally terrifying to imagine having to stand in this place. This is what Job feared. This is the moment when God finally allows Job to present his case—He grants Job's request **without** an advocate. God asks Job a series of questions—only a few of which are, "Where were you when I laid the earth's foundations, fed the animals, and ordered the seasons?" The questions cover creation, the natural world, and the governance of all things, highlighting the vast separation between Job, the clay, and Himself, the Maker of all. Even a righteous man cannot answer or justify himself before the holiness of God. Job's fears from Job 9 become reality: no human words could satisfy or defend against God's perfection.

Now, imagine Jesus standing beside Job as His advocate. Job cannot answer the charges brought before him, but Christ can speak in his place. If the Father were to ask, "Where were you when I stretched the four corners of the earth?" Jesus could rightfully reply, "I was there; through Me, it was done." Scripture repeatedly testifies to this authority. Hebrews 1 declares, "And of the Son He says... You, Lord, created the heavens and the earth." 1 Corinthians 8 and Colossians 1 affirm that all things were created through Him, and John 1 states that nothing was made apart from Him. The Advocate does not remain silent because He is no mere witness. He stands before the Father with full authority, having eternally shared in the Father's work and glory, co-equal with Him in essence and power.

This is the good news John is pressing home to his readers, and the comfort he wants believers to cling to: we have an Advocate in Christ Jesus. He is our Mediator, the One who goes before the Father on our behalf. He intercedes for us so that we may have life. This is our hope. Many Christians fear standing before God, yet Jesus promises that whoever believes in Him does not come into judgment but has passed from death to life (John 5:24). He speaks with confidence because He stands in our place, having paid the penalty for sin at the cross and secured our justification. Our works do not present us before God; Christ does. And if Christ stands as your Advocate for your justification, who then has the authority to bring a charge against you? Scripture answers plainly: "Who shall bring any charge against God's elect?" (Romans 8:33). The Father affirms the Son in all His works and in His resurrection. The only step left is for the sinner to receive Him as Advocate.

Jesus is the one who, in the words of Job, can place His hand on both. These words remind me of the Transfiguration (Matt. 17:1-9). In this moment, the Lord Jesus stood before James, John, and Peter, His face shining like the sun and His robes pure white (v.2). He revealed the majesty that had been hidden behind the flesh He took on for our benefit. Then the Father spoke from heaven, declaring, "This is my beloved Son, with whom I am well pleased; listen to Him" (v.5). The Son stood accepted before the Father, and the disciples, rightly overwhelmed, fell facedown in fear. Yet Jesus stood between the holiness of the Father and the frailty of His disciples. He reached out, touched them, and said, "Rise, and have no fear" (v.7). He is the mediator who can place His hand on both God and man.

We are all guilty, standing before inevitable judgment, like criminals awaiting a verdict. The gospel is Christ entering that courtroom as our representative. If He stands in our place, we do not. To believe the gospel is to relinquish the attempt to plead our own case and to allow Christ to present His finished work on our behalf. Many struggle here, clinging to personal merit and striving to prove worthiness. True surrender is not self defense but trust, placing salvation entirely into the hands of Christ.

Assurance flows from recognizing Jesus as our Advocate before the Father. Confidence is not found in what we might offer God, but in the sufficiency of the One who goes before us. Those who rest in His representation are freed from fear driven obedience. Obedience becomes a response, not an effort to earn acceptance or secure the future. It flows from faith in what Christ has already accomplished at the cross, where redemption was fully secured. Our lives are shaped not by striving for favor, but by trusting the One who has already obtained it.

1 John 2:2 (ESV)
He is the propitiation for our sins, and not for ours only but also for the sins of the whole world.

Jesus is our Advocate, perfectly able to stand in our place before the Father and represent us. Yet even His advocacy does not erase the reality of our sin. We are guilty before a holy and just God, and our sin carries a weight that must be fully addressed. He not only justifies us through His legal representation as the Righteous One who perfectly fulfilled the law, but also satisfies the legal demands of God's justice for our sins. The problem of sin is real, and the solution is found in His propitiation—the atoning work that reconciles us to God.

The term propitiation refers to an atoning sacrifice that satisfies the wrath of God. In Jesus, God's justice is fully upheld, and His mercy is freely extended. This is not a vague gesture or symbolic act. It is a real, objective dealing with sin. Jesus is the propitiation for our sins, and not for ours only but for the sins of the whole world, offering grace to all who will receive Him. His atoning work opens the door for reconciliation with God, removing the ultimate barrier to fellowship.

What does this word mean? John uses the Greek term hilasmos (ἱλασμός), which carries the sense of a sin offering—something that appeases divine wrath. Jesus does not merely stand beside us as our Advocate. He does more than speak in our defense. He steps forward as the payment itself, offering to settle the debt our sin has incurred.

The punishment for sin is death, and as Paul explains in Romans 5, each of us has sinned enough to deserve that sentence countless times over. We cannot pay what we owe. Even with Christ standing in our place as Advocate, a debt remains unless it is satisfied. God is perfectly holy and just; that is what makes the good news so good, but it is also what makes the bad news so terrifying. We are guilty, and there is no escaping the reality that our sin has stored up a righteous wrath that would consume us entirely if we were required to pay it ourselves.

This is why propitiation is necessary. Jesus did not come merely to save us from the world or to rescue us from the devil; He came to save us from the righteous wrath of God. Paul is explicit that apart from Christ, this wrath stands against us (Romans 5:9). Before Christ, we were not merely neutral or misunderstood; we were enemies in active rebellion against our Creator. Yet, Romans 5 makes it clear that it was precisely in this state—while we were still sinners and enemies—that Christ acted on our behalf, demonstrating God's love by reconciling us to Himself through His death (Romans 5:8-10).

Jesus not only stands before the Father for us, He settles the debt before He stands there. At the cross, He drinks the cup of wrath that was stored up for our sin. In doing so, He leaves us with an empty cup—but Christ does not leave it empty. He fills it with His own righteousness. He lived the life we could never live, a life of perfect obedience, storing up righteousness not for Himself, but for us. Our cup of wrath becomes His, and His cup of righteousness becomes ours.

As Paul writes, God made the one who knew no sin to be sin for us, so that in Him we might become the righteousness of God. He clarifies what this means in Colossians 2:13-14: God forgave us by canceling the record of debt that stood against us with its legal demands, setting it aside and nailing it to the cross. Jesus, our perfect High Priest, did not come merely to advocate. He came to pay the fine.

Return again to the courtroom image. Christ meets you before the trial and offers to represent you. He does not deny the charges or pretend they are unfounded. He does not minimize guilt or skirt justice. The accusations are true, and the verdict is deserved. When the charges are brought forward, Jesus does not dispute them; He accepts them and then steps forward and says, "I will pay." The debt is settled, the sentence is satisfied, and you are no longer an enemy of God but reconciled to Him. Unlike the high priests of the old covenant, who first had to make atonement for their own sins before interceding for the people (Hebrews 5:3; 7:27), Christ needs no propitiation for Himself. Only one who is fully righteous and without sin could stand as our advocate and completely satisfy the law's demands on our behalf.

The Atonement

Why is Jesus being our propitiation so important? This is a question often debated in Christian apologetics,[2] and not all Christians agree. I, along with many others, hold to **Penal Substitutionary Atonement**: Jesus Christ paid our fine. He did not die for sin in general; He died for the actual sins of each believer—your sins, my sins, the sins of all who belong to Him—covering every transgression from the first breath to the last. Every record of debt we have incurred, and will incur, is fully satisfied in His sacrifice. There is no charge left unaddressed, and no accusation can ultimately stand against us. By contrast, those who deny Penal Substitution often believe that salvation can be lost, because if Christ's death was not uniquely for us, new charges could always arise. The power and security of the Gospel rests on this truth.

To help visualize it, consider the Judge stamping your entire record of debt—from birth to death—as fully paid. Other views of atonement treat Christ's work more like earned credit: some-

---

2. **Apologetics**: The defense and explanation of the Christian faith through intellectual reasoning. Ron Geaves, "Apologetics," *Continuum Glossary of Religious Terms*, 29.

thing to be applied to your account as needed, but never fully settling the debt once and for all. Penal Substitution, however, declares the ledger closed, the sentence satisfied, the debt cancelled.

Satan's greatest weapon is accusation. If God forgave without an appeasement for our debt, Satan could still accuse us before the Father. Without this payment, the promise of Romans 8—"Who shall bring any charge against God's elect?"—would be undermined. Satan would be justified in accusing us and even God Himself of injustice. This is the power of the atonement: the perfect Judge, who is both Just and Justifier (Romans 3:26), bore our iniquity and drank the cup of wrath reserved for us. God cannot be accused of partiality because He is holy—absolutely Just and separate from human error.

This is why, prior to Christ, animal sacrifices were required: they foreshadowed the ultimate substitution. Sacrifices died in place of Israel when they sinned. If Penal Substitution were not true, one could question whether God demands blood arbitrarily. The debt must be paid in blood, or Christ's death would be unnecessary.

Jesus taking our sin is the epitome of the Gospel's love. John 3:16 declares, "For God so loved the world that he gave His only Son." This does more than show the magnitude of God's love; it reveals the manner—He gave His Son. Christ's sacrifice is the ultimate demonstration of love. Jesus, the eternal Son of God, gave Himself willingly in our place, while the Father poured out wrath on Him for our benefit. This is the great exchange: Jesus, the Righteous, took on our sin so that we might take on His righteousness. He did not die just for the sins of yesterday or today, leaving tomorrow as an open debt. His death transcends time, fully covering every sin and settling the account once and for all.

"Whole World"

When John speaks of the "whole world," he is highlighting the infinite sufficiency of Christ's sacrifice. He is not suggesting that Jesus's sacrifice blindly atones for every single person regardless of faith—a view that leads to the heresy of "universalism," the belief that every single person will ultimately be saved. Rather, John is assuring his readers that this propitiation is not limited to a small elite or a single nation; it is the only and all-sufficient hope for every person under heaven. Whether a person is Jew or Gentile, Christ's work is the singular bridge back to the Father. While the payment is applied specifically to those who believe, the offer of the Gospel is as wide as the world itself.

1 John 2:3 (ESV)
And by this we know that we have come to know Him, if we keep His commandments.

Now comes the part of Scripture where some readers grow uneasy. John says that we know we have come to know Christ if we keep His commandments, and that those who claim to know Him while disregarding His Word are liars. For many readers, especially those new to the faith or unfamiliar with careful study of Scripture, the word *commandments* can immediately raise concern, as it is often assumed to mean the same thing in every context. Scripture, however, uses this term in more than one way, and the meaning is always shaped by context. This is the first of many times in this letter where John references "His commandments," and here he is speaking specifically of the commandments of Christ: to love God and to love your neighbor. Over the next several verses, we will examine this term carefully, from the Law of Moses to the commandments of Christ, so that every reader clearly understands what John means. The focus of John's admonition is not external law-keeping, but the orientation of the believer's heart and life toward Christ.

Read in isolation, this verse can sound like a reversal of everything John has just said. A reader might conclude, *"If obedience is the measure, then where does grace fit? What happens when I fail?"* But this concern only arises when the passage is detached from its immediate context. John has not forgotten what he wrote just a few verses earlier. He has already acknowledged the ongoing reality of sin, and he has already given comfort to believers by declaring that when we do sin, we have an Advocate with the Father, Jesus Christ the Righteous. John does not contradict himself within the span of a paragraph. He does not move from "when you sin, you have an Advocate" to "you are only saved if you never break a commandment." That would require a moment of theological amnesia, and John shows no sign of it.

John's purpose here is not to introduce a new standard that unsettles the assurance he has just given. Rather, he is doing something he will repeat throughout this letter. He draws clear, categorical distinctions between two kinds of people—not between the sinless and the sinful, but between those whose lives are oriented toward obedience through the transforming work of the Spirit and those whose lives are marked by disregard for God's Word. These are not categories of perfection, but of direction. John is not describing flawless command-keeping; he is describing the settled pattern of a life shaped by knowing Christ and being transformed by His Spirit. To claim fellowship with Him while walking in persistent contradiction to His commands is not a struggle with sin; it is a denial of who He is. Conversely, keeping His Word, even imperfectly, is evidence that the love of God is at work, shaping the believer's walk to resemble the life of Christ Himself. This is not a new condition for salvation, but a description of what genuine knowledge of Christ produces.

As we touched on in the "How to Read Scripture" section, it is vital to distinguish descriptive statements from prescriptive commands. Descriptive statements reveal reality; prescriptive statements instruct action. Too often, descriptive Scriptures are mistaken for prescriptive commands. Throughout the New Testament, we see many descriptions of those who know the Lord, yet sadly, some have treated these passages as if they define the requirements for salvation. This brings us back to that vital principle we established in chapter 1, and one I have often said in preaching: do not let someone present the product of salvation and convince you it is the requirement for salvation. Descriptive texts show the work of the Holy Spirit in believers—they are for reflection, not instruction.

For example, I can say, "All humans breathe oxygen." This describes reality, but just because something breathes oxygen does not make it human—a dog or a bird also breathes oxygen. Similarly, a Christian is one who follows the Lord's commands, yet following His commands does not make someone a Christian. What makes a person a Christian is the Spirit of God in them, conforming them to the image of the Son and moving them to walk in His purpose. When Jesus says, "If you love me, you will follow my commandments" (John 14:15), He is not prescribing a condition for love; He is describing the reality of those who truly love Him.

Outward obedience alone does not define a true relationship with God. Even among those who meticulously followed God's commands in Jesus' day, knowing Him was not guaranteed. The Pharisees kept the law, yet Jesus told them, "You do not know the one who sent me" (John 8:19). Paul, too, as a zealous Pharisee, faithfully followed the law, but later recognized that this obedience did not equate to knowing God (Philippians 3:5-7).

These examples show that true obedience flows from inward transformation, not external conformity. As Paul explains in his letter to the Romans, "For no one is a Jew who is merely one outwardly... but a Jew is one inwardly, and circumcision is a matter of the heart, by the Spirit, not by the letter" (Romans 2:28-29). This underscores the point we made earlier: descriptive texts in Scripture reflect the reality of God's transforming work, not prescriptive requirements for salvation. Genuine obedience springs from a heart changed by God.

"By this we know"

John repeatedly uses the phrase, "And by this we know," throughout this letter. It is a call to self-reflection that echoes Paul's exhortation in 2 Corinthians 13:5: "Examine yourselves, to see whether you are in the faith. Test yourselves. Or do you not realize this about yourselves, that Jesus Christ is in you?" Notice that this call is ultimately an invitation to see Christ at work within us. Similarly, John points to the markers of the Spirit—the evidence that God is actively transforming our hearts. When we turn from rebellion and begin to crave the goodness of God, we find the Spirit guiding, shaping, and renewing our desires. This self-examination is not about measuring our own effort or accomplishments, but about discerning Christ's work in us.

Yet, as long as we remain in this flesh, there will always be a tension between our old nature and our new life in Christ. Paul captures this in Romans 7:22-25, expressing both a delight in God's law and a deep struggle with sin: "For I delight in the law of God in my inner being, but I see in my members another law waging war against the law of my mind... Wretched man that I am, who will save me from this body of death?" Here, Paul recognizes sin not merely as an external action, but as a power dwelling deep within human nature. He asks who will rescue him from his own body, yet in the same breath, he proclaims, "Thanks be to God through Jesus Christ our Lord!"

How can Paul move from such raw reflection on his struggle to a proclamation of joy? The answer follows immediately in Romans 8:1: "There is therefore now no condemnation for those who are in Christ Jesus." Before we knew the Lord, we were spiritually dead, completely enslaved to sin and blind to our own wrongdoing. Our hearts were dominated by the flesh, and there was no delight in God's law. But when we are united with Christ, we receive the Spirit of adoption (Romans 8:15). Spiritually, we are no longer slaves; the law of sin may dwell in our flesh, but it no longer has ultimate power over us. What Paul describes as this internal war between the flesh and the Spirit, John characterizes as the difference between walking in the darkness of our old nature or walking in the light of Christ.

This is precisely why Paul describes the frustration of doing what he does not want to do (Romans 7:18–20). This struggle is not a sign of defeat, but evidence that we are spiritually alive. The Spirit awakens a delight in God's law and plants a desire for holiness that was absent before. While the flesh resists, the Spirit is at work, guiding our hearts toward obedience. This ongoing tension demonstrates that sanctification is a process, not an instantaneous transformation. Growth in Christ comes from the Spirit's work within us over time.

Therefore, we do not look to the perfection of our physical actions for assurance. Because the flesh is inherently opposed to God, the law cannot produce perfection in us. Paul summarizes this inner conflict by concluding, "So then, I myself serve the law of God with my mind, but with my flesh I serve the law of sin" (Romans 7:25). He draws a sharp distinction between the inward orientation of the spirit and the outward frailty of the flesh. If the Spirit of God dwells within us, we find our assurance in this new alignment. We look to the fact that our "mind," or our inner being, now delights in and seeks after God's law, even while we groan under the limitations of our mortal bodies.

When John writes, "By this we know that we have come to know him," he is looking for this same inward alignment. He is not prescribing salvation through works; he is calling for honest self-reflection on where our loyalties lie. This echoes the warning from chapter 1: claiming fellowship with God while walking in darkness is a lie. How can someone claim to love the light and yet walk in darkness?

We do not expect those around us to be perfect, just as we are incapable of perfection ourselves. Yet, following Paul's distinction, there is a vital difference between stumbling in the weakness of the flesh and living with a mind that is still settled in darkness. Walking in the light is not about presenting an image of flawless obedience; it is about a life where the "mind" has been captured by Christ. The true Christian both strives to obey Christ's commandments and acknowledges their failures before Him. Those who appear flawless may actually be blind to their own sin, remaining in darkness. Ultimately, walking in the light is as much about seeing ourselves honestly before God—recognizing our shortcomings and relying on His grace—as it is about following His commands. This principle prepares us to consider what John emphasizes in the next verses about knowing Him through obedience and the love that is perfected in those who walk in the light.

"Know Him"

John does not use the specific words *"salvation"* or *"being saved"* in this letter. Instead, he consistently draws a distinction between those who know God and those who do not. For John, this distinction is not secondary or abstract. It is the dividing line between life and death. In the Gospel of John, Jesus speaks about knowing those who belong to Him in multiple places, most clearly in John 10, where He declares, "I am the good shepherd. I know my own and my own know me" (John 10:14). This mutual knowing defines the relationship between Christ and His people.

In our modern use of the word *know*, we often reduce it to intellectual awareness or familiarity. In that sense, nearly everyone "knows" who Jesus is. His name is among the most recognized in human history. But Scripture does not use the language of knowing in this shallow way. Biblically, to know God is to be in a real, living, relational union with Him. It speaks of belonging, covenant, and shared life. In the Old Testament, the word *know* is even used to describe the intimate covenantal bond between husband and wife. Knowledge, in this sense, is not merely information, but communion.

This is why one of the most sobering statements in all of Scripture comes from the lips of Jesus in Matthew 7:23: "I never knew you; depart from me." The issue is not that these people were unaware of Jesus or unfamiliar with religious language. The issue is that they were never in relationship with Him. They were never united to Him.

To be united to Christ by His Spirit is to know Him. Through the prophet Jeremiah, God declares that a man should not boast in his wisdom, strength, or riches, but in this alone: "that he understands and knows me" (Jeremiah 9:24). To know the Lord is to be reconciled to Him, to be brought into fellowship with Him. John will return to this language repeatedly throughout his letter, and it is essential to understand that when he speaks of knowing God, he is speaking of salvation itself.

Jesus makes this unmistakably clear in His High Priestly Prayer when He says, "And this is eternal life, that they know you, the only true God, and Jesus Christ whom you have sent"

(John 17:3). Eternal life is not merely endless existence. It is life in communion with God through the Son. As we move through this letter, we will see that John's primary concern is not merely that we affirm correct doctrine about Christ, but that we truly know the person of Christ. He returns to this theme again and again because nothing carries more weight than this single, life-defining reality. Your assurance, your joy, and your eternal life rest upon this truth: knowing the Father through the Son.

1 John 2:4-5 (ESV)
Whoever says "I know Him" but does not keep His commandments is a liar, and the truth is not in him, but whoever keeps His word, in him truly the love of God is perfected. By this we may know that we are in Him

Think back to chapter 1 of this letter. John wrote, "If we have fellowship with him, but walk in darkness, we lie and do not practice the truth" (1 John 1:6). This is another example of the descriptive text we discussed earlier. John is not instructing how to be saved; he is describing who is saved—who truly knows Him and who has the truth dwelling within. We do not need to worry about losing salvation, but we must examine ourselves honestly. Are we deceiving ourselves? People naturally pursue self-preservation and their own benefit, and eternal life is something everyone desires—even those who do not truly follow Jesus. Consider the parable of the sower (Matthew 13): some hear the good news and respond eagerly, but the seed has no root. They desire everlasting life, yet the Word never takes hold. It is almost like hedging a bet: *"I'll live this life to the fullest, but I'll also go to church and read the Bible so I can secure heaven."* Many pursue their own righteousness or their own imagined version of Jesus rather than truly submitting to Him. Jesus warns that for these, He will inevitably say, "I never knew you" (Matthew 7:23).

Have we become so skilled at self-deception that we forget it is a lie? Do we truly love the Lord, or are we attempting to manipulate Him, as a child manipulates to get what they want? God is not fooled; He does not need to examine our deeds to know our hearts. When John speaks of liars, he is not merely referring to those who lie to others; he is calling attention to those who are deceiving themselves—pursuing their own version of righteousness, their own imagined Jesus, rather than walking in the light. Recognizing this within ourselves is the first step toward genuine fellowship with God and a life transformed by His Spirit. We must reflect and ask ourselves: is the truth in me?

Does this mean that struggling with sin makes someone a liar? By no means. Sin persists in every believer, yet we are protected by our Advocate, Jesus Christ the Righteous. The evidence of a true Christian is seen not in perfection, but in a life shaped by the Spirit. Central to that evidence are two realities: keeping God's commandments and walking in His Word. Love for God expresses itself through obedience and trust in His promises, while love for our neighbor flows from a heart transformed by Him. These are not merely actions or fleeting behaviors—they are the hallmarks of the Spirit's work, the proof that the love of God is being perfected within.

This also helps us understand why John can say both that we have an Advocate when we sin and that "whoever does not keep his commandments is a liar" (1 John 2:4). He is not demanding perfect obedience; rather, he calls for honest reflection on the heart and the direction of one's life. Those who truly know Christ will show evidence of transformation, even amid struggles with sin. John's words give hope and security to believers who are being sanctified, while simultaneously warning those who walk in darkness while claiming to know Him. A life in which love for God and love for neighbor are consistently present reflects what John emphasizes throughout this letter: the Spirit actively shaping our hearts and confirming our fellowship with Him.

Despite the believer's ongoing struggle with sin, the reality that God's commandments are written on the hearts of His children will be evident. God is actively perfecting His love in those who belong to Him, and His commandments are not burdensome. The Christian life, at its core, is shaped by two foundational realities: the believer's faith, trust, and love toward God, from which flows genuine love toward his neighbor. These are the marks John highlights as evidence of true transformation, the patterns we should expect to see in those who walk in the light, and the framework through which we understand how the love of God is being perfected in His children.

Love God

To love God is to trust God. The Shema, Israel's central declaration of faith, commands: "Hear, O Israel: The LORD our God, the LORD is one. You shall love the Lord your God with all your heart and with all your soul and with all your might" (Deut. 6:4-5). This love is not mere emotion; it is a lived reality, seen in how God is the center of our thoughts, decisions, and actions. To truly love Him is to trust Him completely—trusting His promises, relying on His faithfulness, and allowing that trust to shape every aspect of life. Love of God and trust in God are inseparable, because love is demonstrated in obedience, confidence, and reliance on Him rather than in fleeting feelings or superficial devotion.

Many Christians feel their faith is weak, yet when we examine it more closely, their doubt often lies not in God but in themselves. True faith is trusting that God is capable and faithful to accomplish all He has promised. Romans 4:20-22 illustrates this principle through Abraham: "No unbelief made him waver concerning the promise of God, but he grew strong in his faith as he gave glory to God, fully convinced that God was able to do what he had promised. That is why his faith was counted to him as righteousness." Abraham was not perfect. He lied to Pharaoh, took Hagar as a concubine, and fathered Ishmael instead of waiting for God's promised son, Isaac. Yet even in these moments of doubt and sin, he did not allow unbelief in himself to cause him to waver concerning God's promises. His trust was not contingent upon his own obedience, but rested in God's faithfulness despite his failures. As Abraham witnessed God's faithfulness again and again, his confidence in God grew stronger, and that trust naturally shaped his obedience.

Hebrews 11, the "faith chapter," provides further examples. Noah built the ark not on his own wisdom or strength but by trusting God's command, which protected his family from judgment, and Moses did not lead Israel from Egypt by his own plan but by faith in God's ability to save His people. Hebrews 11:1 captures this principle: "Now faith is the assurance of things hoped for, the conviction of things not seen." This is the faith we are called to have. Even in our failures, we can trust that God will accomplish what He has promised. Jesus makes this promise concrete: He is the resurrection and the life; whoever believes in Him, though they die, will live (John 11:25-26). As our Advocate before the Father, He represents us perfectly, and our failure does not hinder His work or our salvation.

Love for God expresses itself in trust—faith in His Word, confidence in His promises, and obedience that flows from that trust. It is not perfection that demonstrates love, but reliance on Him and willingness to follow because we trust Him. This is the first and greatest commandment: to love God, fully trusting in His faithfulness.

Love your neighbor

The second commandment Jesus gives us is to love our neighbor. You may not always act perfectly in this, but the question remains: do you truly love them? Just as love for God is not merely a feeling or emotion, neither is love for your neighbor. As we have seen—and will continue to see throughout this letter—love is selfless. It is the willingness to sacrifice for others, to act without expecting anything in return, and to hope for what is best for them rather than for yourself.

Jesus demonstrated this love supremely when He went to the cross for us while we were still sinners. If Jesus modeled love in this way, we are called to love one another in the same selfless manner. It does not matter how mature we are in Christ or how much we still struggle with the sins of the flesh, as we all do. What matters is whether, when a brother or sister is in need, God's love pours out of our hearts for them. Are we driven by a love that compels us to act sacrificially, even when it costs us?

I know Christians who wrestle daily with lust, addiction, pride, jealousy, gossip, anger, or gluttony. Yet these same individuals will drop everything to help someone in need. In those moments, their own struggles, doubts, or fears fade away—their life is no longer the priority. Their salvation or personal comfort stops being the focus, and what matters most is the person in need. This is the kind of love that can only come from God.

It is this selfless love—rooted in God's Spirit—that fulfills the second commandment and demonstrates His work in the believer's life. Let us now turn to the promise of the covenant and see how God ensures this love, transforming us so that both love for Him and love for our neighbor never waver.

How God Perfects His Love in us

From the earliest days of Israel's history, the Old Testament recognizes a profound problem: the human heart is inherently hard and opposed to God. Moses repeatedly laments Israel's stubbornness and inability to trust and obey God, even in the face of His presence and provision (Exodus 32; Deuteronomy 9:6-7). God Himself identifies their hearts as resistant and rebellious, and the prophets echo the same truth: outward compliance with the law is not enough, because the heart of man is deceitful and inclined toward sin (Jeremiah 17:9; Ezekiel 11:19). Even when Israel keeps the law outwardly, their inner motivations remain corrupt, self-serving, and contrary to God's will. Jesus highlights this tension, showing that obedience to the law without the right heart still violates God's commands: "You have heard it said, 'You shall not commit adultery,' but I tell you, if you even look at a woman with lust, you have committed adultery in your heart" (Matthew 5:27-28). Paul underscores the same reality in Romans 8: the flesh is opposed to God, and our natural desires cannot fulfill His law (Romans 8:7-8). This is why transformation is necessary: the human heart, left to itself, cannot truly love God or neighbor.

What God promises in Ezekiel 36, and accomplishes in Christ, is the radical renewal of the heart through His Spirit. This transformation enables us to desire what is good and to obey God from the heart, rather than from compulsion, fear, or mere external compliance:

"And I will give you a new heart, and a new spirit I will put within you. And I will remove the heart of stone from your flesh and give you a heart of flesh. And I will put my Spirit within you, and cause you to walk in my statutes and be careful to obey my rules" (Ezekiel 36:26-27).

This new heart, received in Christ, is a heart of flesh—a heart reborn and made new by the Spirit. It cries out to God, no longer the heart of stone it once was. Scripture describes the heart of stone as deceitful, wicked, and opposed to God. Even when someone with a heart of stone follows the law outwardly, Jesus warns that the heart may still be far from God (Mark 7:6). This illustrates that people can avoid sinful actions yet remain enslaved to the desires of the heart. Many restrain themselves not out of love for God but out of fear of consequences or social stigma. Their hearts still crave sin, even if their outward behavior does not.

This is why I took us to Paul's reflection in Romans 7 earlier. We see him dealing with this very reality as he describes exactly what it looks like when a new heart of flesh exists alongside the old nature. He provides the clearest picture of the war between the new desires of the Spirit and the lingering resistance of the flesh:

"For I know that nothing good dwells in me, that is, in my flesh. For I have the desire to do what is right, but not the ability to carry it out. For I do not do the good I want, but the evil I do not want is what I keep on doing. Now if I do what I do not want, it is no longer I who do it, but sin that dwells within me. For I delight in the law of God in my inner being, but I see in my members another law waging war against the law of my mind and making me captive to the law of sin that dwells in my members."(Romans 7:18-23)

The heart that once desired only sin is now transformed to delight in God's law, even as the old nature—the flesh—continues to resist. The old and new selves are at war, and this struggle itself is evidence of the Spirit at work. If you find yourself battling with sinful desires while longing to do what is right, this is a sign that God's Spirit is alive within you. Someone with only a heart of stone would not struggle with the intention to do what is right.

His Spirit guides believers to walk in God's statutes and keep His commands. This explains why John can describe obedience as evidence of salvation: it is not the obedient who are saved, but the saved who are obedient. The obedience is not of our own will but the work of God within us. Transformation is ongoing, but the presence of God's love in our hearts—expressed through obedience, trust, and love for others—is the clearest sign that His Spirit is actively perfecting His love in us.

1 John 2:6 (ESV)
whoever says he abides in Him ought to walk in the same way in which He walked.

John again calls believers to deep self-reflection. If you claim to love Christ and to know Him, your life should bear the marks of His character. The word *"ought"* is significant—it is not a checklist for earning salvation or a standard of perfection imposed on us. Rather, it invites us to examine our hearts and ask whether the desire to walk as Christ walked is shaping the way we live. Just as I might tell my son that if he truly wants to be a football player, he ought to work on it daily—not to create the desire for the game, but to see whether that desire manifests in his choices and actions—so too does this *ought* in John's writing point to evidence of a life influenced by God's love.

Of course, one could analyze Christ's life and identify many qualities that marked His earthly ministry. Yet for clarity and focus, four stand out most clearly: love, humility, mercy, and service. While other traits—such as faithfulness—are equally important, they are reflected within these four, providing a practical framework for understanding how Christ walked. This framework helps us recognize the work of God's Spirit in ourselves and in others, guiding us to reflect His life today. With this understanding, the natural question arises: how did Christ walk, and what does it look like to follow Him in these ways?

- **Love** – Jesus demonstrated a perfect and sacrificial love, ultimately brought to fulfillment in His sacrifice on the cross. His love for the Father and for those around Him is evident in every action and word. He was firm yet gentle, and His love was expressed not merely in words, but through tangible deeds. He calls His followers to mirror this love, instructing them, "A new commandment I give to you, that you love one another: just as I have loved you, you also are to love one another" (John 13:34).

- **Humility** – Jesus walked in perfect humility. Though He was worthy of all honor and glory, He never grasped for it, but willingly took the lowest place, modeling the very mind His followers are called to imitate (Philippians 2:5-8). Rather than exalting Himself, He consistently pointed others to the Father. Even when falsely accused, mocked, and abused, He did not defend His innocence or seek vindication, but submitted Himself in quiet obedience. His humility was not weakness, but strength under control, a willing lowering of Himself for the sake of others.

- **Mercy** – Jesus was unwavering in His opposition to sin, yet deeply compassionate toward sinners. Though He alone had the right to condemn, He consistently met people with mercy, seeing beyond their failures to the image of God in which they were made. In doing so, He fulfilled His role as our merciful High Priest, one who is able to sympathize with our weaknesses and extend grace in our time of need (Hebrews 2:17). His mercy did not excuse sin, but it invited repentance, restoration, and hope for those who knew they stood in need of forgiveness.

- **Service** – Jesus embodied service as the outward expression of love, humility, and mercy. He did not lead from a place of comfort or status but willingly took the position of a servant, especially toward the least and the overlooked. He made His purpose unmistakable when He said, "For even the Son of Man came not to be served but to serve, and to give his life as a ransom for many" (Mark 10:45). This posture was not theoretical but lived out in tangible ways, most strikingly when He washed the feet of His disciples, showing that no one is above humble service (John 13:3–15). When the disciples debated greatness, Jesus redirected them by teaching that true greatness is found in lowering oneself for the sake of others, saying, "Let the greatest among you become as the youngest, and the leader as one who serves" (Luke 22:26). In Christ, service is not weakness but the very shape of godly leadership.

This manner of walking, marked by love, humility, mercy, and service, is the visible fruit of abiding in Christ. It is not produced by human effort, but by the transforming work of the Spirit within the believer. As John writes, "But whoever keeps his word, in him truly the love of God is perfected" (1 John 2:5). This perfection is not instantaneous, but formative. Believers grow from spiritual infancy toward maturity as God shapes, disciplines, and conforms them to Christ through the work He has begun in them (Philippians 1; Hebrews 12; Romans 6).

Love gives rise to obedience, and obedience reveals the Spirit's ongoing work in the life of the believer.

To walk as Christ walked, then, is both the calling of the Christian life and its evidence. When love expresses itself through humility, mercy, and sacrificial service, abiding in Christ becomes visible in ordinary, daily life.

1 John 2:7 (ESV)
Beloved, I am writing you no new commandment, but an old commandment that you had from the beginning. The old commandment is the word that you have heard.

John is deliberate and careful with his words, making it clear that he is not introducing new commandments or revealing new truths. What he writes echoes what has been proclaimed from the beginning, reflecting the teaching and example of the Lord Jesus Christ, which John personally witnessed decades earlier. His careful explanation ensures that readers understand the continuity of Christ's message and are not led to assume he is presenting something novel or burdensome.

When many people hear the word "commandments," they instinctively think of the Ten Commandments from the Law of Moses. This is largely due to popular culture and modern language. Yet in the days of the Apostles, Scripture did not commonly refer to the Law given through Moses as the "Ten Commandments" in the way we speak of it today. The Bible itself calls them the "Ten Words" (Exodus 34:28; Deuteronomy 4:13; 10:4), and the familiar title "Ten Commandments" is a later descriptive label. In reality, Moses received hundreds of commands from God, with Jewish tradition counting 613 in total. These laws are often grouped into moral, civil, and ceremonial categories, but these distinctions were developed later and are not categories Scripture explicitly uses. Moreover, the Bible frequently speaks of God's law, commandments, and precepts in a broader sense. For example, in Psalm 119, David refers to the entirety of God's Word as his law and commandments, not merely the Mosaic code. God's commands encompass all that He has spoken for the guidance and flourishing of His people.

It is also important to recognize that when Scripture speaks of "the Law," it does not always mean individual commandments. The first five books of the Bible, Genesis through Deuteronomy, are collectively called the Torah, which simply means "the Law." This is why the Hebrew Scriptures are often summarized as "the Law and the Prophets," referring to the writings of Moses and the prophets. Therefore, when Paul says something like "as the Law says" in passages like 1 Corinthians 14:21 or 34, he is not necessarily pointing to a specific command given at Sinai, but to the broader teachings of the Torah, sometimes even drawing on passages from Genesis.

This distinction matters because many Christians read passages in 1 John or Revelation about keeping the commandments and immediately conclude that Scripture is teaching salvation by law keeping. They assume John is contradicting the gospel by reintroducing the Law of Moses as a requirement for salvation. Yet this misunderstanding comes from importing modern assumptions into the biblical text rather than allowing Scripture to define its own terms.

When Scripture speaks about guarding our ways by God's law, it is not limited to individual commandments, though those certainly play a role. Rather, it refers to the whole word of God as the guiding authority for life. This is similar to how Christians today might say they seek to live their lives guided by the Bible. The emphasis is not on earning salvation through obedience, but on being shaped, instructed, and directed by God's revealed truth. God's word is presented as the means by which we gain wisdom, clarity, and direction in every area of life.

Paul expresses this beautifully in his final letter to Timothy:

"But as for you, continue in what you have learned and have firmly believed, knowing from whom you learned it and how from childhood you have been acquainted with the sacred writings, which are able to make you wise for salvation through faith in Christ Jesus. All Scripture is breathed out by God and profitable for teaching, for reproof, for correction, and for training in righteousness, that the man of God may be complete, equipped for every good work." (2 Timothy 3:14-17)

The Law of Moses

Before we can rightly understand what John means by obedience, commandments, and walking in the light, we must first be clear about what Scripture itself means when it speaks of law. John's language does not exist in isolation, nor would his original readers have separated Christ's teaching from the broader scriptural framework that shaped their understanding of God's will.

Throughout church history, confusion surrounding the law has repeatedly produced fear, legalism, and distorted views of salvation. For that reason, a brief clarification is necessary here, not to divert us from John's message, but to safeguard it. Without this foundation, John's words can easily be misunderstood as a return to the Law of Moses rather than what they truly are, pastoral encouragement rooted in the finished work of Christ.

Therefore, before we speak of the commandments of Christ, we must take a moment to understand the role of the Law of Moses within redemptive history and how Scripture itself teaches us to relate to it. Are Christians under the Law of Moses? No, and this is made clear throughout Romans 2-8 and Galatians 2-3. Yet before examining those arguments, it is important to begin where Jesus Himself began during His earthly ministry. What did Jesus teach about the law? Simply put, the law is good.

The commandments and statutes of God are not something the believer is called to despise or discard. As Paul writes in Romans 3:31, *"Do we then overthrow the law by this faith? By no means! On the contrary, we uphold the law."* The problem has never been the law itself, but how it is approached and used. Paul goes confronts the way many Jews handled the law in Romans 2:23: *"You who boast in the law dishonor God by breaking the law. For, as it is written, 'The name of God is blasphemed among the Gentiles because of you.'"*

This same posture can still be found today, where God's law is used as a means of comparison and self exaltation rather than humility. Some imagine that keeping the law establishes their righteousness, failing to see that the law does not make anyone righteous. Instead, it bears witness to the righteousness of God and exposes our need for grace.

The law was never given so that one could boast in personal righteousness, just as I do not give instructions to my children so they can look down on other children. My rules are given for guidance, not for glory. Yet some approach the law in an either/or mindset: either it is required for salvation, or it is absolutely meaningless. When a Christian says "we are not under the law" they assume we are disregarding the law as if it is now meaningless. If they read the letters to the Romans and Galatians carefully, they would see Paul addressing these misunderstandings. As he writes, *"What then shall we say? That the law is sin? By no means! Yet if it had not been for the law, I would not have known sin. For I would not have known what it is to covet if the law had not said, 'You shall not covet'"* (Romans 7:7). The Law was never given to provide life, but to provide guidance and insight so that we may see the Lord and turn to Him. It helps us recognize our need for a Savior and understand what true righteousness looks like.

The Scriptures even compare the law to a mirror, a mirror that shows us who we truly are. Just as a mirror reveals a smudge on your face or a tangle in your hair, the Word of God exposes the reality of our own unrighteousness. Yet a mirror alone is not enough. No one examines their reflection in a dark room, because without light the mirror cannot reveal what is truly there. In the same way, Scripture is the mirror, and God Himself is the light. When His light shines, our flaws are no longer hidden, and the blemishes of the heart are brought into view. This helps explain how many could possess the law and yet fail to recognize their own sin. The mirror was present, but they were not standing in the light. This is what James warns against when he speaks of those who look into the mirror and then walk away unchanged (James 1:23-24).

I have met many who claim they no longer sin, and to them I often respond that such a claim reveals darkness, not holiness. If someone truly walked in the light, they would see more clearly, not less. The greatest commandment is to love the Lord your God with all your heart, soul, and might. Anyone who honestly looks into the mirror of God's law while standing in the light of Christ will see that they fall short, not only of this command, but of all His commands.

Reflecting honestly on our lives in light of God's commands should drive us to repentance, because it reveals our need for an advocate and a propitiation. We need someone perfect who can stand in the mirror on our behalf, someone who can remove the filth and restore us. That is why we turn to Christ, who fulfills the law perfectly and cleanses us by His sacrifice.

Paul continues this argument in Galatians, addressing a conflict in the early church where Jewish Christians and Gentile Christians debated whether Gentiles were required to follow the Law of Moses, specifically circumcision. Paul strongly rebukes anyone promoting an alternative gospel, emphasizing that salvation is by faith in Christ, not by adherence to the Law. The Law was not given to attain eternal life or the promises of God; it was given after the promise to Abraham to show that salvation comes first through God's promise. He writes, "Is the law then contrary to the promises of God? Certainly not! For if a law had been given that could give life, then righteousness would indeed be by the law. But the Scripture imprisoned everything under sin, so that the promise by faith in Jesus Christ might be given to those who believe" (Galatians 3:21-22).

Paul explains the purpose of the Law further: "Now before faith came, we were held captive under the law, imprisoned until the coming faith would be revealed. So then, the law was our guardian until Christ came, in order that we might be justified by faith. But now that faith has come, we are no longer under a guardian, for in Christ Jesus you are all sons of God, through faith" (Galatians 3:23-26). The law functioned as a guardian, protecting Israel until Christ came. Now that Christ has come, believers are not under the guardianship of the Law, but under the law of the Spirit. This does not mean we forsake the Law given to Moses, because every word from God is beneficial to us. As Jesus Himself quotes in Matthew from the Old Testament, "Man shall not live by bread alone, but by every word that proceeds from the mouth of God" (Matthew 4:4).

You will often hear the statement, "But Christ did not come to abolish the law," in response to the claim that Christians are not under the legal demands of the Law of Moses. This is correct—Christ does not abolish the law. However, those who say this will often omit second half of the Lord's statement. "I have not come to abolish them, but to fulfill them" (Matthew 5:17). It remains in effect, and those who are not in Him will ultimately be judged by it. Yet for those who are in Christ, He fulfills the law on our behalf.

Romans 8 makes this clear: "God accomplished what the law, weakened by sinful flesh, could not do. By sending His Son in the likeness of sinful flesh, He condemned sin in the flesh so that the righteous requirement of the law might be fulfilled in us" (Romans 8:3-4). No one is justified by works of the law (Galatians 2:16), because breaking even one commandment means failing to uphold them all (James 2:10). Therefore, the law is not abolished, but apart from Christ, it brings condemnation.

Jesus, serving as our perfect Advocate, kept the law flawlessly, so that the law's demands would be fully satisfied in Him. If we stand alone before the Father, we are judged by the law and found guilty. But when we stand in Christ, the Father looks upon His Son—faithful and perfect—who represents us. In Him, our sins are paid for, and our righteousness is established. Christ fulfills the law for those who are in Him, and through Him, the law becomes a guide, not a source of condemnation.

"No New Commandment, but an Old Commandment"

Having seen the purpose and fulfillment of the Law, we return now to John's words, where he emphasizes the enduring commandment at the heart of all God's law. John is not introducing new words or commands, but rather expounding upon what his readers have already learned. He reminds them that this has always been the summary of God's commands from the very beginning. This is not a novel teaching; they have heard it before—in the Law, the Prophets, and the teachings of Jesus Christ our Lord. John's careful language underscores that, like the other Apostles, he is not creating new doctrines. This is particularly important in the context of Jewish opponents who might accuse the Apostles of adding to God's revelation. The commandment John emphasizes has been present from the beginning: love one another.

This command is rooted deeply in the Law of Moses. As Leviticus 19:18 states, *"You shall love your neighbor as yourself: I am the LORD"* and "You shall treat the stranger who sojourns with you as the native among you, and you shall love him as yourself." These instructions are not merely ceremonial or civil requirements; they reveal the heart of God's law. Love for others is a central principle that Scripture repeatedly highlights, long before the coming of Christ.

Jesus Himself underscores this command as the most important. When asked which commandment is greatest, He responds: "Love the Lord your God with all your heart and soul, and love your neighbor as yourself. Upon these two commandments, all the Law and the Prophets hang." (Matthew 22:37-40) The words of Christ echo the foundational truth that God's law is fulfilled in love, and this emphasis is carried forward by the Apostles in their teaching.

Paul reinforces this truth in his letters to the early church. Writing to the Galatians, he makes clear that outward rituals like circumcision are meaningless apart from faith expressed through love: "For in Christ Jesus neither circumcision nor uncircumcision counts for anything, but only faith working through love." (Galatians 5:6) He continues, "For the whole law is fulfilled in one word: 'You shall love your neighbor as yourself.'" (Galatians 5:14) Here again, we see that love is the heart of God's law—timeless, unchanging, and now made alive through faith in Christ.

With this understanding, we see that John is not giving a new commandment, but reminding believers of the enduring command that has always been at the center of God's revelation: love one another.

1 John 2:8 (ESV)
At the same time, it is a new commandment that I am writing to you, which is true in Him and in you, because the darkness is passing away and the true light is already shining.

This is where John's language becomes nuanced. He tells us that he is not writing a new commandment, and yet immediately speaks of one. The key to understanding this distinction is recognizing the difference between legal obligation and moral truth. The Law of Moses is good, because it reveals God's righteous standard, but it also carries a legal demand and a sentence of death for those who break it. In Christ, believers are no longer legally bound to that covenant or held liable under its penalties. Yet the moral truths the law declares do not disappear. The Law of Moses and the Law of Christ share real moral overlap, the same values and ethical aims, but they function in different covenantal contexts. One binds the sinner under condemnation, the other operates through mercy and grace. This is how John can say the commandment is not new in substance, yet new in reality, as he explains in verses 7 and 8.

To illustrate this, consider how laws function in different nations. I am a citizen of the United States and therefore bound by its laws. My friend in South Africa is not under U.S. law, and I am not under South African law. Yet we may both refrain from actions like murder or theft, because the moral core overlaps. The difference lies in jurisdiction and consequence. As a U.S. citizen, I live under a specific legal system with its own protections and penalties. In another nation, those legal realities would be entirely different. In the same way, the Law of Moses governed Israel under a covenant of law, while the Law of the Spirit governs those who are in Christ. Both call us to love our neighbor, but the context, consequences, and benefits are not the same. What was once a command that condemned now becomes a command fulfilled in Christ and expressed through love empowered by the Spirit.

Under the Law of Moses, breaking the law brought a curse—ultimately, death. Every transgression brought condemnation. Under the Law of Christ, however, our debt has been paid through Jesus, our Advocate. Verse 2 reminds us: "If anyone sins, we have an Advocate with the Father, Jesus Christ the righteous." In Him, the harsh penalty of the law no longer falls upon us, even as we still strive to obey.

Returning to 1 John 2:8, John explains that this commandment is new because it is now "true in him and in you." This is the pivot point of the new covenant. While the substance of the command—to love—has existed from the beginning, its reality has changed because the "true light" of Christ is now actively shining within the believer. It is no longer an external requirement carved on stone, but a living reality written on our hearts. This is how the old command becomes new: it is now empowered by the Spirit and free from the curse of the law. What was once a burden placed upon a stubborn heart has become a gift realized through a new spirit, moving us from the darkness of mere obligation into the light of a transformed life.

In the flesh, our hearts were too hard to obey God's commands. This was not a minor flaw but a deep-seated resistance. Moses noted that despite seeing God's wonders, the people lacked a heart to understand (Deut. 29:4). By the time of the prophets, this stubbornness had reached a peak; Ezekiel described a "hard forehead and a stubborn heart" (Ezek. 3:7), and Zechariah famously declared their hearts had become "diamond-hard," making them impenetrable to the words sent by God's Spirit (Zech. 7:12).

Yet the promise of transformation was woven into the scriptural narrative from the start. Long before the New Covenant was fully revealed, God promised to circumcise the hearts of

His people so they might truly love Him (Deut. 30:6). We see this longing in David's cry for a clean heart and a willing spirit (Ps. 51:10-12) and in Jeremiah's prophecy of a law written not on stone, but on the heart (Jer. 31:33). Isaiah even points to the outcome of this work: God dwelling with the contrite to revive their spirits (Isa. 57:15). In Christ, these ancient promises move from prophecy to reality. The light that was promised is now shining, and the heart that was once stone is now responsive to the love of God.

This transformation from darkness into light forms the necessary backdrop for what John says next. The evidence of walking in the light is not found in a verbal claim or theological assertion, but in the reality of a heart that has been changed by God. Those who have been transferred out of darkness now live under a different reality altogether. As Paul reminds us, we have been delivered from the domain of darkness and brought into the kingdom of God's beloved Son (Col. 1:13-14). With this in view, John now turns to the visible outworking of that transfer, specifically how the light of Christ is revealed in our love toward others.

1 John 2:9-11 (ESV)
Whoever says he is in the light and hates his brother is still in darkness. Whoever loves his brother abides in the light, and in him there is no cause for stumbling. But whoever hates his brother is in the darkness and walks in the darkness, and does not know where he is going, because the darkness has blinded his eyes.

In these verses, John returns to the sharp contrast he established in the opening of his letter—the distinction between a life characterized by darkness and one that abides in the light. He makes it clear that a verbal claim to be "in the light" is hollow if it is accompanied by hatred toward a brother. Instead of merely repeating a command, John is describing a state of being. Those who love are existing in the light, a reality that provides a clear path for their feet. Jesus reinforced this principle during His ministry, noting that walking in the day prevents stumbling because the light of this world is present, whereas walking in the night inevitably leads to a fall because the light is absent (John 11:9-10). This is a theme that runs deep through the biblical tradition; the wisdom literature of the Old Testament warns that the way of the wicked is like deep darkness, leaving them ignorant of the very obstacles that cause their ruin (Prov. 4:19). Peter likewise cautions that a lack of spiritual fruit leads to a form of blindness and nearsightedness, where one forgets the very cleansing that was meant to define their new life (2 Pet. 1:9-10). For John, the presence of light is not just a concept, but a practical safeguard that enables the believer to see the path ahead.

Walking in the light involves more than moral effort; it is the transforming presence of God revealing what was hidden. Recognition of sin and the practice of confession flow naturally from this light, not from sudden personal improvement.

To picture this, imagine a world of total darkness where everyone has been blind for generations. In this world, people have learned to navigate quite well using only their other senses. They make decisions based on what feels comfortable, what smells pleasant, or what sounds reassuring, entirely unaware of the unseen realities around them. Because they cannot see, they assume their environment is pristine and their own lives are orderly.

When the Gospel enters, it is like a sudden light piercing that darkness. The transformation is not a magic fix; in fact, the first thing it brings is a sense of crisis. Even though the vision of these people is blurry at first, they begin to see the truth about their surroundings and themselves. They notice the decay on the walls they once leaned on for support and the contamination on the very things they thought were clean. The light does not create these flaws; it simply ends the delusion that they weren't there. For the first time, they aren't just guessing based on how they feel—they are seeing based on what is true.

The presence of this light provokes three possible responses. Some react with anger, refusing to believe what the light reveals and suppressing the truth because of their own unrighteousness, as Paul describes in Romans 1:18-21, and as Jesus warned in John 3:19, hating the light because it exposes their darkness. Others experience worldly grief: they acknowledge sin but attempt to fix themselves apart from God, working hard yet never achieving true restoration, because the light is around them but not in them. Godly grief, by contrast, recognizes personal sin and dependence on a Savior, producing a contrite heart that runs to Christ for cleansing and restoration. Those who respond in this way receive the light internally, and while old habits may linger, they no longer walk in darkness. Just as a formerly blind person initially navigates a room with tentative hands, a believer may stumble as they learn to live in the light, but they gradually grow in discernment and obedience.

John's illustration underscores a sobering truth: a person who claims to have sight but continues to live as though blind is a liar. True light transforms a life over time. While believers may stumble, they are now guided by the Spirit, who steadily shapes their discernment, love, and obedience. This is why I return once more to the words of Paul in Colossians, as they provide the definitive legal and spiritual ground for this change: God has delivered us from the domain of darkness and transferred us into the kingdom of His beloved Son, in whom we have redemption and the forgiveness of sins (Col. 1:13-14). We revisit this truth because it is the very engine of the Christian life; we are not merely trying to see better in the dark, we have been moved into an entirely different kingdom. This reality echoes the opening of John's letter: God is light, and in Him there is no darkness at all. Those who walk in the light, though imperfectly, reveal the presence of His Spirit in their hearts, while those who claim fellowship with Him yet persist in darkness demonstrate that the truth is not in them. The visible evidence of this transfer—love for others, confession of sin, and obedience to God's commands—is the fruit of a heart that has truly changed its residence.

Abiding in the Light

Whoever loves his brother abides in the light. His eyes have been opened; he has seen the magnitude of what Christ has done. In this light, he begins to see people for who they truly are—bearers of the divine image—and he sees himself clearly enough to know he has no standing to look down on anyone. Conversely, the man who hates his brother remains entombed in darkness. He is blind to his own wretchedness and his own failures, and thus he believes it is acceptable to withhold the very forgiveness and love he himself requires. He has no love in him because he has no light in him.

Does God's love pour out from you? Scripture is unwavering: all have sinned and fall short of the glory of God. Even as Christians, we continue to wrestle with the remnants of sin. Yet, I often see believers interpret this ongoing struggle as evidence that they are not truly saved. John, however, shifts our focus. His reflection is not centered on the absence of a struggle, but on the presence of Christ's light and love within that struggle.

Rather than fixating primarily on the sin you wrestle with, I ask you to reflect on the love that now remains. Do you find it difficult to show mercy? Do you find it difficult to love? Certainly, we all experience seasons of frustration and anger, but does that anger prevent you from wanting what is best for others? Does it stifle your desire for their good? I challenge you to look past your flaws for a moment and recognize a love within you that cannot be adequately explained apart from the presence of Christ.

To illustrate this, I look at my own life. I battle the flesh just like anyone else. The specific face of that sin may change—shifting from lust or gluttony to coveting or anger—but the true war is with the flesh itself. When people make foolish claims about the faith, I feel a defensive heat rise within me. When I see others with fewer financial burdens, I feel the pull of envy. Yet, the moment I encounter someone in need, my heart stirs to help them, regardless of who they are. My deepest desire is to love people in every aspect.

When someone acts wickedly toward me, my flesh may crave a strike in return, but my heart desires their repentance. There is a war raging within my members—the flesh against the Spirit. My flesh wants to hate, but my Spirit wants to love. We often sense the passions of the flesh and fail to recognize that the very conviction we feel is evidence of God's love at work. The reason we struggle with our decisions is not the absence of grace, but the presence of it.

When I look back to who I was before Christ, there was no battle. There was no regret. I have the words "No Regrets" tattooed on my arm, yet I committed acts that I absolutely should regret. I pursued women solely for sexual gratification, using them with calculated affection only to forget them once I had obtained what I wanted. I did not dread this behavior; I bragged about it. I sold drugs to people who were destroying their lives and felt no guilt. I was involved in violent altercations that left people hospitalized, yet I felt no remorse. The closest thing to regret was the fear of being caught. There was no war within me because there was only my own desire.

Everything changed when the Lord saved me. Early in my walk, the old habits clung to me. I made impulsive decisions and spoke words that later disgusted me. But then I began to experience a new sensation: an internal weight, a personal disgust, a holy regret. Where did this come from? It could only have originated from the Spirit of God. For the first time, I truly understood my own ways. That recognition troubled me deeply, but it also drove me closer to the light.

Ten years later, I am not the man I was before I was saved, nor am I even the same person I was when I first came to Christ. This does not mean I am sinless; I still feel the pull of the flesh toward the actions that once defined me. But I see God's presence in the war itself. Despite my weaknesses, I see Him at work, conforming me. I walk in the light, and that light exposes my flaws daily.

The man who walks in darkness remains like the old man he once was. He does not confess his sins; he claims he has none. He ignores the very things that would now make us sick to our stomachs. He lives comfortably in the dark, while we feel the weight of the darkness that still clings to our flesh.

There are only two standards you should bring into your personal reflection. The first is the Lord Jesus Christ. He is the standard of righteousness. When we keep our eyes on Him, no believer can look down on another, for we all fall short of His perfection. The second standard is the "old man"—who you were before the cross. When I look to Christ, I see that I am in constant need of a Savior. When I look to my past, I recognize that I am no longer that man. My calling is to strive daily to be more like Christ while rejoicing in the fact that I am no longer who I was in my brokenness.

Even in our failures, if we are grieving our sin, we are walking in obedience to the light. We love the law of God because His Spirit dwells within us. The man who walks in the light, though he may fall, rises again. His heart is fixed on God. That Spirit convicts him when he is wrong and reveals the path he ought to take. John's language is intentional; it brings comfort to the faithful and conviction to the unrepentant, always keeping the Gospel at the center of the frame.

1 John 2:12 (ESV)
I am writing to you, little children, because your sins are forgiven for His name's sake.

At this point in the letter, John pauses his ethical exhortations to speak directly to the hearts of his readers. Verses 12 through 14 function almost like a rhythmic hymn or a prayerful interlude, standing out from the surrounding text through their repetitive, almost musical structure. Having just pressed the believer to examine whether they are truly walking in the light, John now pivots to offer the comfort and reassurance of their standing in Christ. By returning to the tender address *"little children,"* he is not merely repeating a greeting; he is embodying the role of an intimate father-figure, carefully wrapping the difficult truths he has just presented in a mantle of pastoral care and encouragement. This affectionate language echoes the words Jesus used to comfort His disciples in the Upper Room (John 13:33), and John employs it here to ensure that his *"little children"* are not overwhelmed by the weighty demands of the Law of Christ, but instead are anchored in the steadfast certainty of the Gospel.

His opening words here also echo and reinforce the foundational truths introduced in the first chapter. He is intentionally grounding the believer once more in the reality that their sins have been forgiven, emphasizing that this forgiveness rests entirely on God's initiative and not on human merit or achievement. In chapter one, forgiveness is tied to the repentant heart that acknowledges sin; in the beginning of chapter two, it is grounded in Christ's intercessory advocacy on our behalf. Now, John reveals the ultimate motivation behind this grace: forgiveness is granted for His name's sake, reminding believers that God's mercy is rooted in His glory, His faithfulness, and His unwavering character.

We can summarize John's progression clearly:
The Repentant Heart explains *who* receives forgiveness.
Christ as our Advocate explains *how* we are forgiven.
God's Glory explains *why* we are forgiven.

This clarification is essential for the believer's peace. You are not forgiven because you walk in the light; rather, you walk in the light because you are forgiven. Obedience is not the requirement for salvation, but the fruit of it. John uses the perfect tense here, indicating that these are completed actions with ongoing results. These are not fragile or temporary conditions; they are settled classifications for those in Christ.

For His Name's Sake

What does it mean that we are forgiven "for His name's sake"? It means God forgives and saves us for His own glory. It is His blood that cleanses, His obedience that is credited to us, His crucifixion that sets us free, and His resurrection that gives us life. From beginning to end, salvation belongs to the Lord.

We are not saved so that we may eventually look at one another and brag about being "impressive Christians." We are a people chosen and saved for the express purpose of bringing glory to Him. Jesus gives us a profound picture of this in His high priestly prayer:

"Father, the hour has come; glorify your Son that the Son may glorify you... I have manifested your name to the people whom you gave me out of the world... All mine are yours, and yours are mine, and I am glorified in them" (John 17:1, 6, 10).

This is the beauty of the Gospel rooted in the Trinity. The Father gives the Son to demonstrate His love; the Son willingly takes on flesh to save those the Father has given Him. The Son saves His sheep so that the Father is glorified, and the Father gives life to the sheep so that the Son is glorified.

Yet this divine work does not stop at the cross or the empty tomb; it is applied and sustained by the Holy Spirit. If the Father originates our salvation and the Son achieves it, the Spirit is the one who secures it within us. He is the one who bears witness to our spirits that we are children of God, silencing the accusations of the enemy. He is the seal upon the believer's heart—a divine mark of ownership that cannot be broken. And He is the faithful guardian of our inheritance, preserving us through every trial until we reach our final home. The Father sends, the Son redeems, and the Spirit preserves. Because the entire Godhead is committed to this work, not one for whom Christ died will ever be lost.

This commitment is not a new theme introduced in the New Testament. The prophets proclaimed this *"for His sake"* motivation long before Christ came, showing that God has always been the primary mover in the redemption of His people:

Psalm 106:8: *"Yet he saved them for his name's sake, that he might make known his mighty power."*

Isaiah 43:25: *"I, I am he who blots out your transgressions for my own sake, and I will not remember your sins."*

Isaiah 48:11: *"For my own sake, for my own sake, I do it... My glory I will not give to another."*

The Security of the Glory

When you grasp that your salvation is a display of God's glory rather than a response to your performance, the beauty of the Gospel begins to shine. You can submit to Him fully—not out of a fear of failing, but out of confidence in His faithfulness. He saves you because He said He would.

The Apostle Paul echoes this in Ephesians 1:13-14, noting that when we believed, we were "sealed with the promised Holy Spirit, who is the guarantee of our inheritance... to the praise of his glory." This seal is unbreakable. If it were not, God's glory would be compromised. Belief is not just acknowledging facts; it is being "fully convinced," like Abraham, that God is able to do exactly what He promised (Romans 4:21).

God is the one who begins the work, and He is the one who completes it (Philippians 1:6). No failure on your part can overturn what He has established for His own sake. When we sin, we are not cast out; we simply return to the light and the Advocate who has already secured our standing.

> *1 John 2:13-14 (ESV)*
> *I am writing to you, fathers, because you know Him who is from the beginning. I am writing to you, young men, because you have overcome the evil one. I write to you, children, because you know the Father. I write to you, fathers, because you know Him who is from the beginning. I write to you, young men, because you are strong and the word of God abides in you, and you have overcome the evil one.*

John's pastoral encouragement is not limited to those young in the faith; it extends to the mature, whom he addresses as fathers. This rhythmic hymn is a gift to every believer, regardless of their stage of life. John knows that his letter contains heavy warnings, and he is aware that there are voices in this world constantly trying to mislead the faithful. While his earlier words drew a sharp line between the children of God and the liars, he does not continue with such weighty language without first offering a consistent reminder of the security we have in Christ. To the faithful, he declares: you know Him who is from the beginning. As we have seen, in John's vocabulary, to know God is synonymous with salvation—it is a deep, relational certainty that anchors this entire letter.

This truth provides necessary peace to those who might be troubled by the exposure of the liars, or by other challenging passages such as Jesus' warning: "Depart from me, I never knew you" (Matt. 7:23). I frequently encounter believers who live in a shadow of fear, wondering if they will hear those words one day. Yet John writes with an almost rhythmic tenderness to assure us that it is possible to know that you know Him. Jesus Himself anchors this security in John 10:27-28:

"My sheep hear my voice, and I know them, and they follow me. I give them eternal life, and they will never perish, and no one will snatch them out of my hand."

If you are in Christ, you need not fear the words "I never knew you." The Lord Jesus is not a liar; He will not tell His sheep, whom He has known since before the foundation of the world, that He never knew them. No one who truly knows Him will perish. This is the promise we are called to trust. In Christ, we have more than a mere hope of forgiveness; we have the assurance that we are known by God and have an Advocate with the Father.

Addressing the Mixed Multitude

While John issues severe warnings to those who walk in darkness, his letter is not intended to keep the believer in a state of perpetual panic. He writes to the little children so they may have confidence in their forgiveness. He writes to the fathers so they may rest in the certainty of Christ's eternal nature. He writes to the young men—those in the heat of spiritual battle—to remind them that they have already overcome the evil one. This victory is not achieved through personal grit, but through the Word of God that abides in them. John does not want those who believe in the Lord Jesus to find fear in his words, even as he exposes the liars among them.

This brings us to a vital observation regarding the balance of the New Testament. Scripture consistently holds together two realities: the absolute security of the believer and the sober warnings against apostasy. When misunderstood, these warnings can be twisted to convince young believers that salvation can be lost or that their seal with the Spirit can somehow be broken. We must remember that most New Testament letters were not written to individuals in isolation, but were read publicly to entire congregations. The Apostles were fully aware that the visible church was a mixed multitude, containing both the faithful and the false.

Jude describes certain people who crept in unnoticed (Jude 4), and Paul warns of fierce wolves arising from within the church itself (Acts 20:29). Because the Apostles recognized this reality, they refused to give a false sense of security to those who were only among the people of God outwardly while denying Him inwardly. Their letters, therefore, offer a double-edged sword: profound comfort and assurance to the true believer, but stern conviction to the religious pretender.

Therefore, when John speaks sharply about those who walk in darkness and then turns to address those in the faith, it is not a contradiction. In 1 John, the author is not concerned that a true believer might lose their salvation; on the contrary, he explicitly states that he writes so that we may have confidence. His warnings are a diagnostic tool meant to protect the peace of the sheep by exposing the nature of the wolf. When John addresses the liar, he is protecting the flock; but when he addresses you—the child, the young man, the father—he is reminding you that your victory is already won. The Spirit who is in you is greater than the one who is in the world, and the Word that abides in you is the very power that has already overcome the evil one. By exposing the nature of falsehood, John provides the tools necessary to discern truth, inviting us to examine our hearts honestly—not to find reasons for doubt, but to recognize the evidence of God's work within us and to rest with total confidence in His presence.

1 John 2:15-16 (ESV)
Do not love the world or the things in the world. If anyone loves the world, the love of the Father is not in him. For all that is in the world—the desires of the flesh and the desires of the eyes and the pride of life—is not from the Father but is from the world.

Here we encounter some of the most timeless and necessary counsel given to Christians past, present, and future. John has just poured out pastoral assurance and affection, addressing his readers as little children, fathers, and young men. Now, as an elder in the faith nearing the end of his life, he delivers a direct and weighty exhortation that every believer must take seriously. This is not a passing remark, but a foundational instruction that demands careful attention.

"Do not love the world."

Early in my walk with Christ, this command unsettled me deeply. What does John mean when he says, "Do not love the world"? Does not Scripture repeatedly command us to love? Is not one of the most familiar verses in the Bible, "For God so loved the world"? And is it not John himself who recorded those words in his Gospel? How can the same Apostle now turn around and tell us not to love the world?

That confusion arose from how I was reading Scripture. Like many young believers, I often approached individual verses in isolation, without giving sufficient attention to their broader context. Read that way, this command can sound contradictory. But when we read John carefully and in context, his meaning becomes clear.

The first question we must ask is simple but essential: what does John mean by "the world"? The Greek word used here is *kosmos*,[3] and it carries several distinct meanings depending on context. One meaning refers to creation itself, the ordered universe. John is certainly not commanding us to despise God's creation. Scripture consistently calls us to marvel at the works of His hands. We are free to delight in a beautiful landscape, a radiant sunset, or the intricacy of the natural world, so long as our delight does not terminate on the gift rather than the Giver.

---

3. **κόσμος (kosmos)** has a range of meanings in the New Testament depending on context:
   (1) the created order or universe, (2) humanity as a whole, (3) the fallen world system in rebellion against God, opposed to His rule and values. — Alexander Souter, *A Pocket Lexicon to the Greek New Testament*, 138–139

Loving creation as an expression of worship toward the Creator is entirely appropriate.

A second meaning of *kosmos* refers to humanity as a whole. This is the sense used in John 3:16, where God's love for the world speaks of His love for people. Clearly, John is not contradicting the command to love our neighbors, our families, our enemies, and even those who persecute us. Scripture repeatedly affirms that we are to love people as Christ has loved us.

The third meaning of *kosmos* is the one John has in view here: the world system in active rebellion against God. This is the world that glorifies sin, exalts pride, celebrates selfishness, and rejects God's authority. This usage appears in statements such as Jesus' words, "You are not of this world, but I chose you out of the world" (John 15:19). It refers not to creation or people, but to the fallen order opposed to God. This is what John commands us not to love. Do not love its values, its priorities, or its rebellion.

John reinforces this point by echoing what he has already taught. Just as one cannot walk in darkness while being in the light, one cannot love a world that is hostile to God while also possessing the love of the Father. Scripture consistently affirms this connection, declaring that "the fear of the LORD is hatred of evil" (Prov. 8:13). If God's love truly abides in you, you cannot cherish the very things that draw the heart away from Him.

To ensure his readers understand precisely what he means, John defines the world he warns against in verse 16. These three categories—the desires of the flesh, the desires of the eyes, and the pride of life—capture the core of worldly temptation and the essence of fallen desire. As we examine them, it is important to reflect not only on how visibly they dominate the culture around us, but also on how persistently they remain within our own flesh.

Notice carefully that John does not say these desires will be absent from the believer. Instead, he tells us not to love them. These desires reflect the ongoing reality of our sin nature. Paul points to these same struggles in Romans 7, describing the impulses that wage war against our minds, and elsewhere emphasizes taking every thought captive to Christ (2 Cor. 10:5). He does not claim these impulses vanish, but he calls believers to resist them, delighting in God's law even as the flesh pulls in the opposite direction.

As we walk through these categories, do not fall into condemnation. You will recognize these desires in yourself, just as every believer does. John has already reminded us that when we sin, we have an Advocate with the Father. His purpose here is not to crush you, but to expose the battlefield so that you may fight wisely. Your spirit has been made new, but your flesh still belongs to this fallen world. All sin flows from these three streams, and therefore we must neither love them nor the world that celebrates them.

The Three Streams of Sin

The first is the **desires of the flesh**, often translated as the lusts of the flesh. This refers not merely to passing interest, but to selfish craving. These desires seek gratification at any cost. They manifest in sexual immorality, gluttony, drunkenness, and indulgence, but they also appear in subtler forms: choosing comfort over sacrifice, ease over love, self satisfaction over service. The flesh constantly whispers that our needs must come first.

We often imagine Satan as our greatest enemy, yet Scripture reminds us that our own flesh is far more dangerous. Satan does not need to force us to sin. Our flesh is fully capable of doing that on its own. In many ways, modern culture does his work for him by constantly feeding our appetites. Endless entertainment saturated with sexuality, advertising that glorifies indulgence, and media that normalizes excess all appeal directly to the flesh.

It is like placing a perfectly prepared meal in front of someone who has just sworn off it after a lifetime of indulgence. The taste is not forgotten overnight. Now imagine that person surrounded by images, stories, and celebrations devoted entirely to glorifying that very thing. It is no wonder the struggle feels overwhelming.

For those who have battled addiction, whether to substances, lust, or other sins, the analogy cuts even deeper. Trying to quit while constantly surrounding yourself with reminders and glorifications of the very thing you are trying to leave behind only intensifies the struggle. Our flesh was not merely entertained by sin; it was enslaved to it.

The second category is the **desires of the eyes**. Here we find coveting, envy, lust, and judgment. We long for what we see others possess. We measure ourselves against others and decide who deserves more and who deserves less. Even when we cannot have something, we still desire it by lingering over it. This feeds the cravings of the flesh and deepens dissatisfaction.

The third and most subtle danger is the **pride of life**. Unlike the first two, which center on desire, this one revolves around self importance. It is the belief that our worth, security, and meaning exist apart from God. It reveals itself in entitlement, self sufficiency, and quiet rebellion. When someone says, "God owes me," whatever follows is the pride of life. When we assume tomorrow is guaranteed, when we view ourselves as more deserving than others, or when we cling to this life as though it were ultimate, the pride of life is at work.

While these three categories are presented individually, they are deeply interconnected. The desires of the flesh fuel the desires of the eyes, while the pride of life convinces us that we deserve the very things we crave. Jesus calls us to deny ourselves and take up our cross, yet the pride of life demands the opposite, insisting that self-preservation and personal fulfillment are our highest aims. This mindset permeates much of the modern world, particularly in cultures obsessed with comfort, success, and personal achievement. In truth, show me any sin, and at least one of these three elements will be present.

Many of us who live in comfort and relative safety can easily fall into the trap of the pride of life, assuming that tomorrow is promised and that our security and well-being are guaranteed. This mindset can lull us into a false sense of control, causing us to cling to the world rather than to God. Yet the reality of the Christian life has always carried cost. In just the last couple of weeks as I am writing this, violence against believers has included over a hundred Christians killed in the Democratic Republic of Congo, an Iraqi Christian murdered in Europe for proclaiming the Gospel, five Christian converts jailed in Iran for leaving the Islamic faith, and public figures assassinated for their beliefs—and by the time this book reaches you, countless more examples will have arisen. Scripture answers this honestly: faithfulness to Christ has always carried a cost.

John himself writes as the last living Apostle. His fellow Apostles were murdered, and his own brother James was executed early on. John was preserved through attempted execution and exile, not because his life was more valuable, but because God's purposes differed. Whether we live or die, all is for the glory of God. To cling to this life as if it were ultimate would be to give in to the pride of life, assuming security and significance apart from Him.

John's warning carries particular weight in times of persecution: do not love this world, do not cling to it. Its value is fleeting, temporary, and ultimately deceptive. Scripture reminds us that what is truly valuable is unseen—the eternal kingdom of God.

Prosperity teachers often promise comfort, wealth, and safety as signs of God's favor. God may grant such things, but never as ultimate ends and never as guarantees in this life. He is not committed to our comfort for comfort's sake. All things, whether prosperity or suffering, or life or death, exist to reveal His glory and to shape His people. The pride of life whispers that tomorrow is promised, that security can be achieved apart from God, but John calls us to renounce such illusions and place our hope wholly in the eternal, unshakable kingdom of Christ.

1 John 2:17 (ESV)
And the world is passing away along with its desires, but whoever does the will of God abides forever.

John's closing words give us the fundamental reason we should not set our hearts on worldly things. The world is passing away along with its desires. The very things people cling to are fleeting and will not endure. Why, then, would we, knowing they are temporary, continue to hold onto them? If I cling to what I confess is perishing, one of two truths must be evident: either I do not truly believe it will pass away, or I love it so much that I am willing to hold onto it until it burns my hand before letting it go. Both reveal the heart of the wicked. Those who bind themselves to what is perishing will perish with it, but whoever does the will of God abides forever. We are not called to treasure what is fleeting, but what is eternal.

Imagine placing two piggy banks in front of you. One can be accessed at any time, its contents immediately available for spending or consumption, while the other remains sealed until the future, untouchable and secure. I then tell you that I will inevitably return and destroy the first piggy bank, erasing everything inside, while the second will last forever, its contents untouched and indestructible. Where would you deposit your money? The answer should be obvious. Why would anyone place even a single penny into the first if they truly believed it could vanish at any moment? And yet, as Christians, we often do precisely that, building up treasures here on earth, fully aware that Christ will return and everything here will pass away. Every dollar we hoard, every convenience we chase, every comfort we accumulate—these are like coins in the first piggy bank, destined to vanish.

Jesus makes this point unmistakably clear in Matthew 6:19-21:

"Do not lay up for yourselves treasures on earth, where moth and rust destroy and where thieves break in and steal, but lay up for yourselves treasures in heaven, where neither moth nor rust destroys and where thieves do not break in and steal. For where your treasure is, there your heart will be also."

This is precisely what John means when he warns against loving the world. If your heart clings to the world, it is anchored there. If it loves the Lord, it is anchored in Him. The first piggy bank represents the world; the second represents the kingdom. You will build your treasure in one or the other.

Does this mean we cannot save money or build anything in this life? Absolutely not. The question is whether what we are building has eternal value. If it impacts nothing beyond the temporal, it is ultimately wasted effort. Imagine looking a thousand years into the future, standing in eternity before your Lord. Would what you are investing your time, energy, and resources into today have mattered at all?

When I say "Christ-centered," I mean that your work, your resources, and your efforts are oriented toward the kingdom of God—toward loving Him and loving others—rather than merely personal comfort, status, or self-satisfaction. Success in itself is not inherently wrong; the problem is the intent of the heart. Just as sin is not only a matter of action but the orientation of the heart behind the action, so too is every earthly effort evaluated by its intent. I know many highly successful people whose work is exemplary—not for personal gain, but because they use their influence, resources, and talents to spread the Gospel, care for the hurting, and build relationships that point others to Christ.

Jesus Himself underscores this principle in Luke 16:9, calling His followers to use worldly wealth to "make friends for yourselves by means of unrighteous wealth, so that when it fails they may receive you into the eternal dwellings." In other words, our time, effort, and even material resources should be invested in relationships and actions that have eternal significance. A Christ-centered life is not opposed to accomplishment or prosperity; it simply reorients the aim of all our efforts toward what will endure beyond this fleeting world. Whether working for a company, building a business, or pursuing a hobby, the guiding question remains: is Christ truly at the center? Are your aims to glorify God and serve others, or are they primarily self-directed?

A Work Trip

Consider this illustrative story, which has stayed with me since I first heard it. Though the details are imagined, the lesson it conveys is profound and eye-opening. A man was sent on a work trip across the country. For two weeks, he would be in another state attending training events. He had never traveled before and was brimming with excitement. Upon arrival, he checked into his hotel and marveled at the room—it was spacious, immaculately clean, and had a view that made him pause. Even though the room had everything he needed for his stay, he began to wonder how he could make the experience even better. He liked to sleep with a fan, so he decided to go to the store and buy one. While there, he saw some bedding on sale and realized he could add even more comfort to his stay. The first night felt extraordinary, as if he had arrived in a sanctuary of comfort.

The next day, however, his focus began to shift. His mind was already turning to how he could make his stay even better. He slept wonderfully with his new fan and bedding, but he began to think about his free time in the room. Training took place only during the day, leaving evenings to himself. He returned to Walmart in search of entertainment, buying a speaker to listen to music. Then he saw an Xbox displayed beneath a large sale sign. He knew he didn't need it, but reasoned it was worth it for a two-week stay.

Over time, his attention drifted further. He became so consumed with maximizing his comfort and entertainment that he skipped gatherings with coworkers, declined invitations for meetups, and spent entire evenings alone in the room. He was entirely focused on optimizing his own enjoyment, prioritizing temporary pleasure over meaningful purpose. By the end of the trip, he had made ten trips to Walmart and spent thousands of dollars on things that provided fleeting satisfaction but no lasting fulfillment.

When it was time to leave, the man began to pack for his trip home, and the magnitude of his mistake finally became clear. Most of his purchases could not travel with him. A wave of frustration and regret washed over him as the reality of wasted money and effort sank in. He could not carry it all back with him; he had no choice but to leave it behind. On the way to the airport, he passed a woman asking for help feeding her child—but he had nothing left to give. Every extra dollar had been spent on temporary pleasures, leaving him empty-handed. On the flight home, the weight of regret pressed down on him, a gnawing awareness of all the opportunities he had squandered. When he returned, he discovered his family's air conditioning had broken, and once again, he had nothing to spare. Every dollar, every hour, every ounce of effort had been poured into comfort that could not follow him beyond the hotel walls.

The man's realization was sobering. The next day at work, when he eagerly tried to recount all that he had learned, his boss instead asked how he had spent time with the other employees. The man admitted he had barely met anyone, having spent most of his time alone in the hotel room. He had taken extra notes and absorbed the training, but his boss's disappointed response cut to the heart of the matter: *"The training could have been done anywhere. I sent you there to meet other people in your position and to build relationships with the people you will be growing this company with. I wanted you to learn with them, not by yourself."* In that moment, he understood that not only had he wasted money and time on temporary comforts, leaving him unable to meet more permanent needs, but he had also missed the very reason he had been sent. Likewise, God places us in this world not to accumulate fleeting pleasures or self-focused comforts, but to invest in what truly endures: the relationships we nurture, the love we give, and the eternal purposes we serve. To live as though this life is all there is, or to prioritize temporary ease over lasting impact, is to miss the very reason we have been sent.

Ladies and gentlemen, the Christian life is a work trip. God is not sending us here to decorate our hotel room or fill it with every comfort we can imagine. Too often, we see Christians who reject fellowship, neglect the church, and attempt to live life on their own terms—reading their Bibles, but living isolated lives. Yet God has placed us in the world to connect with others, to love them, and to cultivate relationships that bear eternal fruit for His kingdom. Reading Scripture without living its truth is not enough; God is not pleased with devotion that stops at the page. Hear me clearly: can you honestly look at your life and say you are investing in things that advance the kingdom, or are you merely focused on making your hotel room more comfortable?

Let us resist loving the world. Every good gift comes from God, yet sin twists these gifts for selfish ends. Let us love what God gives as instruments to honor Him, not as tools for satisfying our desires. Keep your eyes fixed on the Giver, not the gifts, and invest your life in what will endure forever. Every act of kindness, every word of encouragement, every choice to glorify Him over self, is a coin placed in the eternal piggy bank that will never burn, never fade, never vanish.

1 John 2:18 (ESV)
Children, it is the last hour, and as you have heard that antichrist is coming, so now many antichrists have come. Therefore we know that it is the last hour.

John drives home his warning by emphasizing that we are in the last hour. What is the last hour? Clearly, he does not mean this literally, given that he wrote these words nearly two thousand years ago. Rather, in the grand course of redemption, we are in the final stretch. For thousands of years, God's people waited for the arrival of the Messiah, and then He finally came. Today, we await His return, and we live in the concluding phase of this world's existence. When the Lord returns, all of this will come to an end. As John made clear at the close of the previous paragraph, the world itself is destined to perish. John writes this letter after receiving direct revelation, and so he is more aware than ever of what is coming. He has seen it with his own eyes. Now, the enemy is making his final efforts to disrupt the people of God. Now, more than ever, we must remain focused and vigilant. The final hour is upon us.

John then references the coming of the Antichrist, a figure foretold in the prophets of old but now revealed with greater clarity through John's own vision from Jesus. Importantly, John also notes, "So many antichrists have come," signaling that this threat is not limited to a single individual. Instead, there is a rise of many who share the same mindset and spirit of opposition to Christ. This proliferation confirms that we are living in the last hour—the era marked by those who stand against Christ and propagate an antichrist message.

Here John distinguishes between the Antichrist and antichrists among us. The Antichrist is the singular figure prophesied in Daniel, referenced by Jesus, Paul, and John alike. He is described as one who will exalt himself against God, raising himself to divine status, and who will persecute the saints of the Most High. The defining characteristic of the Antichrist is blasphemous self-exaltation. This understanding sheds light on the antichrists who live among us: they share in the same spirit, exalting themselves above God. John warns his readers that, while the ultimate Antichrist has not yet arrived, many antichrists already walk among us. This reality is true today, perhaps more than ever. There are antichrists at work, at school, in the church, and even in places where our children learn.

This warning is not intended to provoke fear or anxiety, but to cultivate vigilance and spiritual discernment. Do not be taken by surprise when you encounter such individuals, for you have been forewarned and equipped with understanding. Do not be swayed or led astray by the subtle lies they speak, for you have been told in advance that they would come seeking to deceive. Awareness does not eliminate the challenge, but it equips us to stand firm in faith, to recognize the spirit of opposition, and to remain unwavering in the truth. By knowing what to expect and whose voice to trust, believers are strengthened to navigate challenges with confidence, clarity, and steadfast devotion.

1 John 2:19 (ESV)
They went out from us, but they were not of us; for if they had been of us, they would have continued with us. But they went out, that it might become plain that they all are not of us.

As I mentioned earlier in this book, John and the other Apostles were not naive to the reality that false brethren existed among the churches. They did not assume that everyone gathered in the visible fellowship was truly in Christ or truly a brother or sister in the faith. Yet John also understands something deeply pastoral. When believers witness someone appear to "walk away from the faith," it naturally provokes questions, fears, and doubts. When people leave the church, others begin to ask, "If he was able to fall away, what if I fall away?" or "How can we speak of assurance if I see people abandon the faith?"

These questions are not limited to the early church. Even today, they surface constantly. We see former pastors renounce the faith. We watch people we once believed were Christians turn to the world and openly reject Christ. When this happens, the question inevitably follows, *"If it happened to them, could it happen to me?"* How can Scripture speak so clearly about hope, assurance, and promise if others appear to have lost their faith?

John addresses this concern directly. He states that such individuals were never truly of us, and then he goes even further by saying that if they had been of us, they would have continued with us. How can John speak with such certainty? Because he understands the role of the Holy Spirit in the life of the believer.

The Apostles were fully aware, from the very beginning, that false believers would exist among the visible people of God. This reality did not take them by surprise, because it was first taught by Jesus Himself. Jesus repeatedly warned His disciples, saying, "Beware of false prophets, who come to you in sheep's clothing but inwardly are ravenous wolves" (Matthew 7:15). Many of

Jesus' parables were given for the express purpose of teaching that there would be those within the covenant community who appeared genuine outwardly, yet lacked true faith inwardly. He taught this truth in the parable of the wheat and the weeds, where both grow together until the time of harvest, and again in the Olivet Discourse through the parable of the sheep and the goats, where the distinction between true and false is finally revealed at judgment (Matthew 13:24-30; Matthew 25:31-46).

This same warning is echoed by the Apostles after Christ's ascension. Paul, when gathering the elders of Ephesus, warned them soberly that "fierce wolves will come in among you, not sparing the flock," and even more alarming, that some would arise "from among your own selves," speaking twisted things to draw disciples after them (Acts 20:29-30). Jude likewise warns the church that "certain people have crept in unnoticed," men who outwardly belong but inwardly deny the truth they profess (Jude 4). These warnings form the backdrop for John's words in this passage. The presence of false believers, deceivers, and eventual departures from the fellowship is not evidence of failure in God's plan, but rather the fulfillment of what Christ and His Apostles clearly foretold.

It is important to note the specific context John is addressing. He is speaking about those who were leaving the faith and embracing the false teachings of Docetism and early Gnosticism, movements well known to his original audience. His readers would not have immediately thought of someone who missed church for a season or struggled spiritually for a time. Rather, they would have understood John to be referring to people who had fully departed from the apostolic faith and aligned themselves with a rival message.

Scripture does not deny that a genuine believer may experience seasons of struggle, confusion, or even temporary separation from the visible body of Christ. This does happen, and it does not automatically mean that such a person was never truly of us. The Lord may be disciplining them, correcting them, or drawing them back through conviction. John's statement is not a license to judge the hearts of those who step away from church for a time. A believer may wander, but the Shepherd is faithful to bring His sheep home.

This reminds me of Paul's words in 1 Corinthians 3:11-15, where he speaks of those who build upon the foundation of Christ with wood, hay, and straw. Paul is clear that no one can remove the foundation, which is Christ Himself. However, each believer is responsible for what he builds upon that foundation. When the fire tests each person's work, some will suffer loss, yet Paul says plainly that the person himself will be saved, though as through fire. There are believers who will lose much because of what they have built, but that loss does not mean they were never truly in Christ.

John's words, then, are not written so that believers can go around declaring that everyone who leaves the fellowship was never saved. Rather, they are written so that believers can understand why some depart permanently and decisively. Their departure does not mean God failed them. It means they were never truly of us to begin with.

When John says, *"If they were of us, they would have continued with us,"* he is reaffirming a consistent biblical truth. Those who walk in the light will be conformed to the image of the Son. Those who possess the Spirit of God will be drawn toward the people of God. The Spirit does not lead believers away from Christ or away from His body. This is not wishful thinking; it is promise. As Paul writes, *"I am sure of this, that he who began a good work in you will bring it to completion"* (Phil. 1:6)

I have had Christians say to me, "I know someone who was truly saved, and then they turned away from Christ and lost their salvation." What they often do not realize is that, in making this claim, they are pronouncing a judgment they do not have the authority to make. Many Christians rightly understand that we are not permitted to condemn someone to hell or declare with certainty the eternal destiny of another person (Matthew 7:1; Romans 14:4). Yet, for some reason, many feel far more comfortable making the opposite judgment. They freely assign heaven to anyone they perceive to be a Christian. They will not pass judgment on the negative, but they will pass judgment on the positive.

Because of this, when someone later "walks away," the assumption is that their original assessment must have been so accurate that the only explanation is the loss of salvation. But John never reasons this way in his letter. Instead, he repeatedly exposes false claims by measuring them against the truth of the gospel. He does not say, "If someone claims fellowship with God and walks in darkness, he has lost his salvation." He says plainly that such a person is lying (1 John 1:6). He does not say, "If someone says he knows God and does not keep His commandments, he has fallen from grace." He says that person is a liar, and the truth is not in him (1 John 2:4). When someone departs from the fellowship and abandons the truth, John does not conclude that salvation has been forfeited. He concludes that they were never truly of us to begin with (1 John 2:19).

John does not presume to know the hidden contents of a person's heart. Rather, he understands what salvation is and what it produces. A man who has been born of God abides in the truth and continues with the people of God (1 John 2:19; 1 John 3:9). If someone walks away for a season and is truly of us, the Lord will bring him back in repentance and restoration, for He disciplines those He loves (Hebrews 12:6). But if someone departs permanently, rejecting Christ and His truth, John teaches us that this departure reveals what was always true. They were never of us.

John presses this point further when he explains that they went out so that it might become plain that they were not of us. Light exposes darkness. Those who walk in darkness while claiming fellowship with God cannot remain hidden forever. Eventually, the light forces a response. They will either come to the truth and repent, or they will depart. These are the liars John has referenced repeatedly throughout his letter. In chapter one, those who claim fellowship while walking in darkness are called liars. In chapter two, those who say they know God while refusing obedience are liars. The pattern is consistent.

Darkness cannot coexist indefinitely with light. Those who persist in darkness will inevitably be exposed and will depart, so that it becomes evident to all that they were never truly of us.

1 John 2:20-21 (ESV)
But you have been anointed by the Holy One, and you all have knowledge. I write to you, not because you do not know the truth, but because you know it, and because no lie is of the truth.

After warning his readers about those who were being led away, John now turns to comfort and reassure the believers. He reminds them of a reality that many Christians today desperately need to recover. You do not need new revelation. Those who walked away were not grounded in the truth to begin with. They resemble the seed Jesus warned about in the parable of the sower, the seed that fell on rocky ground. It sprang up quickly, yet had no root, and when affliction or persecution arose, it withered away (Matthew 13:20-21). There was never true depth. Vain belief was a problem in the first century, and it remains a problem in the church today.

The Apostle Paul, when dealing with a Corinthian church that faced deception from every angle, finishes his first letter by reminding them of the Gospel that saves, and of the word of truth capable of sustaining them: "Unless you believed in vain" (1 Corinthians 15:2). Vain belief is shallow belief. It exists only in words, profession, or emotion, but not in the heart. It does not endure because it was never rooted in regeneration. This is why Paul pushed back so strongly against the Corinthian church's pursuit of worldly wisdom and eloquent speech. He reminds them that when he came to them, he did not rely on lofty rhetoric or human wisdom. Instead, he determined to know nothing except Christ crucified, so that their faith would rest not on the wisdom of man, but on the power of God (1 Corinthians 2:1-5).

These are the people who are always searching for something beyond the gospel. They are drawn to novelty, speculation, and supposed hidden insight because a lingering "what if" remains in their hearts. They are willing to listen to anyone who claims to offer something new. In John's context, this took the form of accepting a false Christ, one who did not truly come in the flesh. The question must be asked, how could they accept such teaching if they truly believed the apostolic witness and the gospel of salvation? John's answer is clear. They were not taught by the Holy Spirit.

Jesus Himself declared, "It is written in the Prophets, 'And they will all be taught by God.' Everyone who has heard and learned from the Father comes to me" (John 6:45). When Peter made the first public confession that Jesus is the Christ, the Son of the living God, Jesus responded by telling him that this confession did not come from flesh and blood, but from the Father who is in heaven (Matthew 16:16-17). True knowledge of Christ is not discovered through speculation or new revelation. It is revealed by God through His Spirit. As Paul writes elsewhere, "No one can say 'Jesus is Lord' except in the Holy Spirit" (1 Corinthians 12:3). The Spirit enlightens the mind, softens the heart, and anchors the believer in the truth of Christ. Because of this, John reminds his readers that they do not need someone to come along and bring them something new.

This warning is just as relevant today. Many people are far more interested in a new word, a prophecy, or a secret insight than they are in the ordinary means God has given. People who have barely studied the Scriptures spend hours scrolling through social media or watching videos in search of something mysterious or hidden. While it may no longer be labeled Gnosticism, it is the same ancient tactic of the enemy. I have met people who have never carefully read the entire New Testament, yet they are eager to discuss non biblical writings, obscure theories, or speculative claims. In doing so, they unintentionally confess that they believe God's Word is insufficient. Yet Scripture testifies that God has given His people everything they need for life and godliness through the knowledge of Him (2 Peter 1:3).

John's reminder to his readers is the same reminder believers need today. You have knowledge. Even if you feel unable to articulate it with precision, you possess it. If you have the Holy Spirit, you have all that is necessary, because He is able to supply what you need, when you need it. More knowledge is not always better, and more information is not always helpful. The Spirit faithfully guides the believer into truth according to God's will (John 16:13).

This is why John says, "I write to you, not because you do not know the truth, but because you know it" (1 John 2:21). God's Word is truth (John 17:17), and those who belong to Christ have been given that Word. They are not dependent on secret revelations, special insight, or new messages. They are grounded in the truth already revealed, preserved, and applied by the Spirit of God.

> *1 John 2:22-23 (ESV)*
> *Who is the liar but he who denies that Jesus is the Christ? This is the antichrist, he who denies the Father and the Son. No one who denies the Son has the Father. Whoever confesses the Son has the Father also.*

Here, John focuses on one of the most essential aspects of the Christian faith: the truth of who Jesus Christ is. This proclamation directly opposes both the early Jewish rejection of Christ and the Gnostic distortions that threatened the churches. The Jews specifically denied that Jesus was the Messiah and the Son of God, rejecting His identity and mission. The early Gnostics, while not necessarily denying Jesus as the Messiah, denied His true Sonship as Scripture presents it. As discussed earlier, Gnostic thought had multiple variations. One sect, known as Cerinthianism, taught that Jesus was merely a man upon whom the Spirit of Christ rested—denying both His full divinity and His true humanity. The other sect, associated with Docetism, claimed that Jesus only appeared to have a body, denying His true incarnation altogether. John's Gospel introduction makes clear the biblical truth: Jesus is the Word made flesh, fully God and fully man (John 1:14).

It is worth asking whether understanding these heresies is necessary. On one hand, a reader is not obligated to memorize every historical heresy. On the other hand, knowing what the Apostles contended with equips us to recognize and resist similar distortions today. Many contemporary errors in the church are not new; they are recycled forms of ancient heresies. Understanding the context of John's letter helps us grasp why he wrote with such urgency and clarity. As the old saying goes, "Those who fail to learn from history are doomed to repeat it." While the details of every heresy can be confusing, grasping the essence of what the early church fought against is critical for discerning truth.

In this passage, John declares a fundamental truth: whoever denies that Jesus is the Christ does not have not God, and whoever acknowledges the Son has the Father also. This statement directly confronts the lie that the departing believers and deceivers were buying into. They were rejecting Christ's identity, either through ignorance or pride, and John warns that such denial aligns them with the spirit of the Antichrist. The lie they followed is precisely that one can reject the Son without rejecting God. John corrects this by emphasizing that denial of the Son is inseparable from denial of the Father. The Spirit of God within believers illuminates this truth, enabling us to discern that these false teachings are lies.

This was not a minor theological disagreement. During His ministry, Jesus explicitly warned the Pharisees that they were not true children of Abraham but children of the devil (John 8:44). John expands on this theme, showing that the denial of Christ is characteristic of those opposed to God. The Jews, in particular, rejected Jesus as both Messiah and Son of God, despite the undeniable evidence of His works. Jesus fulfilled the messianic prophecies through His deeds: healing the sick, giving sight to the blind, and raising the dead. Even Nicodemus, a Pharisee, acknowledged the divine origin of Jesus' ministry when he said, "Rabbi, we know that you are a teacher come from God; for no one can do these signs that you do unless God is with him" (John 3:2). Their rejection was not born of ignorance but of pride. They refused to acknowledge the truth standing clearly before them.

John's warning remains vital for us today. The lie that Christ can be denied without consequence persists in various forms. False teachers, deceived peers, or even personal doubts can tempt believers to compromise the truth of Christ. But the Spirit of God within us—given to all who are truly in Christ—guards our understanding. We know the truth, we discern deception, and we recognize the eternal implications of denying the Son. The Spirit makes the reality of Christ unshakable in the believer's heart, and John assures us that no lie can overturn what God has established.

1 John 2:24-25 (ESV)
Let what you heard from the beginning abide in you. If what you heard from the beginning abides in you, then you too will abide in the Son and in the Father. And this is the promise that He made to us—eternal life.

John calls his readers to hold fast to what they have already heard and known, reminding them not to be swayed by those who seek to sow division. These are the wolves Paul and Jude warned about—those who arise from both outside and within the community, speaking twisted things to draw disciples away (Acts 20:29-30; Jude 4).

Do not allow such people to bring confusion or doubt into your faith. Brothers and sisters, the same warning applies today: do not chase after hidden knowledge or secret revelations that attempt to supplement the gospel. Let what you have heard from the beginning abide in you. If you have believed the testimony concerning Jesus—that He is the Messiah, the Son of God—then you will abide in the Son and the Father.

John reminds us of the promise of eternal life, a promise that is unshakable. Unlike human promises, God cannot lie, and His promise is confirmed by the Spirit, who serves as the guarantee of what is to come (Hebrews 6:17-18; Ephesians 1:13-14). The Spirit ensures that believers remain in the truth, recognize deception, and are guided in righteousness. The lies of antichrists and deceivers cannot undo this reality, because the Spirit works to strengthen, preserve, and sustain those who are in Christ.

Do not listen to those who attempt to bind you with legalism or to deny the identity of Jesus as the Son of God. Hold fast to His words, which are spirit and life (John 6:63), and trust fully in His promise of eternal life. What God has begun in the believer, He will complete by His Spirit (Philippians 1:6). The truth already revealed in Scripture, confirmed by the Spirit, is sufficient for every need of faith and life.

1 John 2:26-27 (ESV)
I write these things to you about those who are trying to deceive you. But the anointing that you received from Him abides in you, and you have no need that anyone should teach you. But as His anointing teaches you about everything, and is true, and is no lie—just as it has taught you, abide in Him.

John makes his purpose explicit. He is writing so that believers may have assurance in the midst of deception. The presence of false teachers is not meant to unsettle the saints, but to drive them back to the source of their confidence. Throughout this letter, John repeatedly contrasts those who deceive with those who abide, and here he reminds his readers where their certainty truly comes from.

Their knowledge of God is not grounded in worldly wisdom, intellectual novelty, or hidden insight. It comes from the anointing they have received, namely, the Holy Spirit. John has already established that true knowledge of Christ is revealed by God, not discovered by human effort. He has reminded them that the Spirit teaches, confirms, and anchors believers in the truth. Now he applies that reality directly to the threat of deception.

When John says that they have no need for anyone to teach them, he is not rejecting the God-ordained role of teachers within the church. Scripture is clear that Christ has given teachers to His body for its edification and growth (Ephesians 4:11–13). John is not contradicting Paul, nor is he undermining the ordinary means God uses to instruct His people. Rather, he is clarifying *how* true spiritual knowledge is received.

There is only one ultimate Teacher, God Himself. Any faithful teacher in the church functions only as an instrument of the Spirit. When a teacher speaks truth, it is the Spirit who applies that truth to the heart of the hearer. Likewise, when a believer receives and understands spiritual truth, it is not because of the brilliance of the teacher, but because the Spirit is already at work within them. Teaching in the church is never a transfer of private wisdom, but a Spirit-led confirmation of revealed truth.

This is why genuine Christian instruction often feels both new and familiar at the same time. Believers hear truth they may not have been able to articulate before, yet it resonates deeply, as though it had always been there. This is not because the teacher has unlocked secret knowledge, but because the Spirit is bearing witness within the believer to what is true. The Spirit who indwells the teacher is the same Spirit who indwells the student. There is no contradiction, no competition, and no dependency created between the two.

John's point is decisive against the claims of Gnosticism. Those who promise hidden revelation, secret insight, or knowledge inaccessible through Scripture alone are exposing themselves as deceivers. This same error continues today under different labels and platforms. Many are drawn to voices that claim special access to truth, implying that Scripture is insufficient without their interpretation or revelation. But this is precisely what John is guarding against.

There is nothing necessary for faith, life, or godliness that is not found in the Word of God and confirmed by the Spirit of God. Teachers may help clarify, organize, and explain what

Scripture teaches, but they cannot give believers anything fundamentally new. The authority rests not in the teacher, but in the truth, and the confirmation of that truth belongs to the Spirit.

John's reassurance is simple and profound. If you have the Spirit, you have what you need. The Spirit teaches you what is true, guards you from deception, and keeps you abiding in Christ. This is not arrogance, nor is it anti-intellectualism. It is confidence in God's sufficiency. The same Spirit who brought you to Christ is faithful to keep you in Him.

1 John 2:28-29 (ESV)
And now, little children, abide in Him, so that when He appears we may have confidence and not shrink from him in shame at his coming. If you know that He is righteous, you may be sure that everyone who practices righteousness has been born of Him.

John ends this chapter with the same encouragement with which he opened it. Abide in Him, find your refuge in Him—He is our safety and our salvation. If we trust in His words, we have no need to shrink back at His coming. If, instead, we place our faith in the words of men rather than in what Jesus has accomplished, we give ourselves cause to shrink back and lose confidence. But when we trust in Him as our righteousness, we can approach that day with assurance.

John emphasizes that everyone who practices righteousness has been born of Him. Notice again the word *practice*. It does not imply that we are righteous by our own power or that we live a flawless life. Rather, it refers to the daily striving to follow Him and walk in His light. The evidence of one's life—the fruit produced by walking in obedience—is how we can discern who is truly of God. Those who actively live out the truths of Christ are His children; apart from Him, we can do nothing.

Chapter Summary

We are not of this world, and we do not walk in darkness. Nothing can strip this from us, and the accuser has no charge that can hold against us. We are called to strive for holiness, to walk as our Lord walked, yet we must remember this: if we sin, we have an advocate with the Father—Jesus Christ. We do not follow the world, but the commandments of Christ, written on our hearts.

We are set apart because we have received His Holy Spirit, who anoints and guides us. We are children of light while the world remains in darkness. Therefore, we must separate ourselves from the world and refuse to walk in its darkness. This is not easy, and we will fail. When measured against the perfect standard of Christ, failure is inevitable, for we are not Him. Yet we cling to the hope that He who began a good work in us will bring it to completion. We can trust Him in all things, even in our stumbles.

Do not doubt the promises of our Lord. Doubt may come for a time, but it is rarely directed at Christ Himself. When believers wrestle with assurance of salvation, their uncertainty is seldom about His power to save; it is about themselves. We know our own untrustworthiness, yet the words of Jesus remain steadfast: His words are spirit and life. They give life to the spiritually dead and sustain our hope until the day He finishes His work in us.

Note to the reader: For the remainder of this book, I will be using the LSB translation. Please refer to the introduction for an explanation of this choice.

Chapter Three

1 John 3

Children of God

Overview

As we move into Chapter 3, the Apostle John shifts our gaze from the battlefield of the world to the household of the Father. If Chapter 2 was about the external dangers of darkness and deception, Chapter 3 is about the internal reality of our new nature. John begins with a breathtaking exclamation: *"See how great a love the Father has given to us!"* This isn't just a sentimental thought; it is a declaration of a legal and spiritual status. We are not merely "followers" of a teacher; we are the adopted sons and daughters of the Living God.

In this chapter, we will explore what it means to possess a "New Identity." We will confront the radical truth that our eternity does not begin when we die—it began the moment we were brought into Christ. This realization demands a response: if we truly possess this hope, we must begin to "purify ourselves" today. We will look at the practical pursuit of righteousness, faith, love, and peace, and we will address the difficult reality of the "mixed multitude"—distinguishing between the believer who struggles with sin and the liar who makes a practice of it.

Throughout this chapter, we will grapple with the tension of our current state: we are already children of God, yet what we *will* be has not yet been fully manifested. We live in the "already but not yet," called to be "vessels of honor" in the Master's house while we await the day we shall see Him as He is.

Note to the Reader: *As mentioned in the introduction and at the conclusion of the previous chapter, all Scripture quotations from this point forward will be from the Legacy Standard Bible (LSB) unless otherwise noted.*

1 John 3:1 (LSB)
See how great a love the Father has given to us, that we would be called children of God; and we are. For this reason the world does not know us, because it did not know Him.

The new life of a believer in Christ is defined by one central reality: sonship. Those who believe in Jesus Christ have been brought into the family of God, not by human lineage, personal resolve, or religious effort, but by the sovereign work of the Spirit. We are no longer children of this age or of the world, but have been called out of it to belong to God Himself. Through faith in Christ, we are born again, receiving a new identity and a new standing before God. As John writes, "But as many as received Him, to them He gave the right to become children of God, even to those who believe in His name" (John 1:12-13). This new birth is not produced by human desire or achievement, but is wholly the gracious act of God.

Scripture consistently reinforces this truth. Paul declares that "in Christ Jesus you are all sons of God, through faith" (Galatians 3:26), grounding our identity not in performance but in union with Christ. This adoption is not merely a change in status; it is accompanied by the indwelling presence of the Spirit. As Romans teaches, we have received the Spirit of adoption by whom we cry, "Abba! Father," and the Spirit Himself bears witness that we are children of God (Romans 8:15-16). Sonship is not an abstract doctrine, but a lived reality, one confirmed inwardly by the Spirit and outwardly by a transformed life.

Do not rush past these words. Pause and behold the magnitude of the love the Father has lavished upon us. This is not a distant or reluctant love, but one that pursued us when we were undeserving, sought us when we were not seeking Him, and rescued us while we were still bound in sin. In Christ, we who were once far off have been brought near. We who were lost have been found. We are no longer strangers or outsiders, but children of God, welcomed into His family and secured by His grace. Few truths shape the Christian life more deeply than this, and John wants it firmly settled in the hearts of his readers.

The Legal Reality of Adoption

This sonship language is not merely rhetorical; it is a foundational pillar of our theology. To understand the weight of being "called children of God," we must consider the concept of adoption as it would have been understood by the original audience. While John does not explicitly use the term adopted in this letter, the reality he describes is the same reality the Apostle Paul articulates with that language. Paul introduces adoption as a theological category to explain what it means to belong to God as sons, and John assumes that same reality when he speaks of being born of God and called His children. In the days of the Apostles, the Roman Empire operated under strict and irreversible adoption laws. In the ancient Roman world, adoption was not a casual or symbolic act, but a formal legal institution with profound judicial consequences. Even though John does not explicitly use the term "adoption" as Paul does, the concept is clearly implied in his discussion of our sonship in Christ.

A Roman adoption (known as *adoptio* or *adrogatio*) transferred a person entirely into the authority and household of the adoptive father.[1] It created a new legal identity. The adopted son fully assumed the name and the inheritance rights of his new family. Under Roman law, the adopted individual was regarded as a legitimate heir, equally entitled to the estate and privileges of the household, while all legal ties and obligations to his previous family were effectively dissolved. This was a permanent bond, not easily reversed, meant to secure an heir and preserve the family line.

When God adopts you, He is not merely granting a title; He is affecting a real and decisive transfer. Scripture tells us that He has "delivered us from the domain of darkness and transferred us to the kingdom of His beloved Son" (Colossians 1:13–14). Your former standing is dissolved. Your old debts are canceled. You now belong to a new household, bearing a new name, secured by redemption and forgiveness. As a legitimate heir of the Kingdom of God, you are permanently bound to your new Father, not by merit or effort, but by sovereign grace.

The World Rejected Him and Rejects Us

Because of this adoption, the world does not know us. Our inclusion in the family of God creates an unavoidable tension with the culture around us. The world does not recognize our new identity, nor does it claim us as its own, because our nature

---

1. Philip E. Goble, Jr., "The Roman Context of Adoption," *The American Journal of Biblical Theology* 22, no. 23 (June 6, 2021)

has been fundamentally changed. We no longer belong to the system from which we have been rescued. Having been brought into the kingdom of God, we now stand in opposition to a world that exists in rebellion against Him.

The world rejected our Lord for the very same reason. He was foreign to everything it valued. What He honored, the world despised. What He condemned, the world celebrated. As Jesus Himself said, "If the world hates you, know that it has hated Me before it hated you" (John 15:18). He did not come operating according to the world's standards of power, success, or self exaltation. Though He came with true authority, He clothed Himself in humility and served rather than seized. The world expects power to be displayed through domination and control, but Christ revealed power through sacrifice, mercy, and obedience to the Father.

Even many among Israel anticipated a Messiah who would conform to worldly expectations, a conquering king who would overthrow their enemies and establish political supremacy. They wanted a ruler who played by the world's rules. Instead, Christ established His kingdom through a cross. He triumphed through suffering and love, overturning every assumption about strength and victory. Because He did not conform to the world, the world did not recognize Him.

The same reality now applies to those who belong to Him. We are driven by the same Spirit, a Spirit oriented toward holiness, love, and eternal things. Our priorities have shifted. Our hopes are no longer rooted in status, gain, or approval. As a result, we appear foreign even to those who once knew us well. John reminds us that this should not surprise us. If the world did not know Him, it will not know the children who now walk in His likeness. Rejection is not a sign of failure in the Christian life, but evidence of genuine belonging to Christ.

> *1 John 3:2-3 (LSB)*
> **Beloved, now we are children of God, and it has not been manifested as yet what we will be. We know that when He is manifested, we will be like Him, because we will see Him just as He is. And everyone who has this hope fixed on Him purifies himself, just as he is pure.**

Already, we can observe the transformative change that God has begun within us. We are now guided by His Spirit. We now know the true nature of love. We now seek after Him. Yet, as profound as this shift is, it is not the finality of our transformation. As John says, "what we will be has not yet appeared." We are currently being sanctified, a process that is ongoing and often messy. But we can rest in absolute trust in God: when He returns, we shall be like Him—our mortal bodies transformed in a moment, "in the twinkling of an eye," as Paul writes in 1 Corinthians 15:52. Our hope is secure, for the Spirit who begins this work in us guarantees its completion and our ultimate glorification.

Jesus is the "firstfruits" of the resurrection (1 Cor 15:20). This designation is profoundly significant: because He has risen, we have a guaranteed hope. His resurrection is not merely an example; it is the anchor of our faith and the assurance that we too will rise and be made perfect. We do not have to wonder in mystery or speculate about what awaits us—Christ's resurrected body shows us what is to come. When Jesus rose, He was clothed in a perfect, glorified body. Death no longer held sway over Him; He was not subject to decay, but possessed life in its fullest abundance. Remarkably, His body still bore the wounds of His sacrifice, yet He was uninjured. He touched the Apostles, proving He was not merely a vision or ghost, but a being who truly occupied physical space. He sat and broke bread in a meal with them, revealing that we too will eat and drink in our glorified bodies. The resurrected body of Jesus shows us that when we are made like Him, we will possess real, tangible bodies and fully engage in the life of the physical world, free from the corruption of sin and death.

Living Your Eternity Now

Everyone who anchors their hope in this, the resurrection and saving work of our Lord, is called to live differently now. John says such a person purifies himself, just as Christ is pure. This is not because purity earns eternity, but because eternal life has already taken root. This is what I mean by "living your eternity now." Scripture presents eternal life not only as a future inheritance, but as a present reality grounded in knowing God and being united to Christ. When we are born again, we do not merely await new life, we enter into it. What will one day be revealed in fullness has already begun its transforming work in us, even as we look forward to its complete and glorious consummation.

When street preaching or ministering online, I often ask Christians a simple question: when does your eternity begin? Too often, eternity is treated as a distant chapter that starts after the grave, while daily life remains fully devoted to the world. Many want the pleasures, comforts, and recognition the world offers today, while reserving obedience, holiness, and devotion for later. Eternity with the King becomes a future hope, while the present is spent chasing what is temporary. This mindset is precisely what John confronts in the previous chapter when he warns against loving the world and the things that are passing away.

John's call forces us to examine our hearts honestly. Are we living today as though the old self is truly dead and the new self is alive? Are we ordering our lives around the reality that eternal life began the moment we came to Christ? Or are we treating eternity as a delayed reward, something we will embrace later, while continuing to live by the values of the present age? If Christ is our life, then our lives should reflect Him now. The question is not why eternity *should* shape us eventually, but why it does not shape us today.

Purifying the Vessel

Notice carefully what John is saying in verse 3: he does not command, "You must purify yourself." Rather, he declares a reality: **everyone** who has this hope fixed on Him purifies himself. Purification is the fruit of faith, the natural outworking of a heart transformed by Christ. It is not a law to obey or a burdensome requirement—it is the reflection of the Spirit at work in a believer.

Consider this: if a blind man is given sight, he will instinctively try to clean the dirt from his face because now he sees it. The act of cleansing is not commanded; it is a natural response to newfound sight. In the same way, purification flows naturally from those whose hearts have been illuminated by Christ. This reality only manifests in one who recognizes two essential truths: first, the recognition of his own imperfection, his sin, and his desperate need for cleansing; second, the recognition of what true purity is—the righteousness of Christ. Only a sinner who sees his need and sees Christ's perfection can truly seek purification. One cannot purify himself without both humility and a vision of true holiness.

A person is only grieved by his sin when his goal is to conquer sin. The person who has no intention of conquering his sin is never grieved by it. I want you to understand that there is a difference between aiming for the bullseye and missing, and not aiming at all. Jesus is the perfect mark of perfection. When you aim for that target, you will miss every time. Sometimes you may land closer than others, but in that missing, we have a continuous Intercessor in heaven, our Lord Jesus.

Those who do not even attempt to hit the target are like a man who claims to have been given sight yet walks around with dirt on his face, never attempting to clean it. They are the ones who are liars. They say they have fellowship with the Lord but walk in darkness. They claim to know God, yet their lives give no evidence of it. To such a person, my words, and the words of the Apostle John, are not for you. These words are for our brothers and sisters in the faith, calling them to begin living their eternity today.

Begin the work of purifying yourself now. This does not imply that you will be one hundred percent successful immediately; we have already discussed the persistent reality of our struggle in the previous chapter. While John's desire is that you do not sin, we rest in the assurance that when and if you do, you have an Advocate in heaven. This provides a message of profound security for those who are actively working to purify themselves. For the believer, purification is not an optional endeavor for those whose hope is fixed on Christ; it is the natural, inevitable fruit of a life transformed by His Spirit.

It is crucial to understand that Jesus is both the author and perfecter of our faith (Hebrews 12:2). He initiates our salvation, sustains it through every trial, and will faithfully bring it to its ultimate completion (Philippians 1:6). Yet, Scripture is equally clear that our response matters. You may wonder: *If God is the one who will ultimately purify me, what role do I actually play?* The answer lies in how we experience the process of sanctification—whether that journey is defined by comfort or marked by avoidable struggle. If we grieve the Spirit and attempt to build upon the foundation of Christ with that which is sinful or dishonorable, Scripture warns that we will suffer loss and may face the discipline of the Lord (1 Corinthians 3:10–15; Hebrews

12:5-11). Conversely, when we walk in obedience and pursue holiness, we position ourselves to experience the fullness of His reward.

I am not contradicting myself by calling you to purify yourself while simultaneously affirming that God is the one who purifies you. These are two sides of the same coin. The call to personal purification is not a demand that replaces God's sovereign work; rather, it is the believer's active participation in sanctification. It is our way of cooperating with the Holy Spirit so that we might avoid unnecessary discipline. To purify oneself is to respond to the work God is already doing in your heart—seeking holiness out of a deep well of gratitude, faith, and dependence on Christ, rather than a religious striving to earn His acceptance.

Vessels for Honor

Purify yourself today. Strive to cleanse yourself from what is dishonorable so that you may be useful to our Lord in this life. This principle is vividly captured by the Apostle Paul in his second letter to Timothy:

"Now in a large house there are not only gold and silver vessels, but also vessels of wood and of earthenware, and some to honor and some to dishonor. Therefore, if anyone cleanses himself from these things, he will be a vessel for honor, sanctified, useful to the Master, prepared for every good work. Now flee from youthful lusts and pursue righteousness, faith, love and peace, with those who call on the Lord from a pure heart." (2 Timothy 2:20-22)

Paul makes it clear that within the Master's house, there are various types of vessels, and not all are utilized for honorable purposes. If this "vessel" imagery feels distant, consider a more modern comparison. In a great house, there are many different plates and utensils. There is the fine china—the gold and silver settings brought out when the Master desires to honor and impress His guests. But that same Master also has paper plates and solo cups kept for common use when nothing significant is taking place.

Likewise, in the Kingdom of Heaven, God will use all of His children in various capacities, but not all of His children function as "golden utensils." Some remain the "paper plates and solo cups." God will indeed use you, but if you desire to be used for that which is honorable, you must possess a desire to cleanse yourself. You must set yourself apart as holy and useful to the Master. Why would He entrust you with honorable work if you are persisting in a walk that does not honor Him?

As a street preacher and missionary, I must consider the practical reality of being spiritually prepared for God's work. If I were still entangled in sin, neglecting prayer, or ignoring Scripture, could God truly use me to shepherd others or proclaim His truth effectively? Preparation in holiness, devotion, and obedience is essential. This doesn't mean God cannot use me, but it demonstrates how He invites us to participate in His plan through faithful spiritual readiness.

If you choose to continue in the same ways as before, refusing to cleanse yourself and grow in your faith, why would He send you somewhere to lead? Why would He send you somewhere where you might dishonor Him? Do you want your Father to look at you and say, "This is my child that I can use for honorable things"? Then why do you not prepare yourself for every good work?

Paul has already shown us in 2 Timothy 2 what this preparation looks like: to purify yourself and be useful to the Master, you must actively participate in your sanctification. This begins with fleeing youthful passions—departing from the things of the world that once enslaved you, including the lust of the eyes, the lust of the flesh, and the pride of life, which we examined in the last chapter. But fleeing alone is not enough. If you depart from your old passions and then remain idle, new desires will arise to consume you.

This is why Paul does not stop at "fleeing"; he immediately calls us to pursue righteousness, faith, love, and peace, along with those who call on the Lord from a pure heart. These four pursuits are not suggestions—they are the practical means Paul gives us to live as vessels prepared for honorable use in the Master's house. Fleeing removes what is dishonorable, and pursuing builds what is holy.

Pursue Righteousness - To pursue righteousness, we must begin with God Himself, for only He is truly righteous (Psalm 11:7). No one besides Him is righteous, and apart from Him, we cannot know what true righteousness is (Romans 3:10-11). Righteousness is not a standard we can discover on our own; it is rooted entirely in His character and revealed in His Word.

Therefore, to pursue righteousness, we must know Him: what He loves, what He hates, and what He desires of us. Study His Word, making it the lamp to your feet (Psalm 119:105). Do not approach the Bible as if preparing for a test or merely seeking a profound revelation to impress others. Open the Scriptures with the intent to know Him. How can I discern what is good or evil if I do not know the standard of Good (Isaiah 5:20)? How can I discern what is right for my life if I do not know what my Creator has purposed for me (Proverbs 3:5-6)? The beginning of our journey to pursue righteousness must start with His Word, and from there we move forward by applying it in our lives. Learn His Word, then live His Word. Righteousness is not merely doing right things—it is conforming our hearts and minds to the standard of God's holiness (Matthew 5:48). As Psalm 119 reminds us, the way to keep our path pure is through His Word, for it alone provides the guidance and standard to live rightly (Psalm 119:9).

Pursue Faith - Live a life of trusting God. Place yourself in situations where you must rely on Him. Do not fear walking in the light. Living a life of faith is the opposite of living in fear. We all know people who live in fear—worried about what others will think if they speak of the Lord, anxious about tomorrow because they watch the news and anticipate every possible danger, concerned about what tomorrow will hold for work, family, and friends. Faith, however, is walking not by sight but by trust in God, eyes fixed on the eternal, knowing that no matter where we may stumble, Christ is victorious. Even if all else fails around us, He will not fail.

Trusting Him in the unknown requires courage. I used to struggle with taking the first step, worried about making the next step perfectly before moving forward. Then I learned, as if I heard God whisper in my ear, that even if I take the wrong step, He is there with me. Use discernment, but know this: in the steps that are right, God guides you, and in the steps that are wrong, He still leads you, showing that to pursue faith is to walk confidently under God's guidance, resting in His sovereignty even when the path ahead is unclear.

Pursue Love - Oh, how I could write an entire book on these two words. Pursue love in a world of hate and darkness. Our world has lost the true meaning of love. We see the word everywhere, yet its reality is rare. Dictionaries define love as strong affection, sexual attraction, or intense feeling. But here in 2 Timothy, Paul uses the Greek word *agape*, and this love is none of those things. Agape is not a feeling—it is a selfless choice. When Scripture tells us God loves us, it is not describing mere affection; it is demonstrating the highest act of selflessness. God is love itself, and He shows that love in action, giving fully of Himself without expectation of return.

God sent His Son to die for us, gaining nothing and yet giving everything, even to those who did not deserve it. This is the standard for how we are to pursue love: selflessly, consistently, and sacrificially. Paul teaches that love endures all things, bears all burdens, and never ceases. Love is not conditional on feelings or convenience; it is a deliberate, ongoing commitment to the good of others. Pursuing love means prioritizing the well-being of those around us above our own desires, serving faithfully even when it is difficult, and obeying God in the way we treat others. Love conquers strife, tempers anger, heals relationships, and reflects the character of God. To pursue love is to walk in the very nature of Christ, whose life was defined by this unending, selfless devotion.

Pursue Peace - Our Lord said to His Apostles in His final moments, "My peace I give to you." Scripture frequently refers to God as "The God of Peace." In Isaiah, He is the one who gives peace; in Romans 5, we are told that by faith we have been justified and now enjoy peace with God. In Romans 12, Paul exhorts us, "If possible, as far as it depends on you, live peaceably with all."

Peace and fear cannot coexist. To pursue peace is to actively cultivate harmony with others, seek reconciliation where there is strife, and avoid situations or influences that foster fear, division, or hostility toward God. It is to live in alignment with His will, trusting Him even when circumstances are uncertain or opposition arises. True peace flows from faith—an inner tranquility grounded in the knowledge that Christ is victorious, that God reigns, and that His Spirit works within us to sustain and guide. Pursuing peace is more than avoiding conflict; it is the intentional work of living faithfully, fostering harmony in relationships, and resting in the assurance of God's perfect sovereignty over every aspect of life. Pursue peace and live in harmony with God, with others, and within your own heart.

The Danger of the Lone Sheep

In your pursuit of righteousness, faith, love, and peace, do not go at it alone if you can help it. Sometimes solitude is unavoidable, but too often Christians isolate themselves by choice. They distance themselves from other believers and justify it by claiming a lack of true believers, or by labeling others as judgmental, hypocritical, or imperfect. The reality is often simpler: they do not want accountability or reminders of their own shortcomings. They want Christianity on their own terms—emphasizing the parts they like and ignoring the parts they don't.

Being alone allows a version of faith without responsibility, reproof, or challenge. Over time, this self-fashioned Christianity can feel like the only "true" way, making fellowship increasingly difficult unless others conform exactly to one's preferences. I challenge you to embrace discomfort. Fellowship is essential. The sheep that strays from the herd is the sheep most vulnerable to the wolf. Satan hunts by isolating God's children from the very people meant to protect, correct, and encourage them. Accountability is not optional; it is a shield.

How can God use you if you refuse to purify yourself? How can He use you to love if you do not pursue love? How can He use you to encourage and build up your brothers and sisters in the faith if you do not intentionally engage with them? Scripture teaches, "Bear one another's burdens, and thus fulfill the law of Christ," which is to "love one another as I have loved you." How can you claim to love God yet neglect your brothers and sisters in Christ? How can you be guided back from darkness if you walk alone? God calls us not only to pursue personal holiness but to do so alongside those who call on the Lord from a pure heart, drawing strength, correction, and encouragement from the community of faith.

1 John 3:4-5 (LSB)
Everyone who does sin also does lawlessness; and sin is lawlessness. And you know that He was manifested in order to take away sins, and in Him there is no sin.

Here we arrive at one of the most frequently misunderstood and misused passages in this entire letter. A small but vocal group isolates these verses and appeals to them to promote what is commonly called the doctrine of sinless perfection. They read John's words in isolation and conclude, "See, a true Christian does not sin. Therefore, if you sin at all, you cannot truly be saved."

This conclusion, however, only arises when these verses are severed from their context. It is not the product of careful reading, but of selective reading. John has already spoken plainly and unambiguously about the ongoing reality of sin in the believer's life. In the opening chapter, he states that if we say we have no sin, we deceive ourselves and the truth is not in us (1 John 1:8). In the very next chapter, he comforts believers with the assurance that when we sin, we have an Advocate with the Father, Jesus Christ the righteous (1 John 2:1). John has not forgotten what he just wrote, nor is he contradicting himself mid letter. The problem is not John's clarity, but the reader's impatience.

What John is doing here in the early verses of chapter three is laying a foundation that he will continue to build upon throughout the chapter. He introduces strong language intentionally, knowing he will define, qualify, and clarify what he means as he moves forward. As we will see later in this chapter, John explains precisely what he means by sin, by righteousness, and by the manner of life that characterizes the child of God. These verses are not meant to stand alone as a blunt theological slogan. They are part of a carefully developed argument that unfolds across the chapter.

When read in context, John is not teaching that believers never commit acts of sin. He is teaching that sin no longer defines them, rules them, or characterizes their life. He is drawing a distinction between a life marked by unrepentant, ongoing rebellion and a life transformed by the new birth. John is not denying the presence of sin in the believer, but the dominion of sin over the believer. To read these verses as a denial of the believer's ongoing struggle with sin is to read John against John himself, something the Apostle never intended.

The Return of an Ancient Error

Before we can rightly interpret John's meaning, we must understand the theological error being imposed upon the text. What is today labeled "sinless perfection" is not new. As Solomon reminds us, "That which has been is that which will be… there is nothing new under the sun" (Ecclesiastes 1:9). This teaching is simply a recycled form of Pelagianism,[2] a fifth-century heresy which denied original sin and claimed that humanity is born morally neutral—capable, by sheer willpower, of living without sin. Such a view fundamentally misunderstands both the depth of sin and the condition of fallen humanity. It reduces sin to outward behavior and salvation to moral performance.

What is Sin?

To grasp John's argument, we must recover a biblical understanding of what sin actually is. Sin is not merely an external act,

---

2. Pelagianism taught that people are capable of avoiding sin and choosing to live righteous lives even apart from God's grace—John D. Barry et al., eds., "Pelagianism," in *The Lexham Bible Dictionary* (Bellingham, WA: Lexham Press, 2016).

nor is it confined to visible behavior. Sin is an inward corruption that gives rise to action, rooted in the desires of the heart.

In Christ, the believer now lives with a real internal conflict: the competing desires of flesh and Spirit. This is not speculation, but apostolic testimony. As we noted earlier, Paul describes this very war within himself, concluding with the confession, "So then, on the one hand I myself with my mind am serving the law of God, but on the other, with my flesh the law of sin" (Romans 7:25). This inner conflict explains why sin remains something the Christian struggles against, even though it no longer defines or governs him.

Scripture consistently ties sin to death, and death still resides in our mortal bodies. Even after conversion, we remain clothed in flesh, awaiting final redemption. As Paul teaches, "Therefore, just as through one man sin entered into the world, and death through sin, and so death spread to all men, because all sinned" (Romans 5:12). Sin is not something we occasionally pick up or stumble into at random; it is a power that once ruled us entirely. It exercised dominion over us and only lost its mastery through our union with Christ (Romans 6:6–14).

This is why Scripture speaks of sin as a power that dwells within us. When God warned Cain that sin was crouching at the door and that its desire was contrary to him, He was not describing an action Cain had yet committed, but a force already at work within him. Sin is not the strike of the fist but the hatred that tightens it. It is not the act of adultery but the lust that conceives it.

This is precisely what Jesus exposes in the Sermon on the Mount. He does not relax the law, nor does He reduce it to outward compliance. He reveals its true depth. Murder is not merely shedding blood, but harboring hatred. Adultery is not merely the physical act, but lustful intent of the heart. External restraint does not equal righteousness. A person may refrain from acting and yet remain guilty in desire.

Jesus reinforces this same truth when He speaks of trees and fruit. A good tree bears good fruit, and a bad tree bears bad fruit. The fruit is not arbitrary, nor is it independent of the tree itself. Fruit is the product of the internal life of the tree. What the tree is determines what it produces. In the same way, sin and righteousness are not first revealed in actions, but in nature. A believer, having been made alive by the Spirit and indwelt by Him, is a good tree. Because he is spiritually alive, his life bears fruit consistent with that new life. An unbeliever, still spiritually dead, remains a bad tree and can only produce fruit consistent with death.

This does not mean unbelievers never do things we would outwardly call good. They feed the hungry, give to charity, and perform acts of kindness. But Scripture does not define goodness merely by external appearance. These actions, though beneficial to others, remain carnal, driven by self interest, reputation, obligation, or personal satisfaction. The root is not faith, love for God, or obedience flowing from a renewed heart. This is why Jesus can say that no good tree bears bad fruit and no bad tree bears good fruit. He is not speaking merely of visible deeds, but of what drives them. The issue is not what is done, but why it is done.

This exposes the fatal flaw in moralistic religion. A person may say, "I have never murdered," or, "I have never committed adultery," and yet stand condemned by the very desires they entertain. The flesh may restrain itself for fear of consequence, shame, or social stigma, but the heart remains corrupt.

This is why claims of moral goodness apart from God inevitably collapse. Even unbelievers who claim virtue do so within cultures deeply shaped by Christian ethics. When consequences and accountability are removed, people no longer restrain themselves. This is why people behave online in ways they never would face to face. The desire did not suddenly appear; only the restraint disappeared.

This distinction between desire and action also explains what might otherwise appear to be contradictions in Scripture. Rahab's lie is a clear example. When the Israelite spies were hidden in her home, Rahab deliberately misled the authorities of Jericho to protect them from death. Bearing false witness violates God's law, yet Rahab is commended for her faith and counted among the faithful because her action flowed not from selfish desire, deception for personal gain, or malice, but from allegiance to the God of Israel and the protection of His people. The same external act can either be sin or obedience depending on what drives it. Sin is not defined merely by behavior, but by intention. It is the orientation of the heart that determines whether an act flows from faith or from the flesh.

This brings us intentionally back to Paul's words in Romans 7, which we explored in chapter 2, because the internal battle he describes is crucial for understanding the Christian life. Paul does not describe an unregenerate man; he describes a man who loves God's law yet finds another law at work in his members. He distinguishes between his true self and the sin that still dwells in his flesh. He desires righteousness, yet is hindered by indwelling sin. This tension is not evidence of a lack of salvation—it confirms it. The unregenerate man does not grieve over sin itself; he may resent consequences, but he does not hate sin. Paul hates what he does because his desire has been transformed, even though his flesh remains unredeemed.

This internal struggle is often overlooked, and many mistakenly assume it is an either/or proposition: either you sin or you do not. Romans 7 demonstrates the complexity of living in mortal flesh until we are ultimately freed from it.

This is the critical distinction John is emphasizing. The Christian is not defined by the absence of sin, but by the fact that sin no longer rules the heart. Sin remains present, but it no longer drives the believer. The direction of the heart has shifted. Even when the believer falls, it is not sin that governs him. John's point throughout the letter is consistent: he is not teaching sinless perfection. Instead, he is clarifying categories—walking in light versus darkness, faithfulness versus deception, the internal change that distinguishes those who grieve over sin from those who accommodate it. The Christian may stumble, yet still walks in the Spirit; the one whose life is defined by sin is revealed by the pattern of unrepentant rebellion.

When John speaks of "the one who does sin", the Greek verb used is ποιεῖ (poiei) in the present tense, which conveys continuous or ongoing action. This is why many translations render it as "practices sin" rather than a simple "does sin," emphasizing that John is referring not to a single misstep, but to a settled, habitual pattern of sin. It is not describing momentary failures or the ongoing struggle of believers, but a life characterized by willful rebellion and persistent disobedience. His aim is not to unsettle the tender conscience, but to expose false assurance.

Understanding this distinction is not merely theological; it calls each believer to examine the heart and the life that flows from it. As we consider John's warning, we are invited to look deeply at our own lives—not superficially, but in practice. What does your life reveal about your heart? Are you struggling against sin, or are you resisting God's commands? This is the critical distinction: the man indwelt by the Spirit battles his flesh, while the man with empty belief battles God's authority. Masks may deceive others, and even ourselves, but they cannot deceive the One who sees the heart.

Self-examination is not about comparing yourself to others or pointing to visible sins to declare yourself righteous by contrast. That is the way of the Pharisee, not the way of faith. True examination turns inward. It asks honest questions: What patterns am I tolerating? What steps am I taking to flee what entangles me? Do I grieve over sin, or do I excuse it? Testing your faith is not a checklist; it is an honest reckoning with the heart. It is easier to ignore these questions and redirect judgment outward, but righteousness demands that judgment begin with ourselves.

John's words are not meant to condemn the struggling believer—they are meant to awaken the complacent one and to bring awareness to the subtle lies of those who would mislead us. Among us are false teachers and the spirits of antichrist, downplaying sin and twisting truth, and John's admonition reminds us to discern carefully and anchor ourselves in the light of Christ.

In Christ There Is No Sin

Christ was manifested to take away sin. He fulfilled the law perfectly on our behalf and bore the penalty for our transgressions, satisfying the demands of justice. In doing so, He has removed the legal power of sin over us. Our sins are fully paid for, and the law no longer stands against those who are in Him. This is not merely a matter of moral instruction—this is a legal reality secured by His righteousness and shed blood.

Because of this, believers are no longer under the authority of the law as a condemning force. While sin still resides in our mortal bodies, it no longer holds ultimate power over us. Christ has satisfied the law's requirements and set us free to walk in the Spirit. The believer's identity is now found in Him, and in this freedom, we can live in the confidence that our debt has been canceled, our record wiped clean, and the penalty satisfied.

We are in Christ, and in Him there is no sin. Through His Spirit, we have been washed, cleansed of all sin, and even when we stumble in these mortal bodies, we have an Advocate interceding on our behalf. One of my favorite passages is Psalm 32, which Paul references in Romans 4: *"Blessed is the one whose transgression is forgiven, whose sin is covered. Blessed is the man against whom the Lord counts no iniquity, and in whose spirit there is no deceit"* (Romans 4:7–8). For those in Christ, God does not continue to count sin against them. Their ledger has been stamped, expunged by the Judge, their debt paid in full.

This is a legal declaration, not a statement about our mortal perfection. Even as believers, we will still sin; our flesh remains prone to selfish desires and failure. Yet in the courtroom of heaven, our sins are not recorded. To illustrate, imagine a basketball scoreboard: every basket requires someone to press a button to count the points. If a basket goes in but no one presses the button, the points aren't counted. In the same way, when we fall short in Christ, our sin is not tallied. God's righteousness fills the cup so fully that there is no space left for our sin.

We have died to the law in Christ; therefore, we are no longer under its condemnation (Romans 6:14). The law's role was to expose sin, but in Christ, the law cannot accuse us. If there is no law applied to condemn us, then in the legal sense, we do not sin. This is not to say that believers live flawlessly; rather, it is a declaration of the legal reality before God. Our righteousness in Christ is imputed to us, and His perfect life covers our shortcomings completely.

Understanding this is crucial. It frees the believer from the fear of legal condemnation while still maintaining the call to holiness. We do not use this as a license to sin, but as assurance that our standing before God is secure. In Him, our failures cannot diminish His work, and our sins, though real in our flesh, cannot separate us from His love or negate His cleansing.

1 John 3:6 (LSB)
No one who abides in Him sins; no one who sins has seen Him or has come to know Him.

What the Apostle has demonstrated from the beginning of this letter is clear: John is not speaking about individual acts of shortcoming or isolated failures. Rather, he is presenting categorical distinctions among people. All men sin, but not all men practice sin. To illustrate, consider a point shared by the late Voddie Baucham, a pastor, author, and one of my favorite preachers of the Word, in one of his sermons.[3]

Let us think for a moment about children. All children disobey at times; even the most well-behaved child will have moments of failure. Yet we instinctively understand that we do not categorize children by isolated incidents. A child's reputation is shaped by the general pattern of their life, not by a single moment caught in isolation.

When a child who is habitually rebellious disobeys, it comes as no surprise. Disobedience is what defines them. They resist correction, disregard instruction, and repeat the same behavior over and over again, often with little concern for consequences. Their actions reflect what they intentionally set out to do. But when a child who is generally obedient disobeys, the response is different. The failure may be real, but it is not deliberate. It is not who they are. They are learning, growing, and striving to do better, even when they stumble. We do not suddenly relabel them as a "disobedient child" because of one failure. Their

---

3. Baucham, Voddie. *Walk in the Light*. Sermon, Grace Family Baptist Church, October 9, 2022.

identity remains intact, even though the action was wrong. The behavior is momentary, not defining.

If a child's identity is shaped by a pattern of obedience, occasional disobedience does not nullify that designation. In the same way, a servant of Christ is an obedient child even when he stumbles. This is why, upon reaching chapter 3, believers should not look back on their failures with paralyzing fear or begin to question their salvation. John is not addressing isolated lapses here. He is confronting heresies that sought to redefine what it means to truly know Christ. He is drawing a categorical line between the believer, whose heart is being transformed from the inside out, and the unbeliever, whose life remains governed by sin.

The reality that believers still sin does not place them back into the category of those who walk in darkness. From the opening lines of this letter, John has been drawing a clear and consistent line between those who walk in the light and those who walk in darkness, between the believer and the liar. Identity, in John's framework, is not determined by a single fall, but by the overall trajectory of the heart.

Scripture affirms this same truth elsewhere. "For the righteous falls seven times and rises again, but the wicked stumble in times of calamity" (Proverbs 24:16). The righteous man is not defined by the fact that he falls, but by the fact that he gets back up. His life is marked by repentance, correction, and perseverance, not by settled rebellion.

The believer may stumble, yet he grieves over his sin and instinctively seeks Christ for restoration. The one who lives in sin without remorse, however, reveals a heart still submerged in darkness. This is the distinction John has emphasized throughout chapters 1 and 2, and it remains his focal point here: categorical lines are drawn by direction, not by momentary actions.

Consider the realities of human temptation. Can I lose my temper and become angry? Yes. Can I be tempted by desire or envy? Yes. Can pride rise in my heart? Certainly. But the question is not whether temptation exists; the question is whether these things define my life. Do I intentionally cultivate anger, lust, jealousy, or pride? No. When sin arises, I grieve it. I confess it. I turn again toward Christ and seek to walk in step with the Spirit. This is the mark of the believer's life: failure met with repentance, not a settled pattern of sin.

John is speaking of those who engage in sin deliberately and without regret. He is not describing the struggling believer navigating ordinary days filled with weakness and failure. He is addressing those whose lives are marked by persistent, unrepentant rebellion. If someone truly knew Christ, His transforming work would be evident, even if slowly. There would be change. There would be conviction. There would be grief over sin.

How can someone who professes belief in the cross continue in the very sins that drove the nails into Christ's hands without remorse? Where is the grief? Where is the conviction? I do not claim perfection. I live daily in the tension between flesh and Spirit. My Spirit longs for righteousness, even as my flesh resists. On my worst days, I fall at the foot of the cross. On my best days, I still stand there. Redemption is not the absence of struggle, but the assurance of Christ's advocacy, the presence of His grace, and the continual call to rise again and walk in the light.

The christian life is not marked by sinlessness, but by repentance. We do not stand because we never fall, but because we know Him, and that knowledge draws us again and again out of darkness and into the light.

> *1 John 3:7-8 (LSB)*
> *Little children, let no one deceive you. The one who does righteousness is righteous, just as He is righteous. The one who does sin is of the devil, because the devil sins from the beginning. The Son of God was manifested for this purpose, to destroy the works of the devil.*

"Let No One Deceive You"

Do not take passages like this out of the letter and let them stand alone. By themselves, passages like this can sound as if the Apostle is claiming that anyone who sins is not truly saved. Yet, context is everything. The Apostle is giving the same warning I wish more Christians proclaimed today, especially in a culture where Christianity has been watered down and made comfortable. If I were to deliver this message personally, it might sound something like this:

"My brothers and sisters in Christ, do not be deceived by anyone who claims to be a Christian. We know that those in Christ walk in the light. Yet, we see so-called Christians attending church on Sunday, confessing to know Christ, and then walking in darkness from Monday through Saturday. We know this is not the lifestyle of a true follower of Christ. How can someone confess to know Christ and yet live in habitual sin? How can someone claim to follow Him while continually choosing what is contrary to His commands? How can someone believe that Christ died for their sins and yet love the very things that drove the nails into His hands? How can one profess love for Christ and simultaneously love the very things that pervert His law?"

Would such a message lead you to believe that struggling with sin means you are not saved? I pray that it would not. This message is not directed at the believer who wrestles with sin in his flesh, striving to walk in a manner worthy of the Lord.

Rather, it is intended for those who feel no grief over their sin. In fact, I would argue that the very people this warning targets would be largely unmoved by it, because they are blind to their sin. We grieve over our sin only because God's Spirit dwells within us. It is by His Spirit that we know Him, and it is by His Spirit that we recognize our sin.

I sometimes hear from young Christians who say, "Mike, I am struggling with [fill in the sin], and I don't know if I am saved." My response is always a question in return: "Were you grieved by your sins before you came to faith? Did you sorrow over your failure to the Lord before you knew Him? When you were dead in your sins, did you ever sit in true remorse over coming short of His standard?" The answer is always no. Before salvation, you may have grieved over the consequences of your sin, or even felt anxiety over the fear of being caught. But you never felt true sorrow for sinning against the Holy and Righteous God of the universe. You did not love Him, you did not know Him, and so the reality of your sin remained hidden. It is only when we know Him that the true condition of our hearts begins to be revealed.

The One Who Does Righteousness and the One Who Does Sin

Before diving into the text, it is important to note a feature of the Legacy Standard Bible (LSB). The LSB is highly literal in its translation, which is why it reads "does righteousness" and "does sin." At first glance, English readers might hear this as a single act or momentary choice. However, as I defined earlier, the Greek verb used here is ποιεῖ (poiei), the term conveys ongoing, habitual action. This distinction is crucial: John is not addressing isolated missteps, but the consistent patterns of a person's life. What someone repeatedly does reveals their category—their spiritual identity—rather than a single failure defining them.

This is the categorical designation we have been emphasizing throughout this chapter. John is not saying "the one who *is* righteous," nor is he claiming the one who does righteousness never stumbles. To illustrate, consider this analogy: If I said, "The one who works out is healthy," I would not mean the person who never misses a gym session, who never slips on their diet, or who never fails to make wise choices about their health. Rather, a person who works out is someone whose life generally reflects a consistent commitment to fitness. The category is determined by the trajectory of the person's practice, not by occasional lapses.

Similarly, Christians may still struggle with sin, yet in the majority of their actions, they strive to live righteously. Their identity is defined by the pattern of their life—the overarching orientation of their heart toward God and obedience—rather than by isolated failures.

On the other hand, the one who lives in rebellion against God is said to be "of the devil." This is not a reference to someone who occasionally stumbles, but to someone whose life is characterized by ongoing rebellion. Just as God is light, the devil embodies darkness. The person whose life is defined by rebellion follows the devil's path, consumed by self-interest, pride, and opposition to God. Outward appearances may deceive, but inwardly, this person remains enslaved to the same destructive patterns the devil has pursued since the beginning.

To make this practical: if your day has been focused on serving the Lord, walking in the light, loving the brethren, and pursuing Christ, yet you experienced a moment of anger, pride, or lust, does that mean you are now someone who "practices sin"? Certainly not. To return to the analogy of the person committed to fitness: if someone works out five out of seven days, eats healthily six out of seven, and consistently makes wise lifestyle choices, we would not categorize them as lazy, gluttonous, or unhealthy based on the occasional lapse. Likewise, the believer's life is assessed by the general trajectory of their practice, not the exceptions.

Is there room for improvement? Absolutely—perfection has not yet been achieved. Yet, as we evaluate our lives, we do not allow fleeting moments of weakness, the failures we are learning from, or short seasons of sin to redefine who we are in Christ. Our identity is determined by the consistent direction of our heart, the pattern of our practice, and the Spirit's work within us, not by isolated actions or temporary failures.

Destroying the Works of the Devil

To understand how Christ destroys these works, we must first understand the nature of the enemy. Sadly, most people's understanding of Satan stems from media and pop culture rather than Scripture. Satan is not a red-skinned monster with horns and a pitchfork. He is not equal to God, nor is he God's "rival" in a dualistic struggle between equal forces of good and evil. Satan does not run hell, and he is not a threat to God's throne.

He was the first heavenly being to rebel—a glorious being created in majesty—yet today he is as insignificant in the presence of God as we are. People often ask, "Why didn't God just kill Satan long ago?" I would respond that Satan's continued existence is actually an insult to him. His existence demonstrates that he is not a threat to God's sovereign plan; if he were, God would have destroyed him instantly. Satan knows this. He knows that God could crush him, and he knows that God will crush him, as promised since the Garden in Genesis 3.

However, rather than crushing him immediately, God allows him to exist to watch the plan of redemption unfold—a plan

Satan is absolutely incapable of stopping. His destruction will come only after that plan is complete. Satan will be forced to see everything set right before he is destroyed in the presence of all God's children—the very people he despises. He will go to his end knowing he didn't stop a single thing God intended to do.

The Nameless Accuser

Who is this devil? The word *devil* comes from the Greek *diabolos*, meaning slanderer or accuser. He is also called *Satan* in Scripture. Neither is a proper name, but a title: the Hebrew term likewise means *accuser* or *adversary*. These titles describe his role rather than reveal a personal identity, helping us understand who he truly is—the enemy of God and His people, the one who opposes righteousness, tempts believers, and seeks to bring accusation and division.

The Old Testament speaks little of Satan and does not explicitly identify the serpent in Eden as him. It is only in the New Testament, through the words of Jesus, that this connection is made clear, revealing the true identity of the adversary behind sin and rebellion (John 8:44).

I believe we do not know Satan's actual name because God has sovereignly blotted it out. Scripture teaches that the memory of the names of His enemies can be wiped from the earth. In the same way, although the devil continues to exist until his final judgment, no one knows his true name. Even those who seek to glorify him cannot speak it.

Many mistakenly claim his name is Lucifer. This arises from a Latin translation of Isaiah, where the term simply means "Light-bearer" or "Morning Star" and functions as a descriptive title rather than a personal name. The Hebrew phrase translated also refers to one who bears light—a designation that could apply to any heavenly being in God's service. Other names, like Gadreel from the Book of Enoch, come from non-biblical sources and have no authority in Scripture.

The point is this: he is the accuser and adversary, the enemy of God, whose ultimate power is limited by God's sovereign will. Titles such as *Satan* or *Light-bearer* reveal his nature and function, not his personal identity. Understanding this helps us recognize his tactics, resist his schemes, and remain focused on Christ, the one who has already defeated him.

Some ask why God has not already destroyed Satan. To that, I offer two answers: first, the greatest insult to him is that God allows him to exist. He is like an ant crawling on the leg of a lion—the lion is unconcerned, demonstrating his utter impotence. Second, God will destroy him at the appointed time, in the presence of all the saints. Rebellion began with him, and redemption will culminate in his final and total destruction.

The Power of Condemnation

Satan is forever known as the accuser, and this title defines his work. To understand his power, we must return to the garden. Satan was created to serve, just as all the heavenly hosts were. Scripture gives us a glimpse of this being as a "guardian cherub"—beautiful, adorned with jewels, the most radiant of the heavenly hosts (Ezekiel 28:14). Yet, pride filled his heart when he saw mankind made in the image of God.

He saw a creation made to exist in close proximity with God for His own pleasure. Knowing that God must punish transgression, Satan deceived the woman into sinning, and she led the man into sin. From that moment, the accuser had a "legal" claim against us. Because God is Just, Satan could challenge God's own righteousness if God allowed us to remain in His presence without punishing our sin.

Satan's goal is to convince you to sin so that he can get you in trouble with your Father. He is like the schoolyard bully who tempts you to break a rule just so he can run to the teacher and accuse you. His power is **condemnation**. Yet, in Christ, that power is gone.

The Disarming of the Enemy

This is the power of the enemy: he convinces you to sin so that he can accuse you of sin. His primary weapon is condemnation. Yet, in Christ, that weapon has been shattered. As Paul writes in Romans 8:1, "there is now no condemnation for those in Christ Jesus." But Paul goes even further in that same chapter to show why the Accuser's mouth is shut. He asks, "Who will bring a charge against God's elect? God is the one who justifies; who is the one who condemns? Christ Jesus is He who died, yes, rather who was raised, who is at the right hand of God, who also intercedes for us" (Romans 8:33-34).

If Jesus is not there to advocate for you, Satan will be there to accuse you. But the enemy cannot successfully accuse you for a debt that has already been ratified and settled in the highest court. This is why the legal language of the New Testament is so vital for a new believer to grasp. You were once a prisoner to your own debt, but Christ performed a divine legal swap.

Consider the triumph described in Colossians 2:13-15. Paul explains that when we were dead in our transgressions, God "made us alive together with Christ, having forgiven us all our transgressions." He did this by "canceling out the certificate of debt consisting of decrees against us, which was hostile to us, and taking it out of the way by nailing it to the cross. When He had disarmed the rulers and authorities, He made a public display of them, triumphing over them in Him."

Satan has been disarmed because the Lord Jesus bore our iniquities. The enemy tried to tempt Jesus in the wilderness, hoping to find a single crack in His righteousness, but he failed. Because Jesus lived a perfectly sinless life, the righteous requirement of the Law can now be fulfilled in us through Him. He condemned sin in the flesh on the cross so that we could be justified by His atonement.

When Jesus was on the cross, He cried out, *"It is finished!"* (John 19:30). The Greek word used there is τετέλεσται (*tetélestai*). In that culture, this was a specific legal and commercial term used to denote that a debt was paid in full, an obligation was met, or a transaction was final. It is written in the perfect tense, which tells us the action was completed in the past with results that continue forever.

Jesus did not die *just* for your sins of yesterday or today. When He paid the penalty, He paid the full price for *all* your sins—past, present, and future. This is why I wanted to bring the words of David and Paul back to your mind after mentioning them earlier. I am doubling down on the power of these words because they define your security:

"Blessed are those whose lawless deeds have been forgiven, and whose sins have been covered; blessed is the man whose sin the Lord will not take into account" (Romans 4:7-8)

Your deeds of yesterday are forgiven, your present failures are covered, and He does not even count the sins of your tomorrow. If you are in Christ, although you still struggle in the flesh, your spirit does not sin. God is no longer keeping a record of your failures because the ledger has been cleared. Those born of God do not "sin" in the legal sense because even when we stumble, we have a permanent Advocate in heaven. The Father looks upon His precious Son, the Lamb who was slain, and does not tally our debt because Christ has already paid the bill in full.

1 John 3:9 (LSB)
Everyone who has been born of God does not sin, because His seed abides in him; and he cannot sin, because he has been born of God.

Now, John begins to show us *why* he can make such a bold claim: why those born of God do not sin in the covenantal, legal sense. This is the moment where the Apostle illuminates what he has been teaching throughout chapters 1 and 2 and the first half of this chapter. He is not suddenly asserting that Christians are morally flawless or walk without failure. Rather, he explains the foundation for why sin no longer defines the believer and cannot be counted against them.

At this point, the importance of reading John carefully and allowing him to unfold his argument should be evident. Earlier, we noted that many misunderstandings in this letter arise when statements are isolated and pressed beyond their intended scope. John is now doing exactly what he promised to do. He is building, clarifying, and defining his own language. These verses were never meant to stand alone. Verse numbers, added centuries later for convenience, can tempt readers to stop too soon, but John expects us to keep reading, to follow his logic, and to let the surrounding context explain his meaning.

As we do, his language becomes clear. John is explaining why sin no longer governs the believer. Whoever has died to sin cannot be charged as a sinner, and if you are in Christ, you have died with Him. This is the foundation beneath everything he has been saying. The reason the believer no longer lives under the dominion of sin, and the reason sin no longer condemns us, is because God's seed, the Holy Spirit Himself, abides in us. His presence is not symbolic, temporary, or passive. He remains in the believer, and because He abides in us, we are no longer under the legal authority of sin or the law.

If God's seed abides in you, then you are cleansed from sin and protected from sin. You are not standing before God in your own righteousness, but clothed in the righteousness of Christ. His obedience has become yours. His death has become yours. His resurrection has secured your life. This is why John can confidently say that those born of God do not sin. He is speaking in covenantal and legal categories. The believer cannot be counted as a transgressor because the charge has already been answered, the debt has already been paid, and the verdict has already been rendered.

The Holy Spirit bears witness within you that you belong to God (Romans 8:16). He guards you from the evil one (1 John 5:18; John 17:15). He intercedes on your behalf according to the will of God (Romans 8:26-27). He teaches you to cry out, "Abba, Father" (Romans 8:15; Galatians 4:6). He testifies to the Father that you are His child and seals you as His own (Ephesians 1:13-14). This reality is not grounded in your consistency, but in God's faithfulness (2 Timothy 2:13). It is not sustained by your performance, but by His abiding presence within you (John 14:16-17).

John is not lowering the standard of holiness. He is magnifying the power of regeneration. A heart indwelt by God is a heart that has been fundamentally changed. Sin may still trouble the flesh, but it no longer reigns over the soul. The believer does not remain in sin because the seed of God produces life, conviction, repentance, and perseverance. What God plants, He grows and preserves.

Prayer of Gratitude

Let us pause and marvel at the grace of God. Oh, what is man that You are mindful of him? Lord, thank You for rescuing, redeeming, and saving me. What a beautiful name it is, the name of the Lord. Let us pray in gratitude for this gift. We thank You, Heavenly Father, for what You have done. We thank You, Lord Jesus, for bearing our sins and dying in our place. We thank You, Holy Spirit, for dwelling within us and walking with us. We deserved hell, yet You have poured out the riches of Your mercy. May we never depart from Your presence, rising each day to fall before You in thanks for every good and perfect gift. We thank You, Lord Jesus, for revealing the Father and serving as our High Priest and Mediator. We thank You, Holy Spirit, for guiding us in Your Light. Amen.

1 John 3:10-11 (LSB)
By this the children of God and the children of the devil are manifested: everyone who does not do righteousness is not of God, as well as the one who does not love his brother. For this is the message which you have heard from the beginning, that we should love one another.

Here the Apostle brings clarity to everything we have been discussing throughout chapters 1-3. John has been drawing categorical distinctions between two types of people: those who belong to God and those who belong to the devil. Now, he gives titles to these categories: children of God versus children of the devil. This language is not new; John is not inventing terminology. He is repeating the words of our Lord, who used the same language in John 8 when He referred to the Pharisees as children of the devil (John 8:44). This is crucial for understanding John's point: these designations are not based on outward appearances or isolated actions, but on the posture of the heart.

In John 8, when Jesus refers to the Pharisees as children of the devil, He explains why they are such: they follow in the same footsteps as the devil, who was a liar and a murderer from the beginning (John 8:44). Jesus is not speaking of actual lineage to

Satan in the flesh, but of a spirit of rebellion and sin. Those who follow in rebellion against God are children of the devil; those who are born of God follow in the way of truth and light. Both categories are spiritual in essence. One could also say that those who are children of the devil are spiritually dead, while those who are children of God are born again and spiritually alive. A dead tree bears bad fruit; a living tree bears good fruit. Those who receive the Spirit of God receive living water, and that water flows out of them in abundance, as Jesus describes in John 7:38.

Again, John uses the words "by this," which, as we covered in the last chapter, appear frequently throughout this letter. This signals to us, the readers, that John is providing descriptive information. He says, "by this" the children of God and children of the devil are manifested, which means revealed. These are the attributes that disclose the true identity of a person. One may put on a mask, pretending to be something one is not, but Jesus referred to such people as hypocrites (Matthew 23:27–28). The word hypocrite means an actor, someone performing a role, pretending to be what they are not.[4]

In our generation, some Christians say, "We are all hypocrites, because we are trying to be something we are not." To this claim, I firmly object. I am not a hypocrite. I am a broken and wretched sinner in need of grace, and by the grace of God and by His Spirit, I live in service to Him. I will fail, but I will rise again. No matter how much I stumble, I will never take my eyes off Christ. I do not wear a mask; I embrace exactly who I am and put my trust in the finished work of the cross. Remember my final

---

4. ὑποκριτής (*hypokritēs*), properly an actor, a hypocrite, one who outwardly plays the part of a religious man to perfection, but is inwardly alien to the spirit of true religion. Alexander Souter, *A Pocket Lexicon to the Greek New Testament* (Oxford: Clarendon Press, 1917), 270.

words from chapter 1: the Gospel is just as much about knowing who you are and what you have done as it is about knowing who He is and what He has done.

A hypocrite pretends he is not who he really is. Like the Pharisees, a hypocrite pretends to care about righteousness, but inwardly is rotten. They are like whitewashed tombs—beautiful on the outside, but dead inside. You cannot staple apples to a dead tree and pretend it produces fruit. The tree needs life, and the fruit it bears reveals the truth of the tree.

Likewise, a child of God or a child of the devil is revealed through actions. Identity is not earned through perfection, but displayed in the intent of the heart. John uses the same word earlier in this chapter when speaking of the Son of God being revealed (1 John 3:5), drawing a theological connection: just as Christ's glory is revealed, so is the reality of a person's heart. This aligns with James's words: "I will show you my faith by my works" (James 2:18). I do not need to announce my faith; my actions demonstrate it. Abraham did not need to say, "I trust God"—his actions demonstrated it when he took Isaac to the top of the mountain. Every example of true faith in Scripture is in action, not words. We are not justified by verbal confession alone, but by genuine faith that is evident in the life it produces.

The hypocrite says, "Look at me, I am righteous; I do this and I do that." But the one who loves the Lord serves Him and demonstrates faith in action. Faith, regeneration, and identity are revealed in how we live—not through flawless perfection, but in the consistent direction and intent of our actions. Children of God are revealed by their love, by practicing what is good, and by a heart consistently oriented toward righteousness.

A child of God may stumble; he may fail daily in the flesh. Yet his life exhibits a consistent pattern of love and obedience. He is motivated by a desire to serve God and pursue what is right, even when executed imperfectly. His love for God and neighbor moves him to confess sin, seek restoration, and persevere in holy living.

By contrast, the child of the devil may appear outwardly righteous, speak knowledgeably about God's law, or even act morally, yet the intent of the heart is absent. Genuine love for God or others is missing. The child of the devil acts as though he is perfect, content with himself, blind to the darkness in which he walks, and therefore unable to perceive or acknowledge sin.

Jesus highlighted this truth in John 13:35: "By this all people will know that you are my disciples, if you have love for one another." Notice the "by this" language—Jesus is telling us exactly how the world will recognize who we are. It will not be by our knowledge of Scripture, not by miraculous works, not by appearances of righteousness, and certainly not by boasting about how good we are. The evidence of our true identity is found in love. Love is the sign, the hallmark, and the visible proof to the world of whose we are. John carries this principle forward in his letter: practicing righteousness and demonstrating love are inseparable. Those who belong to God consistently bear the fruit of His Spirit in acts of love and goodness. Conversely, those who lack love reveal that they do not belong to Him. Love is not merely a feeling; it is the tangible expression of a heart transformed by God, a heart devoted to holiness, righteousness, and mercy.

Outward appearances can be deceptive. Children of God may seem flawed, messy, or weak in human eyes, while children of the devil may appear confident, capable, and morally upright. Yet the ultimate measure lies in the heart: love versus self-interest, obedience versus rebellion, light versus darkness. This is the distinction John has been emphasizing: who we are in Christ is demonstrated by the direction and intent of our hearts, not by perfection or the absence of failure.

In summary, verses 9 and 10 draw together the teaching that has preceded them: the one who practices righteousness belongs to God, the one who does not is not. Love serves as both proof and evidence. Lives guided by the Spirit expose the true condition of the heart. The child of God walks in the light, confesses sin, loves God and neighbor, and strives continually for holiness. The child of the devil walks in darkness, blind to sin, self-centered, and unrepentant. This revelation is not about flawless performance but about the persistent orientation and intent of the heart.

1 John 3:12 (LSB)
not as Cain, who was of the evil one and slew his brother. And for what reason did he slay him? Because his deeds were evil, and his brother's were righteous.

John now turns our attention to the first act of hate in human history—the first murder recorded after the Fall. This is not a digression; it is a direct follow-up to the previous verses. If we are called to love our brothers, John shows why jealousy and hatred are fundamentally opposed to that calling. Cain serves as the first recorded example of a heart turned against God and neighbor. He did not love his brother Abel, but instead allowed jealousy to take root, ultimately driving him to murder.

Jealousy is rooted in a heart focused on self rather than others; it is the fruit of selfishness. Love, by contrast, is selfless, putting the good of others above one's own desires. In this light, the opposite of love is not mere indifference, but selfishness, which manifests in envy, pride, and covetousness. John reminds us that sin originates in the heart, and the child of God resists allowing jealousy, pride, and self-centeredness to dictate his actions, choosing instead the path of love, humility, and service.

We see this principle reflected throughout Scripture. Jesus' parable of the prodigal son illustrates a similar dynamic. While many focus on the lost son, the parable is equally about the older brother, whose heart was filled with jealousy and entitlement. He could not rejoice over the restoration of his brother because he compared himself to his brother, not realizing the blessings he had already received. James echoes this principle in James 4:1-2, pointing out that jealousy and desire stir up sin in the heart. Children of the devil, exemplified by the Pharisees, often mirror this pattern. They expected the Messiah to come to them directly and dismissed His ministry to the broken and lost. Their hearts reveal the same pride and self-focus as Cain.

Cain was not a child of God, but a child of the devil, and his heart reveals the consequences of selfishness. He loved himself and did not love his brother, allowing jealousy to fester and ultimately drive him to murder. Abel, in contrast, approached God with humility and obedience, offering the firstborn of his flock—not as a measure of his own merit, but as an act of faithful submission, returning to God what had already been entrusted to him. His offering, a lamb, foreshadowed the perfect sacrifice of Christ, the righteous Lamb who would reconcile humanity to God.

God accepted Abel's offering because it came from a heart of submission to God, returning to Him what was already His. Cain, however, refused to see beyond himself and resented the favor God showed to Abel. His envy exposed the hardness of his heart and led him to commit the first murder recorded in human history. In this story, John reminds us that the true mark of a child of God is a heart of love, while the mark of a child of the devil is a heart consumed by hatred, jealousy, and self-interest.

The Serpent Seed Heresy

Before we continue with Cain and Abel, I feel compelled—though reluctantly—to address a heresy that has circulated over the past couple of centuries: the so-called "Serpent Seed" doctrine. I do not respect this teaching, nor would I ever want to spend time giving it credence. Yet in an age of information and technology, where falsehoods spread rapidly and widely, it is necessary to confront even the most absurd claims for the sake of truth. Proponents assert that when John calls Cain a child of the devil, he means it literally—that the serpent, Satan, impregnated Eve, making Cain the physical offspring of the devil. This is utterly baseless.

This view fundamentally misreads both Genesis 3 and 1 John 3:12. Genesis 3:15, the first promise of the Gospel, speaks of the enmity between the seed of the woman and the seed of the serpent—a conflict representing the ongoing opposition between God's people and the world, a reality reiterated throughout Scripture, in Jesus' warnings, and in John's letter. Christ is the promised seed of the woman, and all who are in Him share that promise, standing spiritually opposed to the kingdom of the devil. John, like Jesus and Paul, understands "seed" spiritually, not physically. Jesus calls the Pharisees children of the devil (John 8:44) to indicate spiritual alignment, not literal parentage. Likewise, Romans 9 and Galatians 3 show that "seed" is not merely physical lineage; not all of Abraham's offspring are children of promise, but all in Christ share in the blessing of the promised seed. Scripture confirms this: Cain was the son of Adam and Eve (Genesis 4:1: "Now Adam knew Eve his wife, and she conceived and bore Cain, saying, 'I have gotten a man with the help of the Lord.'").

Cain, Abel, and the Gospel

Since John himself draws our attention to Cain, it is worth pausing for a moment to admire the beauty of God's redemptive plan and the way Scripture consistently foreshadows the Gospel. This is not a digression, but a deeper reflection on the very example John uses to illustrate hatred, jealousy, and spiritual opposition. From the earliest pages of Scripture, God is already revealing the conflict between faith and self reliance, love and jealousy, submission and rebellion.

Genesis 3:15 foreshadows the Gospel by declaring that the seed of the woman will crush the serpent. This language is striking, as women are not ordinarily spoken of as carrying seed, yet Eve is told that her seed will triumph. This points us forward to Christ, who would come not from the seed of man, but by the power of God, born of a woman. Immediately following this promise, the account of Cain and Abel unfolds, providing the first prophetic picture of the Gospel in action and the first visible manifestation of the promised enmity. Abel's offering, a lamb, points forward to Jesus, the righteous Lamb of God. Cain's offering, by contrast, was the fruit of his own labor, brought from the cursed ground and rooted in self-reliance rather than humble submission.

The principle is clear. We cannot approach God on the basis of our own works, as though they earn His favor. We must come to Him through the Lamb, trusting in His provision rather than our performance. Abel approached God in faith, acknowledging dependence and giving back what God had first provided. Cain approached God on his own terms, presenting the work of his hands and expecting acceptance on the basis of self effort. When God showed favor to Abel, Cain's heart responded not with repentance, but with jealousy. That jealousy became the seedbed of hatred, and hatred ultimately gave birth to violence.

This pattern reveals that the enmity spoken of in Genesis 3:15 has always been fueled by jealousy. Those who trust in God's provision are opposed by those who trust in themselves. Cain's hatred toward Abel was not merely personal, but spiritual. Abel's life exposed Cain's heart. In the same way, the light of righteousness provokes hostility from those who walk in darkness. Cain's jealousy and resentment exemplify the heart of a child of the devil, while Abel's humility and faith reveal the heart of a child of God.

In this way, the story of Cain and Abel does not only illustrate human sin, it proclaims the Gospel in shadow form. Love rooted in faith stands opposed to jealousy rooted in pride. Submission to God stands opposed to self-interest. From the beginning, Scripture shows us that those born of God walk by faith and love, while those who belong to the devil are driven by jealousy, hatred, and rebellion.

1 John 3:13-14 (LSB)
Do not marvel, brothers, if the world hates you. We know that we have passed out of death into life, because we love the brothers. The one who does not love abides in death.

Do not marvel if the world hates you

It is no accident that John places the account of Cain and Abel immediately before reminding the brethren that hatred from the world is inevitable. He says plainly, "Do not marvel, brothers, if the world hates you." This hatred should not surprise us. It is the same enmity God declared from the beginning, now playing itself out in every generation. The conflict between Cain and Abel was not just personal; it was spiritual. That same hostility continues wherever faith confronts self reliance, wherever light exposes darkness, and wherever Christ is present in His people.

Jesus Himself prepared His disciples for this reality. "If the world hates you, know that it has hated me before it hated you" (John 15:18). He went on to explain why this hatred exists: "If you were of the world, the world would love you as its own; but because you are not of the world, but I chose you out of the world, therefore the world hates you" (John 15:19). The issue is not personality, tone, or presentation. The issue is identity. Believers no longer belong to the world, and the world recognizes that separation. Darkness does not hate the light because the light is unkind, but because the light exposes what the darkness wants to conceal (John 3:19-20).

This is a hard truth that many Christians struggle to accept. We all desire to be liked. We all feel the pull to soften edges, to explain ourselves, to search for a way to live as Christians without offending anyone. Much of modern Christianity is built on the illusion that it is possible to please the world and remain faithful to Christ. But Scripture does not support this hope. If the world hates you because of Christ, the only way they will stop hating you is if you abandon Him. If it is Christ in you that provokes their hostility, then removing Christ is the only way to gain their approval.

This does not mean we should be rude, harsh, or careless. Peter is clear that suffering for sin does not glorify God, but suffering for righteousness does (1 Peter 2:19-20). We are not to repay evil with evil or insult with insult (1 Peter 3:9). We are to live honorably, love sincerely, and walk humbly. But we must also accept this reality: it is perfectly fine if people hate us because of Christ, but it is wrong if people hate Christ because of us. Our concern should not be whether the world approves of us, but whether we are living in a way that reflects our Lord.

We are responsible for our obedience; God is responsible for our reputation.

Passed from Death to Life

John now explains why we do not marvel at the world's hatred. "We know that we have passed out of death into life." Our confidence is not rooted in the world's response to us, but in what God has already done for us. We know where we came from, and we know where we are going. The believer no longer abides in death, and therefore no longer needs the approval of those who do.

This is the same confidence Jesus displayed throughout His ministry. When He was rejected, mocked, and accused, He did not scramble to defend Himself, because He knew who He was and where He came from. Surrounded by unbelief and hostility, He could say without hesitation, "You are from below; I am from above" (John 8:23), drawing a clear line between those who belong to this world and the One sent from the Father. When pressed to deny His relationship with God, He responded, "If I were to say that I do not know Him, I would be a liar like you" (John 8:55). That same settled confidence remained during His trial, when He was struck, mocked, and spat upon, yet did not retaliate or plead His case (Matthew 26:67–68; 27:30). His identity was not shaped by their accusations, because His life was anchored in the Father.

John teaches us that we share in this assurance. We do not need to marvel when the world hates us, because their hatred confirms what has already taken place. We have passed from death to life. The world hates because it abides in death. It does not know God, and therefore it cannot love what reflects Him. Just as we do not marvel when a dead body decays, we should not marvel when those who are spiritually dead respond with hostility toward life and light.

The evidence of this new life is love for the brethren. This love is not sentimental or performative. It is the fruit of regeneration. It is the sign that God's life abides in us. While the world is marked by rivalry, jealousy, and self preservation, the child of God is marked by love, humility, and sacrifice. This love assures us that we belong to Him.

Therefore, we do not plead for the world's acceptance. We do not strive to be understood at all costs. We live for Christ. We love His people. We walk in obedience. And we rest in the knowledge that we have passed from death into life. The world may hate us, but our identity is secure. Our future is certain. And our calling remains unchanged: to live faithfully before God and let our lives bear witness to the truth.

1 John 3:15 (LSB)
Everyone who hates his brother is a murderer, and you know that no murderer has eternal life abiding in him.

John speaks with unmistakable clarity. Hatred is the root from which murder grows, and whoever hates his brother is already a murderer in the heart, because murder proceeds from hatred long before it ever reaches the hands. Our Lord taught the same truth in the Sermon on the Mount, warning that hatred toward a brother places a person in danger of judgment, because sin is not confined to outward acts but originates in the inner disposition of the heart. Cain did not suddenly become a murderer in the field; he was already one in his heart. God warned him that sin was crouching at the door, seeking to rule over him, yet Cain allowed hatred to take possession of his inner life. John's point is clear and sobering: hatred is not a minor flaw, it is evidence of spiritual death. No matter how righteous a man may appear, no matter how religious his speech or behavior, if hatred governs his heart, it does not come from God.

This is a theme John has returned to repeatedly throughout this letter. It is easy to claim love for God, to profess faith, or to speak eloquently about truth, yet hatred exposes the lie beneath such claims. The one who harbors hatred walks in darkness, regardless of how convincing his words may sound. Wisdom, knowledge, and theological precision do not compensate for a heart devoid of love. John's exhortation is therefore practical and discerning: do not attach yourself to those who possess impressive speech but lack love. Instead, associate with the brethren whose lives are marked by genuine love, because love is the unmistakable mark of life in God. Where hatred reigns, death abides; where love is present, eternal life has already begun.

1 John 3:16-17 (LSB)

By this we have known love, that He laid down His life for us; and we ought to lay down our lives for the brothers. But whoever has the world's goods, and sees his brother in need and closes his heart against him, how does the love of God abide in him?

In this letter, I have highlighted the "by this" language and the "ought" language, and here it deserves our careful attention once more. Earlier, John used "by this we know" to encourage self-reflection, showing how the children of God are revealed in their actions. Now, he uses "by this" to demonstrate how God shows His love. This is beautiful because if we know God's love through action, we should show our love to others in the same way we have been shown love: by action. This distinction is vital because we do not know God's heart simply because He says, "I love you." In fact, throughout the vast expanse of the Scriptures, God only uses that specific, direct verbal declaration "I love you" once—in the book of Isaiah, where He tells His people, *"Since you are precious in My sight, since you are honored and I love you"* (Isaiah 43:4).

We do not serve a God of vain words, but a God of action. He does not merely speak of His love; He demonstrates it. While He may only use that specific phrase once, His love permeates every page of Scripture. He affirms it by reminding us of all He has done, all He has forgiven, and all He has provided. This is a profound way to see that love and intent are conveyed by action, not merely by words. This establishes a foundational truth: if love is not acted upon, it does not reflect the love of God.

We know love by Him and Him alone. True love, as God demonstrates it, is foreign to this world. Most love we encounter carries selfish ambition, seeking gain or recognition. God's love, in contrast, is perfectly selfless, expressed in the greatest example imaginable. He teaches us love through His example, and this is why He commands us to love as He has loved. As Jesus said in John 15:12, "This is My commandment, that you love one another, just as I have loved you." He is the Master Teacher, and His curriculum is not a lecture of words, but a life of sacrifice.

We know love because He laid down His life for us. We know love because we have a cloud of witnesses, the Scriptures, that show us time and time again how God demonstrates His love through action. He loved Israel, and He rescued them from slavery—not because they deserved it or did anything to earn it, but simply by His grace. He rescued them from the hands of their enemies. He saved them from their captors, forgave those who repeatedly rebelled, and allowed them the opportunity to repent again and again. We see love most clearly in Christ, who, despite our deserving hell, entered the flesh and laid down His life as a ransom. By His stripes we are healed, and thus we know His love—not by words alone, but because He demonstrated it fully, without hesitation.

Our God has taught us the proper way to love, and it is never limited to words. The atheists who reject the Gospel do not believe God loves them because they do not accept the reality of His actions. In their view, love is verbal, and if that were all it were, their disbelief would make sense. If someone says, "I love you," what does it mean if their actions contradict their words? If I tell my wife I love her every day but then go out and flirt with other women, do I truly love her? If I tell her I love her daily but put her down, abuse her, withhold affection, and fail to support her in need, why should she believe my words? True love, divine love, is revealed in what is done, not merely what is said.

A Question for the Heart

John turns to one of my favorite verses in this entire letter. It is a simple question, yet one powerful enough to leave a person deeply convicted. He poses it not to condemn, but to confront reality. This verse draws a clear parallel with James 2:14-17, which says, "faith without works is dead." James' wording can sometimes feel accusatory, which has led many to misunderstand the passage, thinking he is commanding works as a requirement for salvation. Yet when we read John's question here, we see that they are addressing the same truth from different angles: James focuses on outward expression for others to see, while John calls us to inward reflection, asking us to examine the reality of God's presence within our own hearts.

John asks: *"If you have the world's goods and see a brother in need, yet close your heart to them, how does the love of God abide in you?"*

Let this question sink in. It is not merely asking about what we say or how we appear—it points to the living reality of God's love within us. A heart truly filled with His love will produce intentions that naturally move toward action. I have asked this question of myself and of those I love: How can we claim to know God, to be filled with His love, and to be conformed to the image of His Son, yet fail to extend that love to our brothers and sisters in need?

We can sometimes put on a mask, pretending that circumstances prevent us from acting, offering words of sympathy or regret while withholding true help from a brother in need. This is not about those who are genuinely unable to assist; it is about those who have the capacity to help but hold back out of selfishness or fear. God sees the heart, and so do you. You know when selfishness has kept you from giving, and you know when you have truly given your all. This question pierces the heart of anyone hiding behind a false display of compassion.

These words are not meant to make you feel as though you must go out and help every person in need to prove your faith. Rather, they call for honest self-reflection: when you see a brother in need, why might your heart hesitate? Perhaps there are attachments, distractions, or a love for the world that competes with your love for God and His people. As Paul reminds us, "Each one must give as he has decided in his heart, not reluctantly or under compulsion, for God loves a cheerful giver" (2 Corinthians 9:7). True love and generosity are measured not by obligation, but by the heart that freely chooses to act. Consider the woman in Mark 12:41-44, who gave two small coins at the temple. Jesus commended her, saying she had given more than all the rich, because she gave out of her poverty, from what she truly had, demonstrating that love is not in the abundance we possess, but in the sacrifice we are willing to make for others.

It is easy to give when it costs us nothing, but it is love in action when we share from what little we have, when we prioritize the needs of others over our comfort or convenience. John's question calls us to examine whether the love of God truly abides in us—not in our words, not in our sentiments, but in the reality of sacrificial action.

Now let's hop over to James for a moment. James writes of someone who may say they have faith, verbally declaring it, yet when a brother or sister comes in need, they respond only with words—comfort, encouragement, polite sentiment—without tangible help. This is precisely the reality John confronts: verbal faith, verbal love, unaccompanied by action. James is speaking of someone who *says* they have faith, but their actions do not follow their words. Later, he reinforces this principle when he writes, "I will show you my faith by my works" (James 2:18). Faith is not merely verbal; it is revealed in action. In comparison, John tells us that being a child of God is not simply a label we claim—it is something we demonstrate. Just as you would do anything to help a blood brother, a child of God will desire to do all they can for a brother or sister in Christ.

James' example of someone giving only words—"Go in peace; be warmed and filled"—without practical help illustrates this vividly. So often in American Christianity, faith has become verbal. People are quick to offer comforting words, advice, or to say, "I'll pray for you," yet their support rarely extends further. John and James together teach the same truth from complementary angles: words are not enough; love and faith must flow outward in concrete action. How can someone who has received more than they deserve from God fail to extend His love to others? How can God's love truly abide in you if it does not flow outward in action?

Notice, this scenario is not about someone who is simply in need somewhere in the world. The Apostle gives the example of someone who has the world's goods, who is not in need themselves, yet sees their brothers and sisters in need. There are no excuses in this example. John is not saying, "If you have wealth and see people across the globe suffering, how does God's love abide in you?" He is not calling us to examine every act of global charity in this passage. Rather, he asks a precise and piercing question: how can you, a person blessed with resources, see a brother or sister in Christ in need and yet close your heart?

This is the conviction that struck me when I first read 1 John many years ago—when I truly paused and reflected on it. Do not close your heart. Do not cling to the things of this world more than you cling to love. Do not love the world; love the brothers and sisters of the faith. John's focus here is intimate and immediate: the people you know, the members of your church, the fellow believers in your life. As Peter instructs, "Love one another earnestly from a pure heart" (1 Peter 1:22), and later he emphasizes the priority of this love: "Above all, keep fervent love for one another, for love will cover a multitude of sins" (1 Peter 4:8). The unity and love among the household of God is the defining characteristic of our faith, the evidence for the world to see, as Jesus said in John 13:35: "By this all people will know that you are my disciples, if you have love for one another." This does not diminish our calling to help others outside the faith, but John is highlighting the responsibility to act close to home. The love we show our brothers and sisters in Christ is weighty, tangible, and a true reflection of God's presence in our lives.

How does God's love abide in you? How can it truly dwell in you if it does not flow outward? I meet Christians from every walk of life who measure their faith by how "good" or "obedient" they are, yet they rarely measure it by the love that flows through them. We have already discussed the categorical structure of the believer versus the non-believer earlier in this chapter—what matters most is not your occasional failures, but the condition of your heart. Are you moved, despite your imperfections, to love one another? Are you compelled by something beyond yourself to help your brothers and sisters in the faith when they are in need?

This is the measure I look for in the young believer. This is the proof of God's work within a heart. More than outward obedience, more than ritual or words, the truest evidence of being a child of God is a heart that loves in action. Do you love in word only, or do you love in deed?

In the end, John's question is not a casual suggestion; it is a mirror held up to the heart of every believer. Just as James challenges us to examine whether our faith is only verbal, John challenges us to see whether our love is only spoken or truly lived. A child of God does not merely say, "I love my brothers and sisters," nor do they measure love by what is easy or convenient. True love flows outward, compelled by the reality of God's presence in the heart, unreserved and sacrificial. Our love for the family of God reflects the love we have received from Christ Himself—freely given, fully demonstrated, and unending. Let this question echo in your own heart: if God's love truly abides in you, will it remain hidden, or will it pour out in action to meet the needs of those He calls your family? This is the test, the calling, and the beauty of living a life conformed to the image of His Son.

1 John 3:18 (LSB)
Little children, let us not love with word or with tongue, but in deed and truth.

Let us not be the Christians who say we follow Jesus while walking in darkness. Let us not be the Christians who say we love God while harboring hatred for our brothers. Let us not be the Christians who claim to have faith, yet let that faith fail to move us toward loving one another. Let us not love with words alone, or merely with our tongues; let us love in deed and truth. Let this be the way people recognize you as a servant of Christ. Let it be so evident that I would not need to hear your testimony to know you follow Him.

I was once asked a question I will never forget: If you were being examined in a court of law for being a Christian, would the evidence in your life be sufficient to convict you? Or would it require your own testimony? Yes, our verbal testimony declares who we serve, but the greater testimony is found in our actions. Even more striking, imagine examining a life after someone has passed away, incapable of verbal testimony. Would the life itself reflect a follower of Christ? Would the actions in that life declare love for God?

Consider the example of a sports fan. If someone loves a team, their life will reveal it: they will own the merchandise, set aside time to watch the games, learn about the players, and invest effort and passion into following them. Their actions declare their priorities as clearly—sometimes even more clearly—than their words. The same principle applies to the Christian life. Show me what a person devotes their time, energy, and resources to, and I will show you what truly matters to them.

This principle was perfectly demonstrated in the life of Jesus. Everything He did was for the glory of His Father. His works were not performed to make Himself the Messiah; they were performed to reveal that He is the Messiah (John 5:36; John 10:25). His life bore witness to His identity, His love for the Father, and His love for humanity, showing us that true faith and genuine love are inseparable from tangible action. Loving God with all our heart, soul, mind, and strength (Mark 12:30) cannot be reduced to mere words; it is expressed through devoted, obedient, and sacrificial action.

This is exactly what James speaks of in his letter. Do not be merely a hearer of the Word, someone who listens and talks about it, but be a doer of the Word (James 1:22). James is often quoted for the statement, "Faith without works is dead" (James 2:17), yet the context matters. He gives a scenario in which someone might challenge him: "You say, 'You have faith,

I have works.'" James responds, "Show me your faith apart from your works, and I will show you my faith by my works" (James 2:18). His point is clear: faith is not only declared verbally—it is demonstrated. We do not just tell others we have faith; we show it. We do not simply talk about the goodness of God; we reveal it through our actions. We do not merely say we love people; we show our love in tangible ways.

If the way we know love is because Jesus laid down His life for us, then we ought to show our love to others in a similar, sacrificial manner. How can anyone truly believe words of love if they are never accompanied by actions? How often have you recognized genuine love for yourself—not through words, but through someone stepping outside of their comfort, helping when they barely had enough themselves, or performing other acts of sacrificial care?

I do not write this so you read it and think, "I must do these things to be saved, so I better do them." Remember John's original emphasis: "and he closes his heart to them." The issue is not the actions themselves—it is the condition of the heart. If you act out of obligation while your heart remains closed, there remains a problem. John asks, "How does God's love abide in you?" How can He work in you if your heart is shut to loving a brother or sister whom you have the ability to help? How can you claim to love God and simultaneously close your heart to those He loves? This is not a call to perfection but a call to honesty before God, to examine whether your faith is alive and your love is genuine, or whether it has grown cold, distracted, or self-centered. It is a gentle but firm reminder that the Christian life is relational at its core: love for God and neighbor is the evidence of the Spirit's abiding presence.

This is a question for self-reflection. Only you and the Lord know whether your heart is closed or whether you truly cannot help. Is God's love present in your heart, and you are standing in the way, letting fear, selfishness, or uncertainty hinder it? Or is His love absent in this moment, leaving you unable to act selflessly? The difference matters: one points to a heart resisting God's work and in need of spiritual growth, the other to a heart still in need of His transforming presence.

1 John 3:19 (LSB)
And by this we will know that we are of the truth, and will assure our heart before Him.

By this reflection on our own hearts, we know that we are of the truth. This is not a call to look outward for validation, but inward for evidence. John has repeatedly used this "by this we know" language to guide the believer toward assurance, not anxiety. We seek God's presence within our own lives, and it is by this standard that we find confidence before Him. When I reflect honestly on my life, I can see that God's Spirit dwells within me. Do I still make poor decisions? Yes, of course. But as we discussed earlier, an obedient child may have moments of disobedience, yet we would never categorize him as a disobedient child. His failures do not redefine his identity. In the same way, despite the days where I fail, I cannot deny the love for the brethren that burns within me.

This is precisely what the Apostle Paul calls believers to do when he writes, "Examine yourselves, to see whether you are in the faith. Test yourselves. Or do you not realize this about yourselves, that Jesus Christ is in you?" (2 Corinthians 13:5). Paul is not urging Christians to live in constant fear of their salvation, but to recognize Christ's presence within them. The examination is not meant to produce despair, but assurance. Our flesh is prone to doubt. Our hearts can accuse us. That is why Scripture repeatedly points us back to tangible, Spirit-driven realities that confirm God's work within us.

Peter speaks in a similar way when he describes baptism, clarifying that it is "not as a removal of dirt from the body but as an appeal to God for a good conscience" (1 Peter 3:21). The outward act does not save by its physical nature, but by what it represents inwardly. In the same way, John is not telling us to manufacture love in order to prove something to God. He is calling us to recognize the love that already exists within us as evidence that God's Spirit is at work. This love does not originate from us. It is produced by Him.

This is why John's "by this we know" language is so vital. When doubt creeps in, when our failures loom large, we are not told to look at our perfection, but at the fruit of God's presence in our lives. Do we see His love at work in us? Do we see a love that convicts us, moves us, and grieves us when we fail to act on it? That reflection does not save us, but it reassures us. It reminds us that we are of the truth, and that Christ truly abides in us.

But what if you read these words and do not recognize Christ in yourself? What if you examine your heart and do not see this love, this pull toward the brethren, this grief when love is withheld? For that person, these words are meant to trouble you. John's "by this we know" language comforts the believer, but it confronts the liar. Paul's exhortation cuts both ways. If Christ is not recognized within, that absence should not be ignored or explained away. Scripture does not allow us to soothe ourselves with excuses when God is exposing something far deeper.

My prayer for you is not that you would find immediate comfort, but that you would experience godly grief, the kind Paul describes as producing repentance that leads to salvation without regret (2 Corinthians 7:10). Either these words will bring assurance and peace, or they will bring conviction that drives you into the arms of Christ. Both outcomes are acts of grace. If you find yourself grieved, unsettled, and exposed, do not harden your heart. Let that grief do its work. Let it lead you to repentance, to faith, and ultimately to the same assurance these words give to the child of God. In Christ, both conviction and comfort serve the same loving purpose, to draw us nearer to Him, where true assurance is found.

Agape vs. Worldly Love

Before continuing John's argument, it is necessary to pause and define what Scripture means by *love*. The world has so thoroughly distorted this word that the culture opposed to God often speaks as if it understands love better than God Himself. Slogans like "love is love" reduce love to feelings, desires, and emotional affirmation, all while masking selfish ambition and self gratification. In Scripture, love is not defined by emotion, attraction, or personal fulfillment, but by self giving sacrifice rooted in God's own nature.

The Bible uses multiple words to describe love, but the most significant for John's argument is *agape* (ἀγαπάω). This is not romantic love, emotional attachment, or mutual benefit. *Agape* is the term most commonly used in the New Testament to describe the love of God, Christ's love for us, and our love for Him and for others inspired by that divine love.[5] This is a distinct kind of love, the truest form of love, unstained by the distortions of sin and self interest.

This distinction matters because the modern definition of love bears little resemblance to the love John describes. Even standard dictionary definitions frame love primarily in terms of affection, attraction, admiration, or shared interest. Merriam Webster defines love as strong affection arising from personal

---

5. Alexander Souter, *A Pocket Lexicon to the Greek New Testament* (Oxford: Clarendon Press, 1917), 2.

ties, sexual attraction, or benevolence rooted in admiration or common interests.[6] While these definitions describe human experience, they fall far short of the love revealed in Christ.

The love Paul describes in 1 Corinthians 13, so often quoted at weddings, was not written to define romance or marital affection. Paul is describing the love of God Himself, and the love believers are called to embody as that divine love flows through them. This is the love John has in view, a love that gives, suffers, and lays itself down for the good of others.

With that clarity, we can now understand what John is calling us to look for. He is not asking whether we feel affection, experience attraction, or possess emotional warmth. He is asking whether the sacrificial love of God is present and active in us. This is the love by which we know

The world does not know this love because it rejects His love. We, however, know His love. Remember the words of verse 16: 'by this we know love'—because of what He has done for us. The Lord Jesus came in the flesh to suffer for us. How can we not emulate that same willingness to give sacrificially for others? Life is fleeting—a vapor, a mist. Why hold onto money we do not need? Before Christ, and even early in my walk, greed often dominated me. I pursued the highest-paying jobs, prioritized worldly gain, and sought to maximize every opportunity. But Christ has changed my heart, and through the Spirit, my priorities have shifted.

When we see this love within ourselves and in our actions, a love that does not originate from our flesh, we can have confidence that He is in us and we are in Him. Do not allow failures and shortcomings to overshadow this reality. Do you see God's

---

6. Merriam-Webster, s.v. "love," accessed December 29, 2025, https://www.merriam-webster.com/dictionary/love.

love reflected in your life? Does it stop you in your tracks? Even if you are early in your walk, does it move you to action? Do you feel conviction when you fail to act, grieved by a closed heart in the presence of a need that you could meet?

Remember, change often begins quietly in the heart. Even if you still struggle with selfish desires, greed, or jealousy, the very fact that you are grieved by these things and feel a growing desire to act rightly is a sign that God is at work in you. The inward stirrings of conviction and the yearning to love rightly are the beginnings of transformation, which will gradually flow outward into tangible actions. Progress is rarely instant; God's Spirit works patiently, shaping the heart before it reshapes the hands.

This reflection reassures our hearts before Him. Recognizing the change produced by His love through the Holy Spirit distinguishes the believer from the non-believer. The believer is driven by the Spirit to love; the non-believer acts according to personal passions. Non-believers may do things that seem loving, but their intention is different. Recall your own days before knowing the Lord. How often were your "moral" actions truly selfless and sacrificial? Selflessness implies expecting nothing in return.

Even in my most moral moments before Christ, my actions were influenced by social gain or future advantage. As my friend Taylor Sines writes in his book *Deconstructing Atheism*, "Much of life is simply learning to be a good con artist as long as it does not hurt others." This summarizes all my "good" deeds before Christ. Even in something that may have seemed sacrificial, it was banking social credit for when I would need something in return, or simply to gain recognition, loyalty, or favor. Many people act as if doing good will earn them something in return. They will say things like "The universe paying you back" or "Karma" and in doing this, it only demonstrates that their actions are ultimately self-serving, even when they appear generous or sacrificial.

John is not describing this kind of love. He is describing sacrificial love learned from the Lord Jesus. As he writes, "By this we know love" (1 John 3:16).

One example that opened my eyes to what agape love looks like in a modern and practical sense came from one of my college professors. Consider this scenario objectively: you have been in a relationship for two years and recently became engaged. You have built a life together, shared dreams, and promised your future to one another. Then, one day, your fiancé looks at you and tells you they met someone at work whom they are interested in getting to know. They tell you they still love you, but they admit to an intense desire to explore this new connection. They ask to pause the relationship, to set aside your engagement, so they can pursue someone else.

Your immediate instinct will almost undoubtedly be a defensive cry of: "What about me? What about our two years? What about my heart? How could you do this to me?" That is the natural human response. It is the response of a heart that seeks its own. I get it. That was exactly my response when the professor posed the question. In reality, my immediate thought was, "What in the world?!" I couldn't imagine anyone being capable of reacting any other way. But then the professor continued, and the room grew cold as the truth began to sink in.

True agape love—the selfless, sacrificial love of the Bible—is something entirely different. It would look at that person and honor their choice. Yes, it hurts with a depth that feels like death. Yes, it feels like total betrayal, and it demands that you receive absolutely nothing of what you want. It forces you to be number two. But in the economy of grace, agape love puts their needs and their journey above your own. True selfless love would say, "If you believe this is what is best for you, then because I love you, I want what is best for you, even if it costs me everything."

The classroom fell into a heavy, absolute silence as we all sat and tried to think about it objectively. Even after hearing the answer and knowing in our spirits that it was true, the weight of it was crushing. It felt impossible. Who could actually do that? Who could stand there while their own heart is being torn out and wish the other person well?

But this is the reality of the Gospel. When Christ went to the Cross, He did not do so for people who were cheering for Him or reciprocating His affection. He did so for people who were in the very act of rejecting Him. While we were still sinners—while we were still interested in everything else but Him—Christ died for us (Romans 5:8). He stood in the wreckage of our betrayal and said, "I want what is best for you, even if it costs Me My life."

This is the selfless love that prioritizes the wellbeing of others above our own. It mirrors the sacrificial love we receive from Christ, and it is the very love we are called to emulate toward others, especially the brothers and sisters in the faith. It is a love that does not ask, "What about me?" but instead asks, "How can I serve you?"

1 John 3:20 (LSB)
in whatever our heart condemns us; for God is greater than our heart and knows all things.

The test we rely on is the love of God made visible in our lives. This is what gives us assurance, and it is far more reliable than the doubts that rise up within our own hearts. Our hearts have a remarkable ability to fixate on every fault, every misstep, every failure. It is almost as if they possess a kind of fallen "superpower," magnifying what is wrong and obsessing over our shortcomings rather than resting in Christ's sufficiency.

The Christian often doubts his salvation not because the finished work of the cross is insufficient, but because the heart cannot help but notice repeated failures. It whispers accusations: "You don't deserve grace," "You are a bad Christian," "You are not worthy of His love." And in one sense, those accusations are true.

Yet John reminds us that even when our heart condemns us, God is greater than our heart and knows all things. Our assurance does not rest on the verdict of our heart but on the knowledge of God. Most Christians I meet who struggle with assurance are not doubting God—they are doubting themselves. Their attention shifts subtly from Christ's finished work to their own performance. When the heart whispers, "You don't deserve grace," the instinct is to try to prove it wrong. When it says, "You are a bad Christian," we attempt to correct the accusation by doing more, trying harder, performing better. But this is the wrong battle, on the wrong ground. If you think you can earn your salvation, your heart isn't lying—you are.

The truth is, your heart is right when it says you do not deserve grace. You don't. No one does. Scripture is clear: no one is good but God. Left to ourselves, we deserve judgment, not mercy. But this is precisely why the gospel is good news. We do not quiet the doubts whispered by our hearts with flattering lies about our own worthiness or performance; we confront them with the unchanging truth of God's grace and the finished work of Christ:

> *I do not deserve grace, yet He gives it freely.*
> *I am a bad Christian, yet His work is sufficient.*
> *I am not worthy of His love, yet He has set His love upon me.*

This is John's point. Assurance is not found by denying our sinfulness, but by trusting in the greatness of God who knows all things—including our failures—and still saves us. When the heart condemns, the believer does not argue for his worthiness but rests in God's mercy. God's knowledge of us is not a threat to assurance; it is its foundation.

The verdict of our faith does not rely on the conviction of our hearts but on the Lord Himself. He knows who are His, and He knows you better than you know yourself. This truth is both comforting and sobering. God sees the depths of our thoughts and intentions. He knows the heart that sincerely seeks Him, even amid doubts and unwanted thoughts. He also sees the one who wears a mask, pretending to serve Christ for the wrong reasons. He distinguishes between the person who feels a pull to act but hesitates out of fear, and the one who neglects duty out of selfishness or pride. God searches the heart completely, and those who truly trust Him need not fear their failures. Conversely, those who think they can fool God should tremble, for He will not be mocked.

Our hearts naturally try to condemn us, whispering that we are never doing enough. We may recognize God's love flowing through our lives, yet another voice says, "Yes, but you could be doing more," or "You are a fraud, despite your deeds." Do not allow these thoughts to bring condemnation. God sees beyond our doubts, and He knows the truth of our hearts. As Paul reminds us in Romans 8:26-27,

"And in the same way the Spirit also helps our weakness, for we do not know how to pray as we should, but the Spirit Himself intercedes for us with groanings too deep for words; and He who searches the hearts knows what the mind of the Spirit is, because He intercedes for the saints according to the will of God."

God knows the depths of your heart. When doubts arise, remember that by the love God has placed in us, we can reassure our hearts before Him. Even when our hearts try to condemn us, we reject that condemnation because God is greater than our hearts and knows all things. Therefore, as Romans 8:1 declares,

"There is therefore now no condemnation for those who are in Christ Jesus."

1 John 3:21 (LSB)
Beloved, if our heart does not condemn us, we have confidence before God;

Confidence in Christ

The doubts and condemnation we feel in our hearts are common for Christians, and as we saw in the previous verse, they are a natural response to the awareness of our sin and imperfection. Yet these doubts are not permanent, nor are they the final word. Those who are perfected by the love of Christ have moved beyond the self-condemnation of the heart. Here, the Apostle begins to guide his readers into the confidence we can have in Christ—a confidence not rooted in our performance or worthiness, but in the unchanging reality of who He is and what He has done for us. John reminds us of this truth earlier in his letter:

"But whoever keeps His word, truly in him the love of God has been perfected. By this we know that we are in Him." (1 John 2:5)

When we come to understand His love for us, when we see the fullness of what He has done and recognize that His Word and His love truly abide in us, we are perfected in that love. Doubts, fears, and the whispers of self-condemnation begin to fade—not because we have achieved perfection in ourselves, but because we are secure in the perfection of His love toward us. This is the very reason John writes this letter: to give assurance to believers. It is not simply to remind us who we are, but to point us continually to Christ, so that we might find confidence in Him. The more we grow in the knowledge of His love, the more we are strengthened in faith, and the more the fears that once gripped our hearts are cast out. This is the heart of John's message: as we dwell in the reality of God's love, fully trusting in Him, we are perfected in that love, and the confidence of our salvation becomes a living, sustaining reality.

Trusting His Work, Not Ours

The doubts that arise in our hearts stem from our own failures, but the confidence we gain does not come from our successes. True confidence comes from moving beyond our deeds and looking to what Christ has done for us. The finished work of the Cross is where our confidence rests. Knowing we have been purchased by the blood of Christ is where assurance is found. Knowing that God's promises are sure is where our confidence is anchored.

The believer's confidence is not in themselves. We know that we cannot perfectly keep the law. We know that no human is righteous in God's presence on their own. As Paul writes in Galatians 2:16:

"A man is not justified by the works of the Law but through faith in Jesus Christ. Even we have believed in Christ Jesus, so that we may be justified by faith in Christ and not by the works of the Law; since by the works of the Law no flesh will be justified."

Some find confidence in their own works, and when that confidence falters, they try harder to do more to earn more. Often, these same people compare themselves to others to bolster their self-assurance. Consider the parable of the Pharisee and the Tax Collector we discussed in chapter 1. The Pharisee stood in the temple saying, "At least I am not like this tax collector," comparing himself to another instead of recognizing his own sin before God. The Tax Collector, on the other hand, would not even lift his head but beat his chest, saying, "Have mercy on me, a sinner." Confidence in oneself often comes from a faulty standard—measuring against others rather than against God.

The standard is Christ and Christ alone. Unless we are perfect like Him, we have fallen short of God's glory. Do not place your confidence in yourself—place it in Christ, the perfect High Priest who intercedes for us before the Father. I often encourage believers to meditate on the cross daily, to find themselves at its foot continually. In doing so, our eyes remain fixed on Him, and we are reminded that our salvation is entirely His work, not our own. When we dwell there, it becomes impossible to look down on others or compare ourselves to them, because we recognize that we all fall short and are equally in need of mercy and grace. If Christ is our standard, not ourselves and not anyone else, then our confidence rests wholly in Him. When we trust in what He has accomplished, we can have true assurance of salvation—not because we deserve it, but because He alone is worthy of all our trust.

1 John 3:22-23 (LSB)

and whatever we ask we receive from Him, because we keep His commandments and do the things that are pleasing in His sight. And this is His commandment, that we believe in the name of His Son, Jesus Christ, and love one another, just as He gave a commandment to us.

Not only can we have confidence in our salvation, but when we walk in His will, we can also have confidence that whatever we ask of Him, we receive from Him. This is not to suggest that God is some magical genie who will grant any request on demand. I cannot ask God for a cheeseburger and expect it to appear on my desk next to my computer. The key lies in the important clause of this verse: "Because we keep His commandments and do the things that are pleasing in His sight." This is a condition repeated in multiple places in Scripture regarding prayer. In John 15:7, Jesus says, "If you abide in Me, and My words abide in you, ask whatever you wish, and it will be done for you." When we walk in alignment with God's will, our prayers reflect His purposes, and we can trust that He answers. Conversely, when our requests stem from fleshly desires, we should not expect Him to grant them. As James writes, "You ask and do not receive, because you ask with wrong motives, so that you may spend it on your pleasures" (James 4:3).

One way to understand this is through a parental analogy that many of us can relate to. Children ask for things every day, often without considering whether they truly need them. A young child sees something he wants in the moment, and his request is driven purely by desire. As a parent, I say no—not out of unkindness, but because what he asks for is not beneficial. His older sibling, on the other hand, asks more thoughtfully, requesting only what is necessary and understood to be beneficial. In addition to need, obedience plays a role. A child who refuses to follow rules, constantly misbehaves, or fights with siblings is not rewarded for such behavior, even if their requests seem reasonable. Necessities, like food, clothing, and shelter, are always provided, but extras are granted in alignment with character and readiness.

This analogy mirrors how God responds to His children. As Hebrews 12:10 reminds us, "He disciplines us for our benefit, so that we may share His holiness." God's care is not about granting everything we ask, but guiding us toward what is good and holy. Our prayers are answered according to His perfect will, and sometimes that requires God waiting on us, shaping us, and aligning our hearts before granting requests. Walking in obedience to His Word does not just bring answers; it changes our prayers. Our requests begin to reflect His will, and we learn to pray in alignment with the heart of God.

We Keep His Commandments

Here John emphasizes again, "We keep His commandments." As I noted earlier in this book, back in chapter 2, John often spoke of His commandments, and many readers may have assumed what he meant. Here, he makes it explicit—he defines them clearly. This is important because these commandments are not abstract or culturally assumed—they are the precise markers by which we can recognize the child of God. They are not optional; they are the defining characteristics of those who belong to Christ, the evidence of His life at work in us.

He continues, "And **this** is His commandment: that we **believe** ... and we **love**." These two imperatives are the essence of the Christian life. To believe is to place full trust in the Lord Jesus Christ—His promises, His finished work on the cross, His perfect life, and all that He has done and declared He will do. Biblical belief is not casual acknowledgment or superficial assent; it is wholehearted reliance on Christ, trusting Him completely for salvation, guidance, and life itself. To love, in parallel, is not merely feeling affection or sentiment. It is the sacrificial, obedient love modeled by Christ, a love that seeks the good of others even when it costs us.

These commandments are simple to state but profoundly weighty. He is not referring to the more than six hundred laws of the Torah; he is highlighting the core commands of Christ, the commands that summarize the will of God for His people and mark them as His own. Believe—and trust that He offers rest, provision, protection, guidance, and eternal security as the Good Shepherd. Believe—and rely on Him as the Way, the Truth, and the Life. Believe—and rest in the certainty of His promises: "I will never forsake you," and "It is finished." And Love—love those who oppose you, those who persecute or revile you, those who may not seem deserving. Love God with all your heart and love your brothers and sisters in Christ. Love one another as He has loved you.

John makes the connection explicit: "By this we know love, that He laid down His life for us." The demonstration of Christ's sacrificial love sets the standard for our own. Belief in Him and love for others are inseparable. They are the outward evidence of a heart transformed by the Spirit. When we believe in Christ and love our brothers and sisters, we can have confidence before God. This is the assurance John points to—a confidence not rooted in our own strength, merit, or understanding, but in the faithfulness of Christ and the life-changing power of His love. If we walk in belief and love, our hearts can be reassured before Him, resting in the certainty that we are His.

We Believe

What does it mean, biblically, to *believe*? When the New Testament speaks of belief, it is not merely referring to intellectual acknowledgment or casual agreement with a statement of fact. The word *believe* comes from the Greek term *pisteuō* (πιστεύω).[7] At its core, it means more than simply saying "I think this is true." It carries the sense of placing full trust and reliance on a

---

7. **pisteuō (πιστεύω):** to believe; to trust a person or statement; to place full reliance upon God or the Messiah; to commit one's life to Him; to rely, have confidence, or repose trust with energy of faith. Alexander Souter, A Pocket Lexicon to the Greek New Testament (Oxford: Clarendon Press, 1917), 203.

person or on what that person promises. Biblically, it describes a committed confidence, a total reliance on God or the Messiah, where one entrusts one's entire life to Him. To believe is to repose your trust fully in His character, His promises, and His completed work. It is a deliberate act of commitment and surrender, an active placing of your life upon Christ as stable and trustworthy, energized by faith.

This term *pisteuō* comes from the same Greek root as the word translated *faith* in Scripture, *pistis* (πίστις).[8] Pistis conveys the idea of faith, trust, or reliance, generally understood as the leaning of the entire human personality upon God or the Messiah, with absolute confidence in His power, wisdom, and goodness. In other words, when Scripture says we are saved by faith, it is describing the same trust that is captured in the act of believing. Faith (*pistis*) describes the state or quality of trust, while belief (*pisteuō*) describes the action of placing ourselves in that trust.

So, what does it mean to believe in Him? It is not enough to merely acknowledge that Jesus existed, or that He spoke certain truths, or that He performed miracles. Belief, in the biblical sense, is placing your full confidence in Him—His promises, His words, and His finished work on the cross. Every declaration, every promise, every command of Christ is embraced as true and relied upon for life, salvation, and hope. Saving faith is active and personal: it is trusting in the reality of Christ and His work for your life.

This is why Reformed theology rightly emphasizes that we are saved by faith alone, by belief alone, in Christ alone. Obe-

---

8. **pistis** (πίστις): faith; belief; trust; reliance; generally, the leaning of the entire human personality upon God or the Messiah in absolute trust and confidence in His power, wisdom, and goodness.
Alexander Souter, *A Pocket Lexicon to the Greek New Testament* (Oxford: Clarendon Press, 1917), 203.

dience, good works, and sanctification are not the root of salvation—they are the fruit and evidence of true faith. They flow naturally from a heart that has been transformed and secured in Christ. The Scriptures may describe the product of faith—obedience, works, and righteous living—but these are never added to faith as separate requirements for salvation. They are the inevitable outcome of faith, the evidence that belief has taken root and is alive.

When we speak of being saved by faith alone, we are not referring to a shallow, verbal profession of belief—a faith that exists only in words. True faith drives action; it produces tangible trust that affects how we live. If it does not, then it was never genuine faith to begin with.

Consider this example: suppose a friend is behind on his rent and faces losing his home on the first of the month. You tell him, "I know things are hard right now, and I don't want to see you stressed or forced into desperate measures. I promise to pay your rent on the first." If he truly believes you, that trust will shape his behavior in the days leading up to the first. He will not frantically sell his belongings or scramble for money, because he rests in your promise. But if he spends those days trying to make the money himself, hedging against the possibility that you might not come through, it reveals the truth: he never truly trusted your word. He may have heard your promise and even said he believed it, but his actions betray a lack of true reliance.

In the same way, saving faith is not passive—it transforms our hearts, directs our actions, and demonstrates the reality of our trust in Christ. True faith rests wholly in His promises and is evidenced in a life increasingly aligned with His will.

In your walk with Christ, you will encounter verses and voices that seem to demand additional requirements for salvation. Certain passages describe the fruit of a believer's life—obedience, love, and good works—but these are often misused to suggest that our actions are what save us. The truth is that salvation is always by faith alone; faith is always the requirement. Works and obedience are not conditions for salvation but the natural outcome of genuine trust in Christ. The enemy, much like in the Garden or in the wilderness with Jesus, will try to take God's Word and twist it, using Scripture to confuse, distract, or burden the believer. He quotes truth but seeks to mislead, making it appear that God's promises are contingent on our performance.

Verses that describe the life of the believer—calls to love, obey, and walk rightly—are descriptive, not prescriptive for salvation. They show what faith produces, not what faith requires. Just as a tree is known by its fruit, a life rooted in Christ will bear evidence of trust: love for others, obedience to God, and reliance on His promises in every circumstance. John, Paul, and James all affirm that saving faith is living, active, and transformative. If it does not result in love and obedience, it is not genuine faith but mere intellectual assent.

James makes this distinction clear when he writes:

"You believe that God is one; you do well. Even the demons believe—and shudder!" (James 2:19)

Many people, including demons, believe that God exists. That kind of belief, while true in fact, does not lead to trust, surrender, or obedience. It is merely intellectual assent. Saving faith, by contrast, is rooted in the person and work of Christ—it is belief not only that God exists, but that He is who He says He is, and that He has accomplished our redemption through His Son. It is trusting in His promises, relying on His finished work, and allowing that trust to shape our hearts and lives.

James goes on to clarify that faith without works is dead (James 2:15-17). This is not a contradiction to salvation by faith alone; rather, it is an explanation of the evidence of genuine faith: true faith always produces love and obedience. John makes the same point in 1 John 3:17: a faith that does not lead to giving and sacrificial love is evidence that God's love is not abiding in the heart. Paul likewise calls faith without evidence vain (1 Cor 15:2). Saving faith is never inert; it is alive, active, and always evident in a life increasingly conformed to Christ.

Faith always comes first. Works follow. Confidence rests not in our deeds but in the finished work of Christ, and our actions are the evidence that His Spirit is at work within us. Understanding this frees us from striving to earn salvation and empowers us to live in the obedience and love that flow naturally from trusting Him. To believe is to cast ourselves upon the promises of God, confident that He is faithful, unchanging, and utterly trustworthy.

1 John 3:24 (LSB)
And the one who keeps His commandments abides in Him, and He in him. We know by this that He abides in us, by the Spirit whom He gave us.

The one who keeps His commandments abides in Him, and He in them. John now brings together everything he has been unfolding throughout this chapter and, in many ways, throughout the entire letter. To keep His commandments is not to return to a system of law keeping or to measure oneself by external performance. John has already defined what he means by God's commandments: to believe in the name of His Son Jesus Christ and to love one another. Where belief and love are present, there is abiding. Where abiding is present, there is life.

This is how we examine ourselves. This is how we understand what it means for Christ to be in us. Paul asks the Corinthians, "Do you not realize this about yourselves, that Jesus Christ is in you?" John answers that question here. Christ abides in us by His Spirit. The evidence of His abiding presence is not mystical speculation or emotional experience detached from life, but the visible, ongoing work of transformation produced by the Spirit of God. This is precisely what John has been pointing to from chapter 2 onward. The anointing we have received from Him abides in us. The Spirit teaches us. The Spirit changes us. The Spirit confirms what God has done.

John makes it clear that we know He abides in us "by the Spirit whom He has given us." Salvation is not an object we possess or a status we carry apart from transformation. It is a new identity created and sustained by the indwelling Spirit of God. Where the Spirit dwells, He works. He produces belief that rests in Christ. He produces love that flows outward to the brethren. This is not self generated morality or religious effort. It is the fruit of divine life.

Paul describes this same reality in Romans 8 when he writes that we have not received a spirit of slavery leading again to fear, but the Spirit of adoption by whom we cry, "Abba, Father." The Spirit Himself bears witness with our spirit that we are children of God. This witness is not merely internal affirmation. It is the Spirit testifying through a transformed life. The believer finds within himself a new orientation, a new affection, and a new confidence, not in himself but in God as Father.

John also helps us understand what it means to abide in Christ, language that can sometimes feel abstract or undefined. Jesus used this language in John 15 when He spoke of abiding in the vine. John now clarifies it for us. To abide in Christ is to believe in Him and to love one another. These are not separate spiritual categories. Belief anchors us in Christ. Love flows from Christ through us. Where belief and love are present, abiding is taking place. Where abiding is present, fruit follows.

This also guards us from misunderstanding the source of this love. We do not produce it on our own. Apart from Him, we can do nothing. We are incapable of generating light by ourselves. If light is present in us, it is because He has placed it there. If love flows from us, it is because His Spirit is at work within us. The love John describes throughout this chapter is not natural affection or moral effort. It is the product of God's love poured into us by His Spirit.

Our assurance of salvation, then, does not rest on our strength, our consistency, or our obedience considered in isolation. It rests on God's work in us and His care for us. He is the Good Shepherd who guards His sheep, conforms them to His image, and brings to completion what He has begun. The Spirit's presence is not merely a guarantee of future glory. It is the active means by which God is even now shaping us into what we will one day fully be. As John has already said, when He appears, we shall be like Him.

This is how chapter 3 concludes. Belief, love, abiding, assurance, and transformation are all bound together by the work of the Spirit. The child of God does not look inward to find worth or outward to find security. He looks to Christ, and in looking to Christ, he finds that Christ is already at work within him by His Spirit.

Chapter Summary

We have moved from the battlefield of the world into the household of the Father. This transition is not merely sentimental; it declares a legal and spiritual reality: we are the adopted children of the living God. This new identity is a gift of sovereign grace that the world cannot recognize, just as it did not recognize our Lord. While we are already His children, we live in the tension of the already and the not yet, awaiting the day when His work in us is fully revealed and we see Him as He truly is.

This reality calls for a transformed walk today. If we truly possess this hope, we must begin to purify ourselves—not to earn our place in His house, but because we already belong. We are to distinguish ourselves from the mixed multitude, acknowledging that while sin still struggles within us, we no longer make a practice of it. We are called to be vessels of honor, set apart and useful to the Master, pursuing righteousness, faith, and peace with a sincere heart.

Our assurance does not rest on our own strength or the consistency of our obedience, but on God's work within us. He is the good Shepherd, who guards His sheep and brings to completion what He has begun. Let us not be discouraged by the darkness of the world or the lingering presence of sin, for the Spirit is actively conforming us to the image of His Son. We can rest confidently in this truth: we are loved, we are kept, and we are His forever.

Chapter Four

1 John 4

Love Perfected

Overview

As we move into Chapter 4, the Apostle John turns our attention from the reality of our new identity to the power and perfection of God's love. If Chapter 3 revealed who we are in Christ, Chapter 4 shows us what that love looks like in practice and how it transforms us from within. John emphasizes that love is not merely a feeling or a suggestion—it is the very evidence of God living in us, shaping our hearts, guiding our actions, and revealing the Spirit at work.

In this chapter, we will explore the perfecting nature of God's love: how it matures in us, how it tests and discerns the spirits, and how it both protects and empowers the believer. We will see that true love is inseparable from obedience, humility, and discernment. John challenges us to recognize that the love we experience is not our own but flows from God Himself, and as it grows in us, it serves as a measure of our fellowship with Him and with one another.

Throughout this chapter, we will examine the tests of love that the Spirit brings into our lives, learning to distinguish between what is of God and what is counterfeit. We will confront the tension of living in a world that does not understand or receive this love, yet we are called to respond with the perfect, unshakable love that originates from the Father. As we navigate these truths, we will begin to see how God's love not only transforms us but also equips us to live boldly and faithfully, reflecting His heart to a world in need.

> *1 John 4:1 (LSB)*
> ***Beloved, do not believe every spirit, but test the spirits to see whether they are from God, because many false prophets have gone out into the world.***

Do Not Believe Everything You Hear

After emphasizing the importance of self-reflection for the believer, John shifts his focus back to a warning: be discerning about those who walk among us but live in darkness. He cautions believers to be careful in how they receive others. His original audience was far more isolated than we are today, yet they faced deception just as we do. What is different for us is the sheer abundance of resources and access to God's Word. We live in a generation where Scripture is at our fingertips, an advantage most Christians throughout history never had. The vast majority of followers from the days of the Apostles did not have instant access to all of Scripture—they had to search for it, study it, memorize it, and carefully pass it on.

Yet this very abundance brings a hidden danger: complacency. When information is hard to find, believers are forced to seek, study, and discern. Today, information comes to us effortlessly, often without effort or filtering, and the temptation is to accept the easiest, most engaging, or most attention-grabbing teaching, whether it is true or not. We live in what is called the age of information, but more accurately, it is an age of information overload. Bibles sit on shelves while social media feeds bombard us with opinions, half-truths, and outright lies. Heresies have always existed, but now anyone can broadcast them to potentially millions of people worldwide, often with passion, polish, and compelling presentation, regardless of their accuracy.

As a Christian who teaches online, 1 John 4:1 is always on my mind. Every day, people with thousands or even millions of followers claim authority to teach about God while spreading ideas like: "Paul corrupted Jesus' teachings," "Jesus is the Father," "We can all reach a higher level of consciousness and be Christ," "It is possible for a person to be sinless," or "Jesus didn't exist." Some of these claims are shocking, such as the "serpent seed" doctrine we discussed earlier, alleging Satan had sexual relations with Eve, or the notion that Adam had a first partner, Lilith, who refused to submit, prompting the creation of Eve.

The danger is not always intentional deception. In our generation, ignorance can be just as persuasive. Someone may approach the Bible with curiosity or emotion, and instead of studying carefully, immediately broadcast their opinions and feelings online, claiming insight or revelation. James warns that not many should become teachers (James 3:1), yet today almost anyone with a platform acts as a teacher. The combination of ignorance, passion, and reach creates a perfect storm for misinformation.

This is why John's exhortation is so urgent: do not believe everything you hear. Do not accept every person who claims to bring truth, and do not be lulled into complacency by smooth words or compelling presentation. Discernment is essential. We must sift through information carefully, measuring every teaching against the truth of God's Word and the guidance of His Spirit. The goal is clear: awareness, vigilance, and a refusal to be deceived in a world where misinformation is both abundant and enticing. Solomon reminds us, "The first to plead his case seems right, until another comes and examines him" (Proverbs 18:17). Quoting Scripture does not guarantee accuracy or divine representation; even Satan used God's Word to tempt Jesus in the wilderness. The mere act of quoting Scripture does not prove truth.

Consider the very first deception: when Satan tempted Eve in the garden, he did not lie outright. Instead, he twisted reality. He said, "God knows that when you eat of it your eyes will be opened, and you will be like God, knowing good and evil" (Genesis 3:5). Afterward, God says, "Behold, the man has become like one of us in knowing good and evil" (Genesis 3:22). Satan weaponized truth, distorting God's intent to entice disobedience. To Eve, the serpent may have seemed to have good intentions—and good intentions can be one of the most effective tools of the enemy. As the old saying goes, the path to hell is paved with good intentions.

Over thousands of years, Satan has honed this craft. Scripture describes him as crafty, deceptive, cunning, and wise. His goal is not merely to get people to reject God openly but to pervert His truth. He does not present himself as the enemy; he presents a counterfeit Christ to be served in place of the true Savior.

Sadly, our generation is particularly susceptible to this tactic. Today, someone can step onto a platform, spread heresy, and be defended with claims like, "At least they're trying to share the Word," "Just pray for them," or "Don't judge them." But John does not treat deception—whether intentional or not—with leniency. As we noted, James warns that not all should be teachers, and he adds that those who do will be judged more strictly.

Paul instructs Titus to rebuke sharply those who teach what they ought not to teach (Titus 1:13). It is a sobering reality that society often cares more about the comfort of the wolves than the protection of the flock.

The pride of man wants to believe he is wiser than he is, yet the "foolishness of God" is wiser than man. Eloquence, persuasion, and the appearance of wisdom can mislead even the devout. In the early Corinthian church, Paul observed believers boasting about which teacher they followed—Paul, Apollos, or Peter (1 Cor 1:12). Notice carefully: Peter, Paul, and Apollos were not false teachers. They were faithful servants of Christ. The danger Paul is highlighting is not their teaching, but the human tendency to elevate men rather than God. When believers set their standard on eloquence, style, or the perceived wisdom of teachers, even godly men can inadvertently become idols, opening the door for false teachers to gain influence later.

Paul drives this point home in 1 Corinthians 2:1-5:

"And when I came to you, brothers, I did not come with superiority of word or of wisdom... For I determined to know nothing among you except Jesus Christ, and Him crucified... And my word and my preaching were not in persuasive words of wisdom, but in demonstration of the Spirit and of power, so that your faith would not be in the wisdom of men, but in the power of God."

The principle is simple but profound: if your faith is rooted in a teacher's eloquence rather than the Spirit of God, it is only a matter of time before someone comes who expresses their message more persuasively. I often tell my listeners, "If you trust me simply because of how well I articulate my teachings, it's only a matter of time before someone comes and presents their words more convincingly." This is why Paul warns so strongly: faith must rest in Christ, not in human skill or charm.

The danger goes even deeper. Satan does not simply aim to pull people away from Christ; he presents a counterfeit. As Paul warns in 2 Corinthians, Satan can appear as an "angel of light," and his servants can preach a different Jesus, a different gospel, using persuasive speech to deceive (2 Cor 11:14-15). Elevating men—even godly men—without discerning truth through Scripture and the Spirit creates fertile ground for deception. What begins as admiration for faithful teachers can quickly turn into allegiance to false Apostles and twisted doctrines.

Paul's words echo what John has emphasized throughout his letter: truth is not discovered through human cleverness or charisma, but is revealed by the Spirit of God. We are called to vigilance, to test everything against God's Word, and to anchor our faith in the Spirit's guidance. No matter how convincing a message appears, or how persuasive a messenger may be, ultimate discernment belongs to God, and our allegiance must be to Him alone.

1 John 4:2 (LSB)
By this you know the Spirit of God: every spirit that confesses that Jesus Christ has come in the flesh is from God

Do not let this verse be taken in isolation and applied indiscriminately to every spiritual test. John is addressing a specific heresy—docetism—which denied that Jesus was truly in the flesh. Its adherents believed He only seemed to be human, that His body was an illusion, and that His physical incarnation was not real. This is why, at the very beginning of his letter, John emphasizes that he literally touched Jesus and stood in His presence. His warning confronts this deception directly.

The reality John proclaims, both in this letter and in his Gospel, is that the Word became flesh and dwelt among us. Jesus did not merely appear to be human; He became truly human.

The Son of God, eternal and divine, entered into human history by taking on human nature. By saying He "came in the flesh," John is echoing his own Gospel: the eternal Word, who was with God in the beginning and was God, became fully human. This is a foundational truth of the Christian faith.

Even when considering groups like Jehovah's Witnesses or Mormons, though they may say "Jesus Christ came in the flesh," a closer examination reveals that they deny the full reality of what John is asserting. This statement does not exist in a vacuum; it ties directly back to John 1, which teaches that the Word existed from eternity, was with God, and was God. Jehovah's Witnesses believe that the angel Michael, created by God, came in the flesh and took on the name Jesus. Mormons teach that Jesus is the spirit brother of Satan, a spirit-born son of God like all humans, who later attained divinity through His actions. Muslims consider Jesus a prophet who always existed in human form and had no preexistent divine nature; for them, He did not "come" in the flesh because He was never the eternal Word.

While this verse alone cannot serve as a universal test for all spiritual deception, when considered within the broader theological context of John's writings, it becomes an absolute measure of who Jesus truly is. Public confession of Christ is crucial. Peter's confession in Matthew 16 demonstrates this: "Flesh and bone did not reveal this to you, but only my Father in heaven" (Matthew 16:17). The recognition of Christ's true identity does not come through human intellect, but is revealed by the Spirit of God. John reinforced this in 1 John 2:27, reminding believers that they do not need external teachers to reveal new truths about Jesus. The Spirit within guides them into all truth. Therefore, believers must test every spirit and examine what a person publicly confesses about Jesus.

Satan often mixes truth with lies, but there is one truth he will never confess: the saving Gospel. The Gospel that brings salvation—the truth about who Jesus is and what He accomplished—is Satan's greatest enemy. When a person believes this Gospel, they receive the Spirit of God, who guides them into all truth and protects them from deception. The Spirit's seal on a believer, as Paul describes, is a guarantee of our inheritance and a divine safeguard—the very reality that frustrates Satan's schemes. As Paul writes:

'In Him, you also, when you heard the word of truth, the gospel of your salvation, and believed in Him, were sealed with the promised Holy Spirit, who is the guarantee of our inheritance until we acquire possession of it, to the praise of His glory.' (Ephesians 1:13-14 ESV)

The confession that Jesus Christ has come in the flesh is far more than mere words. It is a declaration that Jesus is the Eternal Word of God, born of the virgin Mary, from the lineage of David, and through Adam. He was truly human, subject to the law, yet fully God. He was "born in the likeness of sinful flesh and, as an offering for sin, condemned sin in the flesh, so that the righteous requirement of the Law might be fulfilled in us" (Romans 8:3-4). The Eternal Son, "who, although existing in the form of God, did not regard equality with God as something to be grasped, but emptied Himself, taking the form of a servant, being born in the likeness of men, and humbled Himself by becoming obedient to the point of death—even death on a cross" (Philippians 2:7-8).

In Christ, the Son of Man and the Son of God are reconciled. He alone bridges the divide between humanity and God, offering redemption and making it possible for man to be restored to fellowship with the Father. Recognizing the truth of His incarnation is not optional; it is central to the faith and a key test for discerning false teachings.

> *1 John 4:3 (LSB)*
> *and every spirit that does not confess Jesus is not from God. This is the spirit of the antichrist, of which you have heard that is coming, and now it is already in the world.*

Defining the Real Jesus

Here is a crucial point: the Name Jesus is only as meaningful as who it describes. When John says to confess Jesus, he is not merely referring to the verbal repetition of a name. He means the full reality of who Jesus is, as He has been revealed in John's Gospel, epistle, and Revelation. Many people claim the name "Jesus" but create their own version of Him. We believe in a different Jesus than groups like the Mormons, yet some argue, "They believe in Jesus, and that's all that matters." To illustrate, I often use an analogy: if someone says, "I love Michael Pagano," and you respond, "Me too," you may think you are talking about the same person. But if that person describes me as 6'4", Hispanic, tan-skinned, with long hair, and you know me as 5'11", Italian, White, with a buzz cut, it is clear you are speaking of two different people. Similarly, you may say you love and follow Jesus, but if your understanding of Him is fundamentally different, you are not following the same Christ. Scripture continually warns of false Christs and false Jesuses, and this is exactly what John is cautioning against.

The use of the term Spirit by John in this chapter is describing influence. It is not speaking of interacting directly with spirits, but rather identifying which spirit is influencing someone. Those who belong to God are influenced by the Spirit of God. Those who stand against God are influenced by anti-Christ spirits. The term "Anti-Christ" here is not a proper title like The Antichrist; rather, it carries its literal meaning: anti, against, Christ. Although we live in flesh and walk in flesh, our battle is not with flesh itself, but with the spiritual influences that shape us (Ephesians 6:12). Everything in the world, including the human heart, is influenced either by God or by that which stands against Him. There is no middle ground in the spiritual realm.

Those who reject Jesus are not from God; they are of the anti-Christ spirit. John warns his readers that this is the same spirit "that is coming" (speaking prophetically of the end), and then emphasizes that it is already present in the world. When John references the one who is coming, he points to the ultimate Antichrist described in Daniel, by Jesus, Paul, and in Revelation, which John wrote before this letter. This is the second time John speaks of the Antichrist and the many antichrists already at work. Both times he uses similar language. He wants his readers to understand that there is one who will come as the ultimate Antichrist, but prior to his arrival, many antichrists are already actively opposing Christ in the world.

To understand why misidentifying Jesus is so dangerous, we need to consider the Greek meaning of the word anti-Christ. The prefix anti doesn't just mean "against"; it can also mean "in place of" or "a substitute for." The spirit of the antichrist isn't always a loud, aggressive enemy of God. Often, it shows up as a substitute for Christ—a counterfeit that looks like the real thing but lacks the substance.

This is why the warning in 1 John 4:3 is so critical. People naturally avoid darkness, but antichrist deception often comes as light. It may sound convincing, look godly, and even quote Scripture, but it is ultimately a replacement for the true Christ. This is exactly what happens when someone claims the name of Jesus but describes a completely different Jesus than the one revealed in the Gospels, in John's writings, and in all of Scripture. Recognizing the difference requires discernment and a Spirit-led understanding of who Christ truly is.

John repeats this warning because the antichrist spirit is already active in the world—a reality his readers needed to grasp in his own time and that continues to be true today. Just as the early church faced deception, so too do we encounter influences that oppose Christ: media that glorifies sin, music and television promoting sexual immorality and pride, and cultural pressures that instill anti-Christ values in children and adults alike.

Even within churches, there are individuals who elevate false Christs—creating personal versions of Jesus that contradict His true teachings. The antichrist spirit seeks to replace Christ with anything the world offers as a substitute: wealth, pleasure, comfort, status, or fleeting gratification. Scripture is often misrepresented or ignored. We must not become complacent. This spirit seeks to influence your children, your spouse, and you.

Our response must be rooted in God's Word: speak it into your life and the lives of your family, teach your children to recognize the Lord's voice, and prepare them, knowing that when they enter the world, they will inevitably encounter the voice of the anti-Christ in countless forms.

1 John 4:4 (LSB)
You are from God, little children, and have overcome them; because greater is He who is in you than he who is in the world.

He Is Greater

Do not fear. Yes, the antichrist spirit is present in the world, and deceivers and false teachers are active around you. John does not shy away from naming these realities; he calls us to vigilance and discernment. Yet, immediately after confronting these dangers, he reminds us of a far greater truth: you are from God. You belong to Him. You are His children, born of His Spirit—a reality John emphasized repeatedly in chapter 3. This is the foundation of our confidence: our identity and security are not grounded in our own wisdom, strength, or ability to overcome, but in the One who has already defeated every power of darkness.

John intentionally uses the language of victory: *you have overcome them.* This is not a declaration of human achievement, but of spiritual reality grounded in our union with Christ. We do not overcome by our own power; the Spirit of God dwelling within us makes us victorious. Notice how John immediately clarifies in Scripture: *because greater is He who is in you than he who is in the world.*

Yes, there is something at work in the world. The antichrist spirit, deceivers, and all forces opposing God are active and seek to influence His children. But here is the glorious truth: the power of God within His children far surpasses any opposition in the world. This reality transforms our perspective. Our overcoming is not in our hands—it is Christ's triumph flowing through us, and it is through this indwelling presence that we participate in His victory.

This structure in John's writing is significant. He names frightening realities—the antichrists, the spirits of deception, the forces opposing Christ—but he does not leave us in fear. Every warning is paired with assurance. Fear is not the aim; awareness is. When John warns about the antichrist spirit and its activity in the world, he anchors our confidence firmly in God. The Spirit in us is stronger than the spirit in the world. The King is in us, and the victory is already won.

This truth also flows naturally from the overarching theme of chapter 3. Being "born of God" is not a one-time event; it is an ongoing reality that shapes who we are and how we live. Our identity as God's children gives us authority and confidence, not because of ourselves, but because of the One whose Spirit lives in us. Our security is not in avoiding deception or perfectly navigating the world; it is in the undeniable truth that the Lord is greater, that His power is at work within us, and that His victory over sin, death, and deception is complete.

Let this settle deeply in your heart: yes, antichrists are in the world, and deception is present; yes, the enemy prowls and schemes. But none of these realities can produce fear in a child of God, for greater is He who is in you. Your King reigns, your Lord is victorious, and you walk in the triumph He has already secured. The Spirit of God is your guide, your power, and your assurance, ensuring that no scheme of the enemy can ultimately prevail against you.

1 John 4:5-6 (LSB)
They are from the world; therefore they speak as from the world, and the world hears them. We are from God. The one who knows God hears us; the one who is not from God does not hear us. From this we know the spirit of truth and the spirit of error.

Not of the World

Those under the influence of the antichrist spirit are those who love the world. John already addressed this clearly in chapter two: "Do not love the world or the things in the world." And what are those things? John defines them precisely, the desires of the flesh, the desires of the eyes, and the pride of life. These are not peripheral issues; they are the very pillars upon which the world operates. In contrast to the kingdom of God, these are the three things the antichrist spirit elevates and feeds. The world is organized around them. Marketing and consumerism thrive by appealing to them. Social media algorithms are engineered to stir them. Entertainment and media are dominated by them. The world hears the antichrist spirit because the world wants what it offers. The antichrist feeds the flesh. The children of

God, by contrast, are fed in the Spirit, by the Bread of Life and the Living Water.

John then turns the contrast directly toward believers: "We are from God." That statement is foundational. To be from God means we are no longer of the world. As the Lord Jesus repeatedly taught, He called us out of the world even while leaving us in it. Like those of the world, we too may have disagreements in the flesh. Yet when it comes to our faith in Christ, something deeper unites us. We hear one another. We recognize one another. There is a shared understanding that cannot be reduced to personality, culture, or background. There is something that draws believers to one another in the Spirit. Even believers you may not naturally like, you cannot help but love. Even believers you disagree with on secondary matters, you recognize them as your family. You know they are your brothers and sisters in Christ.

This discernment does not always develop immediately. Scripture is clear that some believers remain very much in the flesh for a time. Paul addresses this directly in 1 Corinthians 3, describing believers who are infants in Christ, still walking according to the flesh. But as we grow in our walk with the Spirit, our ability to recognize those who are also led by the Spirit matures. John describes this as hearing one another, not audibly, but spiritually. We can speak to the world with clarity, doctrine, and reason, and still be met with blank stares, as though we are speaking another language. No matter how carefully we explain the truth, they simply do not hear us. But when we speak with a brother or sister who is walking in the Spirit, they hear us. They see us. They know us. John tells us that it is by this very reality that we discern the Spirit of truth from the spirit of error.

Ambassadors of Christ

We are in the world, but we are not of the world. This is why Scripture elsewhere describes believers as ambassadors of Christ. Paul tells us plainly, "We are ambassadors for Christ, God making His appeal through us" (2 Corinthians 5:20). An ambassador lives in a foreign land, but he does not belong to it. He represents another kingdom, speaks on behalf of another authority, and answers to a ruler who is not of that land. Though he resides there physically, his allegiance is elsewhere.

This imagery helps us understand much of what John has been describing. We live among those who are of the world, but we are not from the world. We speak while standing in foreign territory, and it should not surprise us when the world does not hear us. An ambassador does not expect the host nation to instinctively understand the values, priorities, or language of the kingdom he represents. In the same way, when believers speak truth, proclaim Christ, or live according to God's Word, the world often responds with confusion, resistance, or rejection. John has already explained why. They are from the world, therefore they speak from the world, and the world listens to them.

At the same time, this ambassadorial identity explains why believers recognize one another so readily. Ambassadors from the same kingdom may be stationed in different lands, cultures, and circumstances, but they know one another by who they represent. There is a shared allegiance, a shared language of faith, and a shared Spirit. This is why John can say, "We are from God. Whoever knows God listens to us." There is a spiritual recognition that transcends personality, background, and secondary disagreements.

This also guards us from misunderstanding our role in the world. An ambassador does not exist to force the laws of his kingdom onto the nation in which he resides. He does not confuse representation with domination. His task is faithfulness, not control. Likewise, Scripture does not call believers to conform the world into the image of the Kingdom by coercion. Rather, we are told, "Do not be conformed to this world, but be transformed by the renewal of your mind" (Romans 12:2). The call is inward faithfulness that results in outward witness, not outward enforcement that replaces the gospel.

Our responsibility is not to make the world behave like the Kingdom of God, but to faithfully represent the King of that Kingdom. We speak the truth, we live the truth, and we embody the love of Christ, trusting that God Himself is the One who opens hearts. Some will hear, because they are from God. Others will not, because they are of the world. This is why Paul exhorts us, "Do not be conformed to this world, but be transformed by the renewal of your mind" (Romans 12:2). Our transformation in Christ—not the shaping of the world—is what allows us to represent the Kingdom faithfully. John tells us this so that we are not surprised, discouraged, or tempted to compromise.

When we understand ourselves as ambassadors, much becomes clear. We know why the world does not hear us. We know why believers hear one another. And we know where our loyalty lies. Our eyes are not set on what is passing away, but on what is eternal. As Paul reminds us, "We look not to the things that are seen, but to the things that are unseen. For the things that are seen are temporary, but the things that are unseen are eternal" (2 Corinthians 4:18).

This clarity shapes every choice we make, every word we speak, and every action we take. We live not to impress the world, but to faithfully reflect the unseen Kingdom we belong to.

1 John 4:7-8 (LSB)
Beloved, let us love one another, for love is from God; and everyone who loves has been born of God and knows God. The one who does not love does not know God, because God is love.

Love is not an option. One cannot claim to love God and yet fail to love the brothers and sisters of the faith, because God is Love. This is not a suggestion or a mere ideal—it is the very essence of who God is, and the evidence of His presence in our lives. We make faith claims, as Paul declares in Galatians 2:20, "I have been crucified with Christ, and it is no longer I who live, but Christ lives in me." But how can we make such a claim and not also bear love for those around us? How can Christ, who demonstrated His perfect love on the cross, remain absent in us, failing to show that same love through our words, actions, and hearts? How can we say we love God, and yet fail to have God's love flowing through us?

John will not drop this message because this is the message. This is the truth. This is the work of the Spirit. The one who does not love does not know God, because God is love. And yet, as believers, we will experience grief, pain, sorrow, shame, and disappointment. These are real and sometimes heavy realities of life, yet Love remains at the core. I grieve because I love. I feel pain because of Love. I sorrow due to Love. I feel shame and disappointment because of Love. Our feelings come and go, but Love—the love of God in us—remains. It anchors us, sustains us, and guides us through every difficulty.

This is why love is not optional. It is the defining mark of life in Christ. Every act, every word, every thought shaped by the Spirit is framed by Love. To deny love is to deny the reality of God in our lives. To walk in love is to participate in God's eternal work, reflecting His mercy, His grace, and His glory to a world that desperately needs to see Him. Love is not merely a command; it is the expression of God's presence, the proof of His Spirit at work, and the heart of our faith.

1 John 4:9 (LSB)
By this the love of God was manifested in us, that God has sent His only begotten Son into the world so that we might live through Him.

John is intentionally repetitive here. Similar words and concepts have appeared throughout this letter, but every word is deliberate. He reminds his readers that our hope and love are not grounded in ourselves. Without God, we would not know Love. Consider the world's understanding of love: it often misleads, promises, and fails. A world quick to say "I love you" yet chooses self-interest over others. A world that exalts personal gain above all else. In contrast, the love of God is what we carry, and it is God's act of Love for us that makes it possible. His love transcends all. He did not merely declare love; He demonstrated it through action, a selfless, sacrificial love that cost Him everything, yet gave without compulsion, even knowing that many would reject Him. This is the love that sustains, transforms, and empowers us.

His Only Begotten Son

This verse is the first time John uses the term "only begotten" in his letter, and it is vital to understand its meaning. Some translations simply say "only," while others use "only begotten," which can confuse readers. The English word *begotten* often carries the sense of being "created" or "brought into existence," as Webster defines it: "brought into existence by or as if by a parent."[1] Unsurprisingly, some argue that this implies Jesus was created.

Dr. James White, in *Forgotten Trinity*, points out the challenges of finite language when speaking of God.[2] Words like "Father" or "person" carry baggage from human experience that can mislead if applied uncritically to God. Similarly, the term *begotten* has limitations when translated into English; it can obscure rather than illuminate.

However, the Greek term John uses, μονογενής (*monogenēs*), is applied uniquely to Jesus. It conveys more than the English "begotten." It is composed of *mono* (only) and *genes* (unique), meaning "one and only," "unique," or "without equal."[3] It is a word that emphasizes radical uniqueness and singularity, not origination in time or creation. John employs this term deliberately to set Jesus apart from all other beings.

John wants to prevent readers from categorizing Jesus alongside the Old Testament "sons of God" (Genesis 6; Job 1) — heavenly beings created by God, commonly understood as angels. These beings are not united with God in essence; they are created and distinct. In contrast, Jesus is the Holy, Unique, One-of-a-Kind Son of God. *Monogenēs* identifies Him as incomparable, unmatched, and singular in His divinity and relationship with the Father.

---

1. Merriam-Webster, "Begotten," *Merriam-Webster.com Dictionary*, https://www.merriam-webster.com/dictionary/begotten (accessed January 1, 2026).

2. James R. White, *The Forgotten Trinity: Recovering the Heart of Christian Belief*, 22.

3. Rick Brannan, ed., *Lexham Research Lexicon of the Greek New Testament*, μονογενής -οῦς, ὁ, 2020.

The term's significance is reinforced in other biblical texts. Proverbs 30:4 asks, "Who has ascended into heaven and descended? Who has gathered the wind in His fists? Who has bound the waters in a garment? Who has established all the ends of the earth? What is His name, and what is His Son's name?" Jesus later quotes this passage in John 3 during His encounter with Nicodemus, a ruler of the Jews. Nicodemus, coming under the weight of Jesus' teaching and miraculous works, admits that Jesus must be from God, for no one could perform such signs apart from divine authority (John 3:2). Jesus engages him in a conversation that both instructs and astonishes, bringing Nicodemus face-to-face with truths about heaven, God, and the Messiah.

In this dialogue, Jesus invokes Proverbs 30:4, asking, "Who can ascend into heaven and descend?" Nicodemus would have been aware of the fuller context of the passage: it continues to speak of God's sovereignty over creation, asking who can gather the wind, bind the waters, and establish the ends of the earth, concluding with the question, "What is His name, and what is His Son's name?" By referring to the beginning of this Scripture, Jesus draws Nicodemus' attention to its ultimate focus — the Son of God — and then explicitly identifies Himself as that Son, saying, in effect, "It is the Son of Man who does this." Through this, Jesus inserts Himself as the unique fulfillment of Proverbs 30:4, revealing that the one spoken of in Scripture is none other than He who has come from God. The title *Son of Man*, which He uses frequently throughout His ministry, underscores both His divinity and His God-ordained Messianic role, linking the Old Testament prophecy directly to His person and mission.

Immediately following this, Jesus delivers one of the most familiar statements in all of Scripture: "For God so loved the world, He gave His only begotten Son" (John 3:16). The placement is no coincidence. After alluding to an Old Testament passage about God and His Son, Jesus presents Himself as that very Son, the one uniquely sent from God to bring salvation. In Greek, the text could be rendered: "God so loved the world that He gave His one and only, unique Son" — emphasizing that the Son is not simply a child among children, not one created like the angels or one of the many "sons of God" referenced in the Old Testament, but the singular, incomparable, unique Son of God. The weight of this statement is staggering: the world's hope, love, and life itself is grounded in the singularity of Christ, God's only Son, whose love is demonstrated in action, not merely in words.

John's usage is exclusive. No other New Testament author applies *monogenēs* to Jesus. Even David is called a "son of God" symbolically, but John draws a clear line: Jesus alone is the unique, eternal Son of God.

A similar usage appears in Hebrews, where Isaac is called the *only begotten son* of Abraham. Isaac was not the firstborn (Ishmael preceded him) but was the promised, unique seed of Abraham. The word identifies Isaac as distinct from others and highlights his singular status. In the same way, John uses *monogenēs* to distinguish Jesus from any other being. It is not a term of creation, but of incomparability and divine uniqueness.

Son of Man & Son of God

I have used the term *Son of Man* a handful of times in this book, and it is important to help you understand why this title is significant. For newer believers, you may wonder why I insert it when discussing the Son of God. At first glance, the term *Son of Man* can seem contrary to *Son of God*, but it is not. In fact, *Son of Man* is the title Jesus used most frequently to refer to Himself in Scripture. It is a profoundly Messianic title, rich with meaning. The Jews of His day understood its weight, which is why the high priest and the chief priests considered it blasphemy and tore their robes when Jesus claimed it during His interrogation (Matthew 26:63-65, Mark 14:61-64).

The title *Son of Man* originates in Daniel 7, when Daniel has a vision of someone "like a son of man" coming with the clouds of heaven (Daniel 7:13-14). This imagery is deeply divine, for the clouds are associated with God Himself, as seen in Exodus 13:21 and Psalm 104:3. Daniel sees this figure approach the Ancient of Days — God — and is given "dominion, glory, and a kingdom, that all peoples, nations, and languages should serve him; his dominion is an everlasting dominion, which shall not pass away, and his kingdom one that shall not be destroyed" (Daniel 7:14, ESV). The phrase *like a son of man* conveys both divinity and humanity — a being in the image of a man, yet clothed with eternal authority.

Jesus explicitly applies this title to Himself. He tells His disciples that they will see "the Son of Man coming on the clouds of heaven with power and great glory" to gather His elect (Matthew 24:30-31, cf. Mark 13:26). By claiming this title, Jesus identifies Himself as the fulfillment of Daniel's vision — the one who bears both the authority of God and the likeness of humanity. He is fully God and fully man, the perfect Mediator who entered our world in flesh to redeem it.

The *Son of Man* title complements the *Son of God* title. As *Son of God*, He is divine, eternally begotten, the unique Son who is fully God. As *Son of Man*, He is incarnate, fully human, sharing in our nature yet without sin (Hebrews 4:15). Together, these titles reveal the mystery of the incarnation: Jesus is both the sovereign Lord and the compassionate Savior, the eternal God who entered time and space to save His people.

> *1 John 4:10 (LSB)*
> *In this is love, not that we have loved God, but that He loved us and sent His Son to be the propitiation for our sins.*

He Loved Us First

We did not love God first. God's love is not a response to ours, and no one is saved because they loved Him. He did not sacrifice Himself for those who already loved Him; He gave His life for those who had actively sinned against Him. As Paul writes, *"But God demonstrates His own love toward us, in that while we were yet sinners, Christ died for us"* (Romans 5:8). What did we do to deserve such love? Nothing. What did we do to earn it? Nothing. And yet, in His mercy, He loved us anyway. *(See also our discussion of propitiation in 1 John 2:2.)*

This is the same theme that runs like a lifeline throughout the first three chapters of John's letter. No matter where he takes the reader, John consistently brings us back to this truth: it is God's love, not ours, that is the foundation of our hope, our life, and our fellowship. This recurring emphasis reminds us that we are never operating in a vacuum of our own efforts or emotions. Love does not begin with us — it originates entirely with Him.

The verse emphasizes that God's love is not abstract or theoretical; it is personal and active. He sent His Son as the propitiation for our sins — not merely as a general gesture, but as the one who would bear the punishment we deserved. Christ did not come to die for the righteous, for there were none; He came to die for the guilty, the rebellious, the unworthy. While we were estranged from Him and under the weight of His just wrath, He intervened, taking that penalty upon Himself. This is the true heart of divine love: it is sacrificial, costly, and undeserved, flowing toward us even when we are at our lowest and least lovable.

This is the love that now abides in the believer. It is not conditional on our performance, our emotions, or our spiritual maturity. It is the love that sustains us in our daily lives, that covers our shortcomings, and that enables us to love others in ways we could not naturally achieve. This is God's love — active, unearned, and transformative — and it is the very presence of God with us, the source of hope, joy, and abiding fellowship in Christ.

1 John 4:11 (LSB)
Beloved, if God so loved us, we also ought to love one another.

If God was willing to love us in such a radical, sacrificial way, then we too ought to love one another in the same manner. This "ought" is not a ritualistic command or a legalistic expectation; it is a reflective challenge. John is calling us to examine our hearts. How can we withhold love from someone when we ourselves were undeserving of God's love? We were sinners, undeserving in every way, yet He poured out His love without reservation. The measure of God's love for us sets the standard for how we are to love others in the faith.

What is remarkable in John's writing is how often he returns to this theme. Across the span of just three chapters, he repeatedly emphasizes the necessity of love among believers. In chapter 2, he stresses that love is essential for walking in the truth. In chapter 3, he reminds us that love is the evidence of being born of God. And now, in chapter 4, he reiterates this truth, linking it directly to God's sacrificial love for us in Christ. John's repetition is intentional — it is pastoral, designed to impress upon the reader that love is not optional. Love is the hallmark of God's children; it is the foundation of the Christian life.

This love is not merely compassion or acts of charity, though these are expressions of it. It is also the love that gently corrects error. John's letter consistently intertwines encouragement and correction, yet both are always rooted in love. His warnings are not cold admonishments; they are acts of care. His corrections are paired with uplift and exhortation. This is the love that sustains the letter's tone — a love strong enough to confront error, yet tender enough to nurture spiritual growth. John's example reminds us that love must frame all of our engagement in the faith.

Love must be the foundation of all things we do in the faith. It is not merely a virtuous suggestion or a sentimental additive; it is the structural integrity of the entire Christian life. Paul writes in 1 Corinthians 13:

"If I speak with the tongues of men and of angels, but do not have love, I have become a noisy gong or a clanging cymbal. And if I have the gift of prophecy, and know all mysteries and all knowledge; and if I have all faith, so as to remove mountains, but do not have love, I am nothing. And if I give all my possessions to feed the poor, and if I surrender my body to be burned, but do not have love, it profits me nothing." (1 Cor 13:1-3)

Take heed of the absolute nature of Paul's words: without love, the greatest spiritual gifts are reduced to irritating noise. The deepest knowledge of mysteries becomes hollow intellectualism. Even a faith that moves mountains, if void of love, results in a person who is spiritually "nothing." Every act of service, every sacrifice of the flesh, and every theological insight becomes utter vanity if love is not the animating force.

Love is the fuel that drives the car; without it, you do not possess a vehicle—you only have a large, expensive paperweight.It becomes a machine useless and incapable of fulfilling its intended purpose. This is the indispensable key to our faith. Without love, we will gain nothing for the kingdom and achieve nothing for His glory, regardless of how busy we are with religious activity.

Christ did not call you to be a mercenary to win worldly battles, a conqueror to seize land, or a herald to demand glory for yourself. Christ called you to love. In the economy of heaven, love is the only currency that never devalues. It is the power that conquers all because God Himself is love. To live without love is to live without God. If we miss this, we have missed the very heart of Jesus Christ and the Gospel He came to bring.

1 John 4:12 (LSB)
No one has beheld God at any time; if we love one another, God abides in us, and His love is perfected in us.

No One Has Beheld God

I do not want this to confuse you. You may read this and think, how can no one have beheld God at any time? After all, John opened this letter stating that the Apostles had seen Him with their own eyes, touched Him, and walked with Him. When John now says no one has beheld God at any time, we must understand the context of his broader writings. When we look closely at his Gospel and this letter, John nearly always uses the term God when speaking of the Father. At the same time, he speaks of Jesus being in perfect unity with God, one with God and sharing in His glory, as we see throughout all of his writings — most clearly in the introduction of John 1: "And the Word was God." He uses the term God to refer to the fullness of the divine essence — the unapproachable, infinite, and eternal nature of the Father.

No human, in his natural state, can behold the fullness of the Father. God made this clear to Moses in Exodus 33:20: "You cannot see my face, for man shall not see me and live." Paul reinforces this in 1 Timothy 6:16, specifically speaking of the Father as He who "dwells in unapproachable light, whom no one has ever seen or can see." This is the infinite gap between the Creator and the creature; our finite and mortal eyes were never designed to gaze directly upon the raw, unshielded glory of the Godhead in its entirety.

This is why John uses almost identical language in his Gospel to clarify the distinction: "No one has ever seen God; the only God, who is at the Father's side, He has made Him known" (John 1:18). Here, John draws a clear line between God the Father, whom no one has ever seen, and God the Son, who perfectly reveals Him. Jesus Himself confirms this in John 6:46: "Not that anyone has seen the Father except He who is from God; He has seen the Father."

Man can only behold God in the way that God reveals Himself, supremely and exhaustively in His Son. There is a profound beauty in this unity: beholding the infinite fullness of God is not necessary through any other means because Jesus reveals the Father perfectly. As Jesus told Philip, "Whoever has seen me has seen the Father" (John 14:9). This is possible because Jesus is in the Father and the Father is in Him. Paul tells us in Colossians 2:9 that the entire fullness of the Godhead dwells bodily within Jesus.

Therefore, when the Apostles saw Jesus, they were indeed seeing God, but they were seeing Him in a way that allowed them to comprehend Him. He is the image of the invisible God (Colossians 1:15) and the radiance of the glory of God, the exact imprint of His nature (Hebrews 1:3). Although we cannot look upon the unapproachable light of the Father's essence, we do not miss any part of Him when we look at the Son. Jesus is the revelation of God Himself. Any time someone in history has truly "seen God," they have seen the Son, who alone bridges the divide and makes the invisible Father known to our finite hearts.

Throughout Scripture, the presence of God in the Old Testament often manifests in the person of Jesus. When God walked in the Garden with Adam and Eve, it was Jesus. When God met Abraham, it was Jesus. When God wrestled with Jacob, it was Jesus. John, reflecting on Isaiah's prophecy, notes in John 12:40 that Isaiah "saw His glory" and spoke of Him — the One who would come as Jesus. Even in Isaiah 6, when the prophet sees God on His throne, he is beholding Jesus, the Son of God, in glory.

We do not need to see God in His fullness to love Him. We walk by faith, not by sight. We behold His hand in the miracles He performs. We behold His love manifested in Christ. We behold the fruit He produces in our lives. As Jesus says in John 20:29: "Blessed are those who did not see, and yet believed." Our love is empowered and sustained by what we have already seen and experienced in His Son, not by direct sight of God's total essence.

If we love one another, we see God's love made tangible among us. His love abides in us, and through us, it is perfected. We become living evidence of the God we cannot fully behold.

We Bring God to People

Although John does not explicitly say this, there is a profound beauty in these words. Jesus is the image of the invisible God. He is the full revelation of God and His love. God came to man in the flesh so that we could see and touch Him. Now, as His children and ambassadors of Christ, we continue the mission He began.

We bring the light of Christ into the world. We manifest the revelation of His love through our lives. The Father sent the Son to save us, and the Son sends us, empowered by the Holy Spirit, to reach the lost. Paul describes believers as "fellow workers" in

1 Corinthians 3:9, and as temples of God where His Spirit dwells. Today, the meeting place for God is no longer in a building, behind the veil, or in the tabernacle — it is in His children, in us, who bear Christ within.

In a world shrouded in darkness and deception, you might be the only true image of Jesus someone ever encounters. Every encounter with a child of God is an opportunity to reflect God's love and light. Just as Jesus revealed the Father to us, we are called to be the living revelation of Jesus to others — through our love, our deeds, and the way we walk in His Spirit.

1 John 4:13 (LSB)
By this we know that we abide in Him and He in us, because He has given us of His Spirit.

His Spirit, Our Assurance

This verse echoes the conclusion of chapter 3, reinforcing a truth that John wants his readers to grasp deeply: this is the assurance of our faith. We abide in Him, and He abides in us, not through our own effort or through any outward display of piety, but by the work of the Spirit. This is the fruit of God's regeneration in us — the Spirit indwelling us, producing His love within our hearts. John carefully guides the reader here, as he does throughout his letters, never allowing us to think that we are the origin of these things. He repeatedly draws us back to God as the source, ensuring we understand that it is His love, His Spirit, and His initiative that make all of this possible. The believer is never the cause; we are the recipients of His work, and in that, we find true assurance.

It is by this love — God's love manifested in us — that we can know with confidence that we are in fellowship with Him. John's repeated use of the phrase "By this we know" is intentional. I point it out deliberately so the reader sees what John is pressing upon our hearts: our assurance never rests on our performance, our abilities, or any outward display, but on God's love and Spirit at work within us. Some today, unfortunately, try to place conditions on this certainty. You may hear claims like, "You must speak in tongues to know you have the Holy Spirit." This is unbiblical and entirely contrary to the witness of Scripture. The indwelling Spirit is not validated by the exercise of a particular spiritual gift, but by the presence of God's love in the believer's life. Love is the mark of true union with Christ, and by this love, the world recognizes those who belong to Him (John 13:35).

Ironically, those who elevate certain gifts above others often cling to passages in Acts or Paul's first letter to the Corinthians while ignoring the broader teaching of Scripture. Paul addresses this directly in 1 Corinthians 12, explaining that there are varieties of gifts, but the same Spirit distributes them according to His will. These gifts are given for the building up of the church, not as proof of salvation or spiritual status. Later, in 1 Corinthians 13, Paul emphasizes that these gifts are temporary, but love is eternal: "Love never ends" (1 Cor 13:8). Love endures because God Himself is love.

If love is eternal, and we will eternally dwell with God, then love must be the truest and most enduring sign of our union with Him. It is not a fleeting emotion, a ritual, or a display of spiritual ability — it is the Spirit's work within us, the tangible evidence of His indwelling presence. By this love, we have confidence. By this love, we know we abide in Him, and He in us. By this love, we see the proof that we are children of God, now and forever. This is John's point: repeated, intentional, and unshakable.

> *1 John 4:14 (LSB)*
> *We have beheld and bear witness that the Father has sent the Son to be Savior of the world.*

No one has beheld God, the Father, but the Apostles have seen Him, walked with Him, and bear **firsthand witness** to the Love of the Father, testifying not to stories they've been told or rumors they've heard, but to the reality they experienced with their own eyes. They witnessed the Father's love in action, revealed supremely in the sending of His Son to be the Savior of the world. Love is at the very heart of the Gospel. Love is at the very heart of God.

Love & The Trinity

I want to take a moment to demonstrate why God's triune nature is so crucial to what we believe. John was confronting gnosticism, and much of his letter addresses those who deny that Jesus truly came in the flesh. While this heresy is less common today, another heresy has resurfaced in many circles: the denial of the Trinity. Among these errors, one that has gained notable traction is Modalism (also called Oneness theology). Modalists assert that Father, Son, and Holy Spirit are not three co-equal, co-eternal persons, but merely different modes or manifestations of God. Under this belief, the Father "became" the Son when He took on flesh, and Jesus is nothing more than a temporary mode of God whose purpose was solely to act as Savior.

Surprisingly, many who identify as Evangelical Christians fall into this trap. With the weakening of biblical teaching on the Trinity, a variety of analogies, illustrations, and explanations are often used to describe God. One popular example is the analogy, "God is like water; water can be ice, liquid, or steam." While intuitive to some, even this single analogy can inadvertently create an image of a God who changes forms depending on His purpose—misrepresenting His eternal, unchanging, and relational nature. This is just one example; in weekly preaching, in music, and in countless other analogies and teachings, similar errors appear, all of which subtly undermine a biblically faithful understanding of God's triune nature.

Of course, Scripture contains countless proofs and direct statements from Jesus that decisively refute such heresies. I will not attempt to exhaust them here—doing so could fill an entire book. For those seeking to build a deeper, biblical understanding of the Trinity, I highly recommend *Forgotten Trinity* by Dr. James White for a modern, accessible approach. For those who want to engage with classical theological writings, Athanasius's *On the Incarnation* and Augustine's *De Trinitate* remain timeless, robust resources that have shaped orthodox understanding of God's triune nature. These works, ancient and modern alike, provide the depth and rigor necessary to grow in both knowledge and conviction regarding the triune God revealed in Scripture.

However, for our purposes, I want to focus on God's love and why His triune nature is essential to understanding it. The Gospel is not only about God's love for His creation—though that love is real and active—it is ultimately about the love that eternally exists between the Father and the Son, perfectly revealed within the Godhead. John has stated repeatedly that "God is love" (1 John 4:8, 16). But love, by its very nature, requires an object; it is always expressed outwardly, selfless, and relational. True love cannot exist in isolation—it must be directed toward another and witnessed, and in the Trinity, that love is fully eternal, self-sufficient, and complete.

If God's love were directed only toward creation, one could ask: Did God love anyone before creation? And if creation were to cease, would His love also cease? Could God's love be self-sufficient if it depended on anything outside Himself? Scripture provides the answer: the Father eternally loves the Son. This eternal love demonstrates that God's love has no beginning and no end. His love does not depend on creation. It is fully self-sufficient and eternally expressed within the Godhead.

Love also requires a witness. Even in human relationships, marriage demonstrates this: love exists between two people and is witnessed by others. Within the Trinity, the Father loves the Son, the Son loves the Father, and the Holy Spirit testifies to this love. Love exists perfectly, eternally, and relationally within God Himself. He is fully self-sufficient in His love, and this eternal, triune love is why God can truly be described as Love. By nature, God is relational. By essence, God is love. And by existence, God is triune: one Being, eternally existing as three co-equal persons.

If Modalism were true, the love between the Father and the Son that Scripture repeatedly affirms becomes artificial—a performance for creation's sake rather than a reflection of God's eternal character. But Jesus affirms the genuine, eternal nature of this love throughout the Gospels:

- *"The Father loves the Son and has given all things into His hand" (John 3:35)*

- *"For the Father loves the Son and shows Him all that He Himself is doing" (John 5:20)*

- *"For this reason the Father loves Me, because I lay down My life that I may take it up again" (John 10:17)*

- *"As the Father has loved Me, so have I loved you" (John 15:9)*

- *"You have loved Me before the foundation of the world" (John 17:24, speaking to the Father in the High Priestly Prayer)*

This is not a superficial or performative love. It is real. It is eternal. It is the love that exists between the Father and the Son from eternity past, fully revealed in Jesus Christ. God is love, and His love is inherently triune. To deny the Trinity is, ultimately, to deny the eternal, relational, self-sufficient love of God.

1 John 4:15-16 (LSB)
Whoever confesses that Jesus is the Son of God, God abides in him, and he in God. And we have come to know and have believed in the love which God has in us. God is love, and the one who abides in love abides in God, and God abides in him.

This confession is the very rock of our faith. Peter was the first to make it when Jesus asked, "Who do you say I am?" Peter responded, "You are the Christ, the Son of the living God" (Matthew 16:16). Jesus' response underscores the divine origin of this revelation: "Blessed are you, Simon Bar-Jonah, for flesh and blood did not reveal this to you, but my Father who is in heaven" (Matthew 16:17). Peter did not arrive at this confession on his own; it was the work of the Spirit of God, poured out by the Father. This confession of who Jesus is—the recognition that He is the eternal Son of God, the Christ—is the foundation upon which the Church is built. It is for this reason Jesus changes Simon's name to Peter in this moment: the Church is founded not on human insight, opinion, or merit, but on the divinely revealed truth of Christ's identity.

As Paul reminds us, "No one can say, 'Jesus is Lord,' except by the Holy Spirit" (1 Corinthians 12:3). This is not merely about the words we speak; it is about the truth we acknowledge in our hearts. To confess Jesus as Lord is to recognize Him as YHWH, fully God, co-eternal with the Father, not simply as a title, a role, or a mode. Many may claim to confess Jesus as Lord or Son of God, but their words may carry a different meaning than what Scripture teaches. They may see Him as a great teacher, a prophet, or a spiritual example, yet miss the eternal reality of His divine Sonship. True confession recognizes Jesus as the uncreated, eternal Son, the Word who was in the beginning with God, the Word who was God, the perfect image of the invisible God, Loved by the Father, in perfect unity with Him from before the foundation of the world (John 1:1, Colossians 1:15, Hebrews 1:3).

Those who confess this truth do so by the Spirit of God, and through this confession we know that God abides in them, and they abide in God. This is not theoretical knowledge; it is relational, experiential, and transformative. We believe in the infinite love God has for us. We see that love displayed supremely on the Cross, and we witness it in every promise He has made. In response to this love, our hearts are drawn upward, and by His Spirit, our love for God grows. The love of God, planted within us by His Spirit, expands as we behold His glory, meditate on His truth, and obey His commands. In this divine cycle of giving and receiving, we come to know that the Spirit, the Word, and the Father dwell in us, and that His love is perfected in our lives.

1 John 4:17 (LSB)
By this, love has been perfected with us, so that we may have confidence in the day of judgement, because as He is, so also are we in this world.

Confidence in the day of judgement.

The more we learn of His love, the more we are perfected in His love. And the more His love is perfected in us, the stronger and steadier our confidence becomes. John is now beginning to draw his letter toward its conclusion, and as he does, he brings the central aim of everything he has written into full view. This has been his purpose all along. We can have real assurance of our faith and genuine confidence in our salvation. The Christian life is not meant to be lived under the shadow of constant uncertainty, fear, or endless "what ifs." Our confidence is not rooted in ourselves, but in what God has already done.

If we know that God has given us His Spirit, and if we know that we are His children, then we are not left to speculate about our standing before Him. We are not guessing. We are trusting in what He has accomplished. When we rightly understand the work of God on our behalf, our confidence extends even to the day of judgment itself. This is not arrogance. It is faith in the sufficiency of Christ.

Jesus states this plainly and without qualification in John 5:24: "Truly, truly, I say to you, he who hears My word, and believes Him who sent Me, has eternal life, and does not come into judgment, but has passed out of death into life." Notice the certainty of His words. Eternal life is not merely promised for the future, it is possessed in the present. Judgment is not looming ahead for the believer, it has already been addressed. Death is not our destination, it is our past.

We hear the promises of Christ. We believe that the Father sent the Son. We trust in the Father's love, made visible and tangible in the sending of His Son into the world. And because of this, judgment no longer stands against us. Christ has already taken it upon Himself. When Jesus went to the cross, He did not merely make salvation possible. He paid the full debt of our sin. The record of our guilt was nailed to the cross with Him.

In the courtroom of heaven, our case has already been settled. Jesus stood in our place. The verdict has been rendered. The sentence has been carried out. There is no future court date awaiting the believer, because the fine has already been paid in full. When Christ cried out, "It is finished," He was not expressing exhaustion. He was declaring completion, finality, and victory.

When this reality takes hold of our hearts, fear of future judgment loses its grip. We do not look ahead with dread or uncertainty, but with confidence, because we know exactly what has happened. Jesus entered the courtroom for us. He bore the judgment we deserved. He satisfied divine justice. And because of that, we can stand before God, not trembling in fear, but resting in assurance, fully confident in the finished work of Christ.

1 John 4:18 (LSB)
There is no fear in love; but perfect love casts out fear, because fear involves punishment, and the one who fears is not perfected in love.

The Fear of Judgment vs. the Fear of the Lord

Do not misunderstand the apostle's words here. John is not denying the fear of God. Scripture is unequivocal on this point. "The fear of the Lord is the beginning of knowledge" (Proverbs 1:7). "The fear of the Lord is the beginning of wisdom" (Proverbs 9:10). "The fear of the Lord leads to life" (Proverbs 19:23). These are not isolated statements, but a consistent testimony echoed throughout both the Old and New Testaments. The Bible never dismisses the fear of the Lord, rather, it exalts it as foundational to wisdom, life, and true understanding.

What John is addressing here is not the fear of God's majesty, holiness, or authority. He is addressing a different fear entirely. He is confronting the fear of judgment, the fear of condemnation, the fear of punishment that belongs not to sons, but to criminals.

Healthy Fear

Everyone fears fire. You may not consciously think of yourself as fearing it, but you do. You can sit near a fireplace, light a candle, or cook over a stove without trembling, not because you lack fear, but because the fire is contained and controlled. Yet if that same fire were to spread, surround you, or escape its boundaries, fear would immediately set in. And no matter how tame or controlled that fire appears, you will not place your hand into it, because you understand what it is capable of doing.

This is a healthy fear. It is not panic, but recognition. It is the awareness of power. It is respect. This is the kind of fear Scripture speaks of when it calls us to fear the Lord.

God is described as a consuming fire (Hebrews 12:29; Deuteronomy 4:24). Even though He is gracious, merciful, and loving, we do not forget who He is. Just as we are comforted by the warmth of a fireplace while never forgetting its destructive potential, so we rest in God's grace without losing sight of His holiness, power, and authority. This recognition of who God is, His awe inspiring majesty and strength, is the beginning of wisdom. A wise man does not stand proudly before God. He falls on his face and pleads for mercy.

This fear is not unhealthy. It is necessary. It produces humility, reverence, obedience, and worship.

Fear of Judgment

When John writes that "fear involves punishment," he is not speaking of reverent awe. He is speaking of condemnation. This is the fear of the criminal standing before a judge, knowing he is guilty, knowing the judge has the authority to sentence him. This fear is not rooted in love, but in guilt.

A child, however, fears his father in a completely different way. A child knows his father will discipline him, not destroy him. Punishment is the end for the criminal. Discipline is a means of correction and growth for a son.

We do not fear judgment because Christ has taken our punishment. We do fear God, because like any good Father, He disciplines His children. But punishment and discipline are not the same thing. Scripture is clear. "For those whom the Lord loves He disciplines" (Hebrews 12:6). And again, "For the moment all discipline seems painful rather than pleasant, but later it yields the peaceful fruit of righteousness to those who have been trained by it" (Hebrews 12:11).

Discipline hurts, but it heals. Punishment destroys. Our Father in heaven does not punish His children for their failures. If He did, none of us would survive. He disciplines us to strengthen us, refine us, and conform us to the image of His Son.

No Fear in the Day of Judgment

As I mentioned in my exposition of 1 John 4:17, the Lord Jesus Himself made a promise in John 5:24. He said that the one who hears His word and believes the Father who sent Him does not come into judgment. This is not a vague hope or a theological inference; it is a direct promise from Christ. This is precisely why we do not fear judgment, because our Lord has already spoken with absolute clarity. The day of judgment is not for the children of God.

The courtroom scene has already taken place. The case has already been heard. The verdict has already been rendered. Jesus Christ stood in our place. The charges against us were brought forward in full, and the entire legal demand of the law was satisfied on the cross. Justice was not ignored; it was fulfilled.

Wrath was not postponed; it was poured out. Judgment was not avoided; it was executed—upon Christ.

Therefore, there is no remaining judgment left for those who are in Him. To fear future condemnation is to forget that Christ already entered the courtroom on our behalf and declared, "It is finished." The believer does not await a trial; we stand on a finished verdict secured by the promise of Christ Himself.

The only way fear of judgment could return is if new charges could be brought against us. Yet Scripture asks, "Who will bring a charge against God's elect?" (Romans 8:33). And John has already reminded us earlier, "If anyone sins, we have an advocate with the Father, Jesus Christ the righteous" (1 John 2:1).

This is the confidence we have, grounded in the love God demonstrated on the cross. "Therefore there is now no condemnation for those who are in Christ Jesus" (Romans 8:1). We are no longer enemies of God, but children of God (Galatians 3:26). And as children, "you have not received a spirit of slavery leading to fear again, but you have received the Spirit of adoption as sons, by whom we cry out, 'Abba, Father'" (Romans 8:15).

A Pastoral Appeal

If you still fear judgment, it is not because God's love is insufficient, but because that love has not yet been fully settled in your heart. If you still fear condemnation, you may not yet be resting in the fullness of the Gospel and what Christ has already accomplished on your behalf. This is not a rebuke meant to drive you away, but an invitation to draw nearer to the cross, where fear is swallowed up by grace.

My prayer is that anyone who has read this far has felt that fear begin to loosen its grip. And if it has not, I do not want you to withdraw or despair. I want you to look again, more closely, at what Christ has done. From the beginning of this letter, John has pressed this truth upon us again and again: who Jesus is, what He has done, the love He has demonstrated, the judgment He has borne, and the grace He has freely given. By now, you have seen the depth of His sacrifice, the certainty of His promises, and the overwhelming love poured out at the cross.

To say that love has not yet been perfected is not to say you are cast out, but that there is still more peace to be found, more assurance to be embraced, and more freedom to step into. God is not calling you to prove yourself, but to trust Him. He is not asking you to overcome fear by effort, but to let His perfect love do what it was always meant to do: drive fear away.

If you still find yourself asking, What if I mess up? What if I fail? What if I am not good enough? What if I do not believe enough? Then hear this clearly. These questions do not arise because Christ's work is uncertain, but because we so often turn inward and begin to measure ourselves instead of resting in what He has already accomplished. We begin to live in hypotheticals we construct in our own minds rather than in the finished reality of the cross. Do not overcomplicate the Gospel. The Gospel is simple, yet we are remarkably skilled at making it difficult. It is easy because it requires nothing of you. It is hard because it requires nothing of you. We struggle to let go. We struggle to trust.

And this is where childlike faith becomes essential. Trust is the heart of the matter. It is the quiet confidence of trusting your Father with what you do not understand, just as a child trusts his own father far beyond his ability to reason. My youngest son does not spend his days stressed or anxious, wondering if a single mistake will cause me to abandon him or disown him. He does not wake up worried about how the bills are paid or how food appears on the table. He is my child in his good moments and his bad, and I love him regardless. I do not love him because of the good he does, and I do not lose love for him because of his failures. My love for him is deeper than his actions because it is rooted in his identity as my son.

This is the safety of the household of God. My son rests because he trusts his father. I could walk upstairs right now, lift him while he sleeps, and carry him through the entire house without him ever opening his eyes. He would remain completely at peace, unaware and unafraid, because his father's arms are a place of absolute safety. If we truly understood our identity as children of the Father, we would find that same rest, knowing that we are being carried by a Love that does not let go.

Now imagine a stranger trying to pick you up while you slept. How quickly fear would rise in your chest. How fast you would wake in panic, struggling to break free. The difference between resting in peace and waking in terror is not a matter of your own strength; it is entirely a matter of trust. And that is exactly what this world has stolen from us.

This broken world has trained us to keep our eyes open and our guards up. We have been lied to, disappointed, hurt, scammed, and betrayed. Often, it was the very people we loved and depended on the most who failed us, leaving wounds that make the very idea of "resting" feel dangerous. I understand why trust feels difficult, even impossible. But hear me clearly: God has never failed anyone, and He will not begin His record of failure with you.

Today is the day of salvation, and you must anchor your soul in this reality: you will not be the first person God lies to. You will not be the first person He abandons or forgets. He is not like the broken men and women who have crossed your path. He is trustworthy. His Word is truth. Jesus Christ is able to save, and He is fully capable of doing exactly what He promised.

He said He is the Good Shepherd and that He will lose none of His sheep. He is not a liar. I may fear failing God, but I do not fear God failing me. If I fail, I know He will discipline me—and it may hurt for a season—but He does so only to strengthen me and lead me back into righteousness. I can rest in the middle of my own weakness because I know He will not forsake me or abandon me. That is His unbreakable promise: "I will never leave you nor forsake you" (Hebrews 13:5).

You are not being held by your own ability to hang on; you are being carried by the One who has already overcome the world. In those arms, you can finally afford to close your eyes and rest.

1 John 4:19 (LSB)
We love, because he loved us.

The Priority of Love

I can trust all of His promises because He loved me before I ever loved Him. That means His love for me is not contingent on my successes or failures, because He loved me before any of those successes or failures ever occurred. As a father, I have learned this through my own children. As parents, we will often say things like, "I love my children despite their failures," but that is only half of the truth. I also love them despite their successes.

I loved my children from the moment I was aware of their existence. My love for them transcends their personalities, their traits, or their accomplishments. My love for them is not grounded on things that happened after their birth; I loved them before they ever left their mother's womb. Likewise, the Scripture proclaims that God loved us before we were born. He loved us first. We do not love and trust God first; we love and trust God because He loved us first.

Known at the Cross

When Christ went to the cross, He did not go for a mysterious, nameless number of people whom He did not know yet. Jesus knew the name of each and every one of His sheep while He hung on that tree. He went to the cross for you. This is not a generalized love; it is a specific, covenantal, and personal devotion.

When Jesus prayed the High Priestly prayer in the Garden of Gethsemane, He was not just praying for His Apostles and disciples who were alive at that moment. He was praying for each and every one of us who would eventually believe in Him. He explicitly stated: "I do not ask on behalf of these alone, but for those also who believe in Me through their word" (John 17:20).

An Unanswerable Petition

Consider the weight of that moment. He prayed those words after asking the Father to "Keep them in Your name" (John 17:11), "Keep them from the evil one" (John 17:15), and "Sanctify them by the truth" (John 17:17).

Do we truly believe the Father, who has loved the Son before the foundation of the world, would deny His Son's petition? We have already seen that the Father loves the Son and gives Him all things. Therefore, we can have absolute confidence that Jesus's prayer to His Father on our behalf will not go unanswered. If Christ has asked the Father to keep you, and the Father always hears the Son, then you are kept by a power that cannot be broken. Your security does not rest on your ability to stay sanctified, but on the Father's commitment to answer the Son's prayer.

> *1 John 4:20-21 (LSB)*
> *If someone says, "I love God," and hates his brother, he is a liar; for the one who does not love his brother whom he has seen, cannot love God whom he has not seen. And this commandment we have from Him, that the one who loves God should love his brother also.*

The Anatomy of a Liar

John finishes this section of his letter by way of reminding us of what he has said several times already: the one who says he has fellowship with Him but walks in darkness is a liar. Someone may say, "I love God," but if those words are spoken by a heart that hates his brother, he is a liar. He could have easily repeated his words from chapter 3: If you hate your brother, "how does God's love abide in you?" But instead, he sharpens the point.

If you hate the very ones whom God loves, how can you claim to love God? If you hate God's children, how can you claim you love the Father? Now, does this mean you have to like your brothers at all times? Not at all. I don't always like my brothers. I don't even always like my children. Sometimes my children act stubborn or greedy, and I don't like them in that moment. Yet, I always love them. Love is a covenant of the will and a fruit of the Spirit; "liking" is often just a matter of the moment. Love remains even when affection feels strained.

The "Lord, Lord" Deception

John has no fear of switching from his gentle language to directly calling people liars. It is actually an act of love that he does so. He does not soften his words to comfort those who need to hear the sharp truth. Personally, I would rather find out I have been lying to others and to myself now, than find out on that final day when I say, "Lord, Lord," only to hear, "I never knew you."

When Jesus says the words "I never knew you," He is calling the self-proclaimed believer a liar. These are not merely believers who fail at loving perfectly; they are those who have pursued a false version of Jesus—one of their own making, a Jesus crafted to serve their own agendas or satisfy their own desires. The self-proclaimed Christian says, "Lord, I did so many things in Your name," but Jesus says, "No, you did not." The self-proclaimed Christian says, "I love You," and Jesus says, "No, you do not." Jesus said, "If you love Me, you will keep My commands" (John 14:15), and we know His commandment is twofold: to Believe and to Love. If you do not love, then you are a liar when it comes to your claim of belief.

For love to be genuine, Scripture tells us that we must hate what is evil and cling to what is good. Romans 12:9 makes this clear. Love does not ignore evil. Love names it. If someone hates his brother while proclaiming how much he loves God, John says plainly that he is a liar and that the truth is not in him.

The Proximity of Proof

The one who refuses to love the brother who stands before him cannot love the God who seems far away. How many people loudly proclaim a love for God whom they do not see, who dwells in the highest heavens, while their brothers and sisters, whom they can see and touch, receive none of that love? It is easy to say "I love you" to someone five thousand miles away. There is rarely a moment when that love must be demonstrated. You are not required to bring them a meal in their time of need, to lift them up when they fall, or to sacrifice your time and resources for their good.

In the same way, verbally proclaiming love for God is the easiest thing a man can do. It costs nothing more than breath. It requires no sacrifice, no endurance, no strength. Yet when a brother stands in front of him in need, suddenly that love cannot be found.

The Law of Christ

This is the commandment of our Lord, what Paul calls the Law of Christ: "Bear one another's burdens, and so fulfill the law of Christ" (Galatians 6:1). Do not misunderstand what is being said here. This is not a law you keep in order to be saved. You cannot fulfill it in the flesh, and that is precisely why the person who does not love is called a liar. John does not say, "If someone says he loves God but hates his brother, he is in danger of losing his salvation." He is not warning believers that they may fail to keep the Law of Christ.

Instead, John points to a reality he has emphasized throughout the entire letter: if you are a child of God, born of the Spirit, and God abides in you, you will love. If love is absent, then the claim of being His is false. This is not a matter of trying harder, striving in the flesh, or climbing some moral ladder. The answer is not found in human effort—it is found in God Himself. You need Him to dwell within you, to bring His presence, to guide your heart, and to produce life and love through His Spirit.

These words are not meant to drive a man into self-effort. They are intended to wound the heart in order to awaken godly grief. As Scripture reminds us, "Godly grief produces a repentance that leads to salvation" (2 Corinthians 7:8). True conviction does not crush or condemn; it reveals the reality of who we are apart from God and points us toward Him who transforms.

John ends this chapter exactly where he began, with truth that exposes, love that saves, and a Spirit-driven reality that proves God is at work in the hearts of His children.

Summary

We have transitioned in this chapter from the foundation of our identity into the active perfection of God's love within us. This love is not a passive sentiment or abstract idea, but a powerful and discerning reality. It enables us to distinguish between the Spirit of truth and the spirit of error. Because we are born of God, we are given spiritual ears to hear the voice of our Father and spiritual discernment to recognize the counterfeits that seek to substitute themselves for the true Christ. We stand as ambassadors in a foreign land, grounded in the assurance that the One who dwells within us is infinitely greater than the one who is in the world.

The hallmark of this chapter is the revelation that God Himself is the source and origin of all true love. We do not love in order to gain His favor. We love because He first loved us, setting His covenantal love upon us before we ever drew breath. This divine love is perfected in us when it moves beyond the inner life of the heart and expresses itself through our hands and lives, becoming visible in the way we treat the brothers and sisters who stand before us. While the Father's essence remains unapproachable in its fullness, His love is made tangible, visible, and comprehensible through the person of Jesus Christ and through the lives of His children who abide in Him.

Our confidence, then, is anchored not in our performance but in the finished work of the Son and the faithful intercession of our Great High Priest. We are not preserved by the strength of our own grip, but by the sovereign hand of the Father who hears and answers the petition of His Son to keep those who belong to Him. As this chapter comes to a close, John reminds us that a mere verbal claim of faith is empty if it is not accompanied by the fruit of love. If we find our hearts lacking, the answer is not self effort or spiritual striving, but godly grief that leads us back to the source of life itself.

We rest in the promise that we are indwelt by the Spirit, carried by the Son, and perfected by a Love that does not falter, does not fail, and does not let go.

Chapter Five

1 John 5

That You May Know

Overview

John now brings his letter to its close, but he does not do so by introducing new ideas. Instead, he gathers everything he has already declared and presses it firmly into the heart of the believer. Chapter five functions as both a summary and a seal. What has been taught throughout the letter is now restated with clarity, repetition, and purpose, so that the believer does not merely understand these truths but rests in them.

Throughout this epistle, John has drawn clear and unavoidable distinctions. He has contrasted light and darkness, truth and error, love and hatred, the child of God and the liar. He has given his readers both assurance and discernment, assurance for those who are born of God and discernment to recognize those who merely claim faith while denying it in life or doctrine. John has exposed false Christs, warned against deceiving spirits, and reminded the church that confession, obedience, and love are not separate marks but inseparable fruits of genuine faith.

Now, in this final chapter, John gathers these themes and drives them home with pastoral urgency. He wants the believer to know, not to guess, not to hope vaguely, but to know that they have eternal life. He reinforces that faith in the true Christ produces new birth, that new birth results in obedience and love, and that this life is sustained not by human effort but by the testimony of God Himself. John anchors assurance not in emotional experience or outward performance, but in God's witness concerning His Son and the Spirit's work within the believer.

Chapter five is John's final appeal to confidence. It is the culmination of everything he has been saying from the opening lines of the letter. The believer is not left in uncertainty, fear, or self-examination without end. Instead, John presses the truth upon us so that we may rest, fully assured, that eternal life is found in the Son, that those who are born of God overcome the world, and that God's testimony is greater than every voice that would seek to unsettle or deceive.

This chapter does not call the believer to strive harder, but to believe rightly, love faithfully, and live confidently in what God has already done. This final movement is not merely a conclusion; it is an invitation to rest. John has taken us through the fires of testing and the call to sacrificial love, but here, he provides the anchor for the soul. He understands that a heart plagued by uncertainty cannot effectively love or obey. Therefore, he removes every shadow of doubt, showing us that the life we possess is held not by our own strength, but by the unwavering testimony of God Himself. It is John's final word to the church—not of doubt, but of settled assurance grounded in Christ alone. As we step into these verses, we are stepping onto the solid ground of divine certainty.

1 John 5:1 (LSB)
Everyone who believes that Jesus is the Christ has been born of God, and everyone who loves the One who gives new birth loves also the one who has been born of Him.

The Nature of Saving Belief

As John begins the final chapter of his letter, he returns to the most fundamental question of our faith: Who do you say that Jesus is?

When John speaks of believing that Jesus is the Christ—the Anointed One—he is not referring to mere acknowledgment. It is crucial to remember what we have already established earlier in this letter concerning saving belief. Biblical belief is not simply recognizing that a god exists. In fact, prior to the modern era, it was exceedingly rare for anyone to deny the existence of a god or gods. Historically, the term *atheist* often described someone who rejected a particular deity, not the reality of God altogether, which is why the Romans actually called the early Christians "atheists" for rejecting the pantheon of gods. When Scripture speaks of unbelief, it is not primarily addressing atheism as we understand it today.

We have a tendency to read the word *unbelief* through a modern lens, instinctively equating it with atheism because disbelief has become more visible in contemporary culture. But this assumption imports a present-day concern back into an ancient text. When Scripture is read in its historical and theological context, it becomes clear that the biblical writers are not confronting denial of God's existence. The issue they confront is far more pervasive and far more dangerous: a refusal to trust the God whom they claim to believe in.

The Bible reserves its strongest language for the person who says there is no God at all, calling such a person foolish: "The fool says in his heart, 'There is no God'" (Psalm 14:1). But when Scripture addresses unbelief, especially throughout both the Old and New Testaments, it speaks of something far more subtle and far more common: a failure to trust God's word, God's promises, and God's provision.

When Israel is rebuked repeatedly for unbelief, it is not because they stopped believing that God existed. They believed God was real, but they did not trust Him. They turned away from reliance upon Him and sought provision, security, and deliverance elsewhere. This unbelief often manifested in idolatry, false gods, political alliances, or self-reliance. When Jesus marvels at Israel's unbelief, it is not disbelief in God's existence that astonishes Him, but a life lived contrary to trust in God.

Unbelief, then, is not merely intellectual. It is practical. It is lived out in the details of our daily lives. To illustrate, consider something closer to home. If I tell my son that I will be home at five o'clock and bring dinner with me, but I arrive to find him already eating because he assumed I would not come through, the issue is not that he doubts my existence. The issue is that he did not trust my word.

Or if I warn my son not to engage in sexual immorality because it will bring consequences and pain into his life, and he ignores that warning and later suffers those very consequences, the issue is not ignorance. It is unbelief. He did not trust the truth of what was spoken. Every time we live contrary to God's Word, we are expressing a form of unbelief. We may confess Him with our lips, but our actions reveal where our trust truly lies.

The Christ: The Capable One

All throughout the Old Testament, God promised the coming of an Anointed One, the Christ. This promised Christ would be worthy of our confidence because He would be fully capable of saving and delivering His people. To believe that Jesus is the Christ is not merely to affirm a title. Too often, people repeat the word "Christ" as if it were merely a last name, without realizing the weight of what it signifies. It is a declaration of everything He fulfilled, the One anointed by God, the promised One who accomplishes God's purposes and brings salvation to His people. It is to confess that Jesus is the One promised throughout Scripture, the One capable of fulfilling every messianic promise, the One in whom absolute trust is justified.

John emphasizes this truth repeatedly, echoing what he established in 1 John 2:22, where he confronted those who denied that Jesus is the Christ. Then, as now, his point is clear: the identity of Jesus is not a minor detail, a theological abstraction, or a philosophical claim. It is the foundation of salvation itself. To reject who He is is to reject the work He came to accomplish.

When John says, "Everyone who believes that Jesus is the Christ has been born of God," he is not establishing a checklist by which someone earns new birth. He is describing the inevitable result of regeneration. This confession is not the cause of being born of God; it is the evidence of it. No one arrives at this confession apart from the work of the Spirit of God. Spiritual sight always precedes spiritual confession, and faith in the Christ is the natural outflow of the Spirit's work in the believer.

Born of God, Loving God's Children

John's purpose here is to give assurance and clarity to the believer. He emphasizes two things: first, that everyone who believes in Jesus as the Christ has been born of God; and second, that everyone who loves the One who gives new birth naturally loves those who have been born of Him.

To be born of God is not about performance, morality, or self effort. It is the work of God in a person's life, bringing spiritual life and a new nature. Faith in Jesus is the evidence of this new birth, the outward confession of what God has already done inwardly. Those who have been born of God have life because God has acted; their love and obedience flow from His work, not their own striving. This truth protects the believer from both pride and despair, because new birth rests entirely on God's grace and not human ability. It leaves no room for boasting and no reason for fear, because what God begins, He sustains. Assurance grows not by looking inward at our performance, but by looking outward to God's faithfulness.

John immediately connects this new life with love. Everyone who loves the One who gives new birth, everyone who loves God, also loves those who have been born of Him. This is not an abstract principle; it is the practical outworking of the commandments of Christ. Loving God produces love for God's people, because they share the same Father, the same life, and the same hope. As we saw at the close of chapter 3, the commandment is simple and unmistakable: we love God, and we love one another. In this love, the believer finds both evidence of new birth and the comfort of belonging to God's family.

1 John 5:2-3
By this we know that we love the children of God, when we love God and do His commandments. For this is the love of God, that we keep His commandments; and His commandments are not burdensome

The Evidence of Action

We know that we love the children of God by how we live, not merely by what we say. Anyone can claim to love his brothers, but love is not proven by words alone. Love is known by action. It is revealed in conduct, not in volume or vocabulary. I know that my wife loves me not simply because she says so, but because she is faithful to me, selfless toward me, and present when I need her. I know that my friends love me because they show up when it matters, standing with me in trials, offering encouragement, and sacrificing their own comfort for my well-being. Love is practical; it is tangible; it manifests in the ordinary and extraordinary rhythms of life. This is not a complicated concept in everyday experience, yet when we encounter it in Scripture, confusion often sets in, as though spiritual love were meant to exist only in abstract sentiment rather than lived reality.

John repeats much of what he has already emphasized earlier in his letter. Likewise, it may cause me to echo the same themes in this commentary. But this repetition is intentional. It draws the reader's focus to the most vital truths of the faith, ensuring that the core principles—believing in Christ, being born of God, and loving one another—are deeply understood and not easily overlooked. This is one of the first of several moments in this chapter where repetition serves to reinforce the heart of John's message.

Some may object, asking, "But aren't we saved by grace through faith, not by works? Isn't John saying here that we must keep commandments?" No. John is not giving us a ladder to climb toward salvation. He is not prescribing a way to earn new birth. Rather, he is saying, "By this we know." This language repeated throughout the letter: it is the mirror by which believers reflect on their own lives, the evidence that God's work is at hand. The commandments, the life of love, the fruit of faith—these are not prerequisites for salvation, but the signs that reveal who already belongs to God.

A Tale of Two Fathers

Consider this illustration. Imagine two fathers. One father is loving, truthful, and just. He teaches obedience, humility, compassion, kindness, and self-control. The other father is rebellious, deceitful, violent, and proud. He teaches selfishness, dishonesty, manipulation, and lawlessness. Now imagine that each father has ten children—twenty children total—gathered together in one place. You do not know which child belongs to which father.

But as you watch how they speak, how they treat one another, how they respond to authority, and what they pursue, you would likely be able to identify which children belong to each father. Not because the children are perfect, but because they resemble the one who raised them.

This is exactly how John speaks throughout his letter. By this we know the children of God and the children of the devil. God's commandments are clear and have already been defined repeatedly by John: we are commanded to believe in the One whom He has sent, that Jesus is the Christ, and to love one another.

And what about the children of the devil? Jesus Himself addressed this directly when speaking to the Pharisees. He said, "You are doing the deeds of your father" (John 8:41), and again,

"If God were your Father, you would love Me" (John 8:42). Later, Jesus makes His meaning unmistakable:

"You are of your father the devil, and you want to do the desires of your father. He was a murderer from the beginning and does not stand in the truth, because there is no truth in him. Whenever he speaks a lie, he speaks from his own nature, for he is a liar and the father of lies." (John 8:44-45)

Jesus identified them as children of the devil because they did not obey God; instead, they followed in the footsteps of their father, the murderer and liar. Their lives lacked both love and belief, and this absence of spiritual fruit revealed their true origin. We know that those who are born of God love one another and believe in the Lord Jesus Christ. A child learns from and follows his father's guidance. This does not mean you follow that guidance perfectly—just as my own children do not keep my instructions without fail. But the direction of the life reveals the nature of the father.

Not a Burden

When John writes that "His commandments are not burdensome," he is not referring to the 600-plus ceremonial and civil laws given to the nation of Israel. He is speaking specifically about the commandments he has defined in the previous chapter—the same commandments that run throughout the entirety of Scripture: Love and Believe. These are not heavy, oppressive rules to weigh you down. They are the pathways of life, the outworking of God's grace in the heart of His children.

Love does not boast; it forgives, it is gentle, and it is kind. Belief in Jesus naturally leads to obedience, a desire to turn away from darkness, and a longing to walk in the light. This is why Jesus declared that the entire Law and the Prophets hang on two commands: loving the Lord with all your heart, soul, and mind, and loving your neighbor as yourself. Everything else in the Christian walk flows from these two pillars.

Christ's words offer this comfort directly: "Come to me, all who labor and are heavy laden, and I will give you rest. Take my yoke upon you, and learn from me, for I am gentle and lowly in heart, and you will find rest for your souls. For my yoke is easy, and my burden is light" (Matthew 11:28-30). The commandments of God, then, are not burdensome because they are not imposed as an external weight but are the natural fruit of a heart born of God. To love Him and believe in Him is to live under a yoke that is life-giving, not life-draining, and to experience the rest and freedom that Jesus came to provide.

The Fuel of Faith

Faith and love are inseparable. Paul writes that the only thing that counts for anything is "faith working through love" (Galatians 5:6) and that "the whole law is fulfilled in one word: 'You shall love your neighbor as yourself'" (Galatians 5:14). Do not fall into the trap of treating the command to love as a "work" you must manufacture. Rather, love is the *product* of the faith you possess.

John has already shown that it is not our own love that we bear; it is His love in us, poured into our hearts by the indwelling of the Holy Spirit. This is a matter of cause and effect: faith is the cause, and love is the effect. These two are inseparable because God Himself is Love. The one who has faith has God, and the one who has God has Love. Love is not something added on later; it is the natural fruit of God's presence in the believer's life. Where faith lives, love inevitably follows.

Consider a fire: you cannot have a burning flame without it producing heat. The flame is the source, but the heat is the inevitable proof that the fire is alive. If a man claims to have a roaring fire in his fireplace, yet the room remains freezing, he is deceiving himself and others. The heat is not an optional byproduct; it is the essence of a fire's life. The fire does not strive to warm the room—it simply does so because that is what fire is.

Likewise, if a man claims to have faith, yet shows no love, he is a liar. Faith is the flame, and love is the heat. You cannot claim to be set ablaze by the Spirit of God and remain cold toward the people of God. Love is the visible evidence of an invisible fire; where the Spirit dwells, love will inevitably follow.

The Life of the Tree

If a man or woman has the Spirit of God in them, they *will* love, because "the fruit of the Spirit is love, joy, peace, patience, kindness, goodness, faithfulness, gentleness, and self-control" (Galatians 5:22-23). Does this mean every single believer's fruit will always look and taste the same? No. The quality and sweetness of the fruit depend on the maturity of the walk. Just as an immature tree may produce fruit that is small or tart, a young believer may still be learning to yield fully to the Spirit. Yet, if the tree is healthy and possesses the life of God, it will produce good fruit.

The fruit is not a "work" of the tree; it is the natural product of the tree's internal life. We cannot see the complex internal processes taking place inside a trunk or a branch, but we know they are happening because we see the nourishing results.

When you were dead in your sins, you were a dead tree—rotten on the inside and incapable of producing anything good. You may have looked healthy on the outside, but the internal death was eventually revealed by the lack of fruit. There was nothing you could do to produce fruit, just as there is nothing a man can do to make a dead tree grow. But while you were dead in your sins, God made us alive together with Him. He poured out the Living Water into our hearts and gave us life. Now, His Spirit is at work within you—and that Spirit *will* produce fruit. As you mature in Him, that fruit becomes more evident and more nourishing to those around you. You are no longer striving to grow fruit to prove you are alive; you are bearing fruit because the Spirit has made you alive.

> *1 John 5:4-5 (LSB)*
> *For everything that has been born of God overcomes the world; and this is the overcoming that has overcome the world—our faith. Who is the one who overcomes the world, but he who believes that Jesus is the Son of God?*

Eternal Security

Everything that has been born of God overcomes the world. There is no room in this statement for the idea that someone born of God could die again and require another birth. We did nothing to be born the first time, and we do nothing to be born a second time. In our first birth, we were born into sin, and therefore into mortality and death. As Scripture declares, "sin entered into the world and death through sin, and so death spread to all men, because all sinned" (Romans 5:12). But those who are born of God are not born again into sin; we are born of the Spirit, set free from sin, and "born again not of perishable seed but imperishable" (1 Peter 1:23).

This is the promise of Scripture—the promise of God Himself: that He will lose none of those who belong to Him and that He gives them eternal life (John 10:27-30). When we speak of eternal security, the focus is not on ourselves but on Him who saves. Some refer to this belief as "Once Saved Always Saved," or OSAS. I am not a fan of that term because it has been misused and misunderstood in so many ways. To be clear, affirming eternal security does not mean that salvation rests on the mere recitation of a prayer or a momentary profession of faith. It is not a verbal stamp of approval or a label one can claim without evidence of transformation. As we have already addressed in this letter, and throughout Scripture, John consistently rebukes a faith that is only spoken and not lived—a profession that lacks the fruit of obedience, love, and the Spirit's work. True eternal security is grounded in the person and work of Christ, and it is evidenced in a transformative faith, not in fleeting words or superficial declarations.

I confess and teach the eternal security of the believer as we see repeatedly throughout this letter. In fact, the very purpose of this book is to demonstrate from Scripture that we can have assurance of our salvation and know, with confidence, that it is secure.

Many opponents of eternal security argue that this teaching gives believers license to sin without consequence. This is a strawman. We do not affirm the eternal security of the believer to grant freedom to sin; rather, we affirm it because it is the promise of God and the guarantee of Christ's finished work. Eternal security is not a defense of human effort—it is a defense of the saving work of Christ. As we have already discussed in chapter three, the children of God do not seek permission to sin. On the contrary, a true child of God hates sin and grieves over it. Anyone who claims to belong to God yet embraces sin without repentance or sorrow is not a child of God; John plainly identifies such a person as a liar (1 John 1:6-7, 2:4). Eternal security does not excuse sin; it secures the believer in Christ while the Spirit transforms the heart, producing genuine holiness and godly desire.

Over the last two hundred pages, we have explored the reality of the Spirit's transforming work. The child of God is sealed by the Spirit, transformed by the Spirit, and preserved by the Spirit. The atoning work of Christ on the cross guards us. Scripture declares that He Himself preserves and protects us. Peter writes, "who by God's power are being guarded through faith for a salvation ready to be revealed in the last time" (1 Peter 1:5), affirming that our inheritance is promised and secured until the day of redemption. Ephesians 1 confirms that we are sealed by the Spirit of promise: "In Him you also, having heard the word of truth, the gospel of your salvation—having believed, you were sealed with the promised Holy Spirit" (Ephesians 1:13). And 2 Corinthians 1 describes the Spirit as God's guarantee: "who also sealed us and gave the pledge of the Spirit in our hearts" (2 Corinthians 1:22), demonstrating the certainty and faithfulness of His work within us.

Are there liars among us? Yes. John has made that clear. Can someone who claims to belong to the church fall away? Yes—but as John explains in chapter 2, those who fall away were never truly of us. They were never born of God; they were always outsiders. True believers, on the other hand, have the Spirit of God guarding and keeping them. Their salvation rests not on their fluctuating faithfulness but on the unshakable promises and preservation of God Himself.

Eternal security, then, is not a casual theological statement. It is a declaration of divine faithfulness, rooted in the finished work of Christ, confirmed by the indwelling Spirit, and guaranteed by the promises of God. Consider the words of John: *"Everything that has been born of God overcomes the world"* (1 John 5:4). How could something born of God ever lose its salvation without contradicting this absolute declaration? If even one child of God could fail and be lost, then not *everything* born of God overcomes the world. Eternal security is grounded not in human effort, but in the Father's unchanging promise and the Son's victorious work. The child of God cannot fail, for the Father does not ignore the intercession of His Son. Jesus Himself prayed, *"Holy Father, keep them in Your name, which You have given Me, that they may be one, even as We are one"* (John 17:11). Does the Father neglect this prayer? Hardly. Scripture reminds us that *"the Spirit helps us in our weakness. For we do not know what to pray for as we ought, but the Spirit himself intercedes for us with groanings too deep for words"* (Romans 8:26). Does God ignore the Spirit's intercession on our behalf?

Nor does eternal security rest on mere providence or chance. As Romans 8:28 declares, *"For those who love God, all things work together for good, for those who are called according to His purpose."* And as Paul writes, *"He who began a good work in you will bring it to completion at the day of Jesus Christ"* (Philippians 1:6). Everything born of God is encompassed in this promise, preserved, and perfected by Him. The victory over the world is not conditional, tentative, or fragile—it is absolute, guaranteed by God's faithfulness, Christ's finished work, and the Spirit's sustaining power. Those who are born of God cannot be lost—not because of anything they do, but because of everything He has already done.

If eternal life is an act of grace, given precisely because we are incapable of attaining it, then the argument that salvation can be lost through human failure collapses under its own weight. Jesus did not die on the cross to give you another chance at inevitable failure; He died to save you despite your failures. To claim that salvation can be forfeited by weakness is to suggest that you can lose grace for the very same reason you required grace in the first place. This reasoning is a theological contradiction. The incapacity that made grace necessary at the start does not disappear after conversion. If grace were sufficient to initiate salvation but not to sustain it, then salvation would ultimately rest on human consistency rather than divine faithfulness. Scripture teaches the opposite: eternal life is God's work from beginning to end. It is granted, secured, and preserved by Him. Therefore, your security rests not in your performance, but in the unwavering faithfulness of God.

The Impossibility of Losing Eternal Life

If we have been born again of imperishable, incorruptible seed, how can this new life be lost? How can it ever come to an end? Our first life was born of the corruptible, bound to mortality, decay, and ultimately death. But those who are born of God—born of the Spirit, born of imperishable seed—are fundamentally different. This new life is not subject to the failures of the flesh, the shifting circumstances of the world, or the fleeting nature of earthly hopes. It is eternal in its very nature; it cannot perish, it cannot decay, and it cannot be undone. To imagine that this eternal life could end is to call God a liar, for Scripture repeatedly affirms His faithfulness and truth. Eternal life is incorruptible because it is a divine gift, secured by Christ's atoning work, and maintained by the Spirit who cannot fail. Those who are in Christ belong to Him; their victory is complete, their inheritance imperishable, and their hope irrevocable.

This victory is exclusive to those in Christ and cannot be manufactured through human effort or secured by worldly affection. It is not the self-righteous who overcome the world, for they remain dead in their sins. It is not those who love the world and the fleeting things of the world who overcome, for their hope is perishable. Nor is it those who trust in their own works, for they remain enslaved to what they were born into. As the Apostle Paul explains in Romans 6, we were once slaves to sin. This was not a casual or superficial entanglement—it was absolute dominion. Sin produces death, and under its bondage, we were enslaved to death itself.

1 JOHN 5

Some opponents of eternal security concede that salvation cannot be lost, but argue that it can be forfeited. "God doesn't remove our free will," they say. "A believer could walk away if they choose." To this objection, Scripture gives a clear answer: the believer is not merely a free agent in isolation but a transformed child of God, a bondservant of the living God. The Greek word *doulos*, used in Romans 6 and elsewhere, denotes someone who is legally bound to their master, whose life, purpose, and inheritance are fully under the authority of that master.[1]

Early Christians, including Peter, Paul, James, and Jude, often referred to themselves as doulos, bondservants, of God. This language may seem foreign to modern readers. Today, much of Christian culture sensualizes and romanticizes our relationship with the Lord with phrases like "My Jesus" and "inviting Jesus into our hearts," emphasizing personal choice, emotional experience, or casual participation. Faith is often presented as an optional relationship or a lifestyle preference rather than a total, life-defining allegiance. In contrast, these early believers understood their relationship with God in radically different terms. They saw themselves as fully owned and pledged to their Master, bound in covenant, whose life, purpose, and future were inseparably His.

This understanding of bondservant identity shapes everything about how one lives and perceives salvation. It is not merely about whether you have "accepted Jesus" in a moment of decision; it is about recognizing that you belong to Him completely, that your freedom, your will, and your loyalty are now aligned with the will of your Lord. Modern phrasing often emphasizes human choice, but the early Christian understanding

---

1. *doulos* – Rick Brannan, ed., *Lexham Research Lexicon of the Greek New Testament*.

emphasized divine ownership and permanence: once given, the bond is irrevocable, secured by covenant, and honored eternally by God. Recognizing oneself as a bondservant of God transforms the believer's identity—from seeing faith as a voluntary activity to seeing it as an existential reality. This is why eternal security is not optional or fragile; it flows naturally from the reality of belonging to Christ as His fully claimed, indwelt, and sealed servant.

This identity has deep roots in Scripture. In the Old Testament, the law concerning bondservants (Exodus 21:2-6) shows that a servant who willingly submits to a master could choose to remain with that master indefinitely, and the master was required to honor that choice, retaining the servant forever. The key point is that the permanence of the bond was contingent on the servant's deliberate decision to commit; once made, it was legally and relationally binding, not symbolic or superficial. In the same way, when a believer exercises their will to submit to God—to trust Christ and accept His lordship—this choice is honored by God eternally. The believer now belongs to Him fully, and that submission is permanent, grounded in covenantal love, divine sovereignty, and the reality of God's unbreakable promises. Our freedom is not removed, but it is transformed: the choice to belong to Christ becomes the foundation for a secure, irrevocable life in Him.

Paul makes this divine logic explicit: "But now having been freed from sin and enslaved to God, you have your benefit, which leads to sanctification, and ultimately to the end—eternal life" (Romans 6:22). We did not overcome sin on our own, and just as we could not release ourselves from the dominion of sin, so we cannot release ourselves from the dominion of righteousness. The guarantee of eternal life does not come from our effort, our will, or our performance; it comes from the work of God in us, the Spirit who secures, preserves, and transforms us. God does not remove our autonomy; He gives us a new will, a will alive with the desire for Him, so that we cannot stay away from the source of life. In Ezekiel 36, God declares that He will give His people a new heart and put His Spirit within them, causing them to walk in His statutes. This is not coercion—it is divine life, enabling obedience because the believer now wants God.

Even in moments when our flesh rebels or our faith falters, Scripture assures us of God's immovable faithfulness: "If we are faithless, He remains faithful, for He cannot deny Himself" (2 Timothy 2:13). This is the powerhouse of truth: we are in Christ, Christ is in us, and for Him to fail to preserve us would require Him to deny His own identity and the work of His own flesh. Galatians 2:20 reminds us that it is no longer we who live, but Christ who lives in us. Because we are incorporated into His body, our inseparability from Him is ontological, not optional. The Spirit guarantees that what God begins in a believer will be brought to completion.

This is the reality of the "forfeiture" objection: a believer cannot simply "give back" their salvation. The new birth gives a transformed will that cannot, and will not, ultimately reject God, even in brief moments of rebellion. Our freedom after salvation allows for choices that affect sanctification, joy, and reward, but it does not affect the security of the eternal life God has given. John emphasizes this point in chapters 2 and 3: the children of God are distinguished by the new will, by the Spirit's intercession, and by obedience that flows from transformation, not mere words. Those who abandon Christ in appearance were never truly born of God.

The Spirit within the believer functions like oxygen to the body: we may attempt foolishly to withhold ourselves from it, but our body inevitably responds. So too, the Spirit compels the believer's heart to Christ, pleading even when we rebel. Peter's confession in John 6:68—"Lord, to whom shall we go? You have the words of eternal life"—illustrates the certainty of this work. The believer cannot ultimately walk away because the Spirit has given knowledge and desire for Christ, and the soul cannot survive apart from Him.

Paul reinforces this security in 1 Corinthians 3: he laid the foundation in Christ, and no one can lay another. A believer may build upon it poorly, foolishly, or in sin, and the result may be loss or suffering in this life, but the foundation remains secure. The eternal life of the believer is preserved; the building may burn, but the person is saved. Freedom comes after salvation, not from it. How one builds matters, but it does not determine whether salvation stands.

In short, eternal life is truly imperishable. It cannot die, it cannot be lost, and it cannot be forfeited. The believer has a transformed will, a Spirit who intercedes, and a Savior who cannot deny Himself. Those who are born of God belong to Him, and all that is His—their inheritance, their life, their victory—is secure, eternal, and irrevocable.

Our Faith: The Instrument of Victory

In 1 John 4:4, John reminded us that we have already overcome the world. That is not a claim to human ability, but a declaration of the reality for all who are born of God. Now, in 1 John 5, he shows us exactly how this victory is experienced and maintained. It is not by our own strength, effort, or wisdom, but by the power of Christ Himself. John makes clear that the overcoming of the world is exercised through faith—the believer's reliance on Him who has already conquered every power, every temptation, and every trial.

Faith, then, is the channel through which we participate in Christ's triumph. It is not an abstract concept, nor is it a one-time declaration; it is the practical, daily trust in Jesus that enables us to walk in victory. The world, with its shifting values, alluring pleasures, and oppressive trials, does not overcome those who cling to Him. We do not overcome by might, merit, or moral effort; we overcome by holding fast to Christ, the One who has already overcome the world.

John's emphasis is striking: victory is not theoretical. It is a lived reality, activated by faith. Faith is both the instrument of our salvation and the means by which we continue to experience victory over the world. It is the channel by which the power of Christ flows into the life of the believer, transforming weakness into strength, fear into courage, and doubt into assurance.

This faith also shapes the way we engage the world around us. It does not make the challenges of life disappear, but it changes how we face them. Trials are no longer paralyzing threats; they become opportunities to trust God more deeply. Temptations no longer have the final word; they are moments to lean harder on Him. Even when circumstances seem impossible, faith keeps our eyes on the One who has already won, reminding us that the ultimate outcome is secure, and that no power of the world, flesh, or enemy can undo what Christ has accomplished on our behalf.

This is the faith that secures the believer, enabling them to endure trials, resist temptation, and stand firm even when the world seems to prevail. It is faith in Him, not in ourselves, that makes victory possible. As John explains, it is our trust in Him who overcomes that allows us to overcome: by His power, not our own.

In short, the Christian life is not a struggle to conquer the world in our own strength; it is a continual reliance on Christ. Our faith is not passive—it is active, confident, and enduring. It is the very instrument by which God's promises are realized in our lives, allowing us to share in the triumph of the One who has already overcome all that opposes Him.

1 John 5:6 (LSB)
This is the One who came by water and blood, Jesus Christ; not with the water only, but with the water and with the blood. It is the Spirit who bears witness, because the Spirit is the truth.

Came by Water and Blood

Jesus's introduction was by water. He was baptized at the beginning of His public ministry, and in that water He was revealed to the people as the Son of God. The Father spoke from heaven, and the Spirit descended upon Him. He came by water to bring living water, to purify His people by the washing of regeneration. In the Old Testament, water was consistently associated with purification, and Jesus Himself declares that He brings living water. He tells the Samaritan woman, "If you knew the gift of God, and who it is who says to you, 'Give Me a drink,' you would have asked Him, and He would have given you living water" (John 4:10). He later proclaims, "From his innermost being will flow rivers of living water" (John 7:38), echoing the promises of Isaiah that God would pour water on the thirsty land and bring refreshment and renewal to His people (Isaiah 44:3; 55:1; 58:11).

The water represents the washing of regeneration and the new life of purity brought by the Spirit of God. Throughout Scripture, water consistently serves as an image of God's cleansing work, not merely external washing, but inward renewal accomplished by Him. It speaks of cleansing, renewal, and the sovereign work of God in making a people holy for Himself. As Paul explains, God saves us "by the washing of regeneration and renewing by the Holy Spirit" (Titus 3:5). This is not a human work, but a divine act, where God removes what is defiled and brings forth new life. To say that Christ came by water is to say that He came to cleanse, to renew, and to restore His people by the life-giving work of the Spirit.

John is careful to emphasize the words of verse 6: Jesus Christ "did not come by water only, but by the water and by the blood." This distinction is intentional. Jesus did not come merely to wash, renew, or restore. He also came to atone. Cleansing without sacrifice would leave sin unpaid, and forgiveness without transformation would leave the work incomplete. Christ came with both purposes fully in view.

Not only are we washed and purified by water, but our sins are paid for by His blood. In His baptism, Jesus was made known to us as the Son of God. In His death on the cross, He was revealed as the Son of Man, fully God and fully man. The Son of God stood in the water as the Father spoke from heaven and declared, "This is My beloved Son, in whom I am well pleased" (Matthew 3:17 LSB). At the cross, the Son of Man suffered and died as a propitiation for our sins, bearing the penalty we deserved (1 John 2:2).

John's language here reaches back across the entire letter. From the beginning, he has emphasized both the atoning work of Christ and the transforming work that flows from it. Jesus came to purchase a people for Himself by His blood and to purify them by His Spirit. Scripture speaks of this purpose clearly: Christ "gave Himself for us to redeem us from every lawless deed, and to purify for Himself a people for His own possession" (Titus 2:14). Redemption and purification are never separated.

"Not with the water only, but with the water and with the blood." At the cross, Jesus was pierced in His side with a spear, "and immediately blood and water came out" (John 19:34 LSB). John records this detail intentionally. The one who cleanses His people also redeems them. The blood speaks of propitiation, forgiveness, and purchase. The water speaks of renewal, life, and transformation. Together, they summarize the heart of John's message.

Jesus did not come to display His glory for its own sake. He did not come to demand worship or prove His identity through spectacle. He came with a purpose: to purchase a people for His own possession by His blood and to wash them clean by the life-giving work of the Spirit. As John brings his letter toward its conclusion, he wraps these truths together with rich theological imagery. Jesus Christ came by water and by blood, accomplishing fully what neither could accomplish alone.

Baptism and the Lord's Supper

The blood and the water are profound and inseparable images within the Christian faith. In fact, the two most significant ordinances practiced in Christianity today—baptism and the Lord's Supper—are visible proclamations of these very realities. Every time baptism is administered and every time the Lord's Supper is observed, the gospel is not merely remembered, it is proclaimed.

In baptism, the believer goes into the water as Christ went into the grave and comes out of the water as Christ came out of the grave. The water signifies the washing of renewal, while the act itself portrays passage through judgment and into new life. This imagery is not invented by the church; it is woven throughout Scripture. Noah and his family were brought safely through the waters of judgment in the ark, and Israel passed through the Red Sea as God delivered them from bondage. The flood functioned as a baptism for Noah and his household, and the Red Sea was a baptism for the people of Israel. Paul makes this connection explicit when he writes, "Our fathers were all under the cloud and all passed through the sea; and all were baptized into Moses in the cloud and in the sea" (1 Corinthians

10:1-2). Baptism thus symbolizes not only death to sin but also participation in God's deliverance and covenant, an outward sign of an inward transformation that only God can accomplish.

Yet Christ did not come by water alone. Noah passed through water, and Israel passed through water, but both still bore the weight of their own sins. Cleansing without atonement was never enough. Jesus came by water and by blood. Because of this, we also look to the Lord's Supper as a continual and solemn reminder of what Christ has done for us. The bread and the cup proclaim His body given and His blood shed for the forgiveness of sins. As Paul writes, "For as often as you eat this bread and drink the cup, you proclaim the death of the Lord until He comes" (1 Corinthians 11:26). The Supper is more than ritual; it is a living testimony to the sufficiency of Christ's sacrifice, a proclamation to the world and a renewal for the heart of every believer.

It is the Spirit who bears witness to these truths. It is the Spirit of God who reveals who Jesus is to His people. The Spirit descended upon Jesus at His baptism. The Spirit of God raised Jesus from the grave. The Spirit of God brings to remembrance all that Jesus has done and all that He has accomplished. Jesus promised this when He said, "I will ask the Father, and He will give you another Advocate, that He may be with you forever, the Spirit of truth" (John 14:16). He further declared, "The Advocate, the Holy Spirit, whom the Father will send in My name, He will teach you all things, and bring to your remembrance all that I have said to you" (John 14:26).

These ordinances, therefore, are not mere symbols. They are divine encounters. Each baptism reminds us that death, judgment, and sin have been conquered in Christ. Each Lord's Supper calls us to stand in awe of the blood that cleanses, to participate in the victory that Christ has secured, and to renew our faith in Him who alone gives life. Together, water and blood proclaim the gospel in full: the promise of forgiveness, the reality of transformation, and the assurance of eternal life. They invite believers to step into a daily reality of grace, remembrance, and reliance on the One who has overcome sin and death.

1 John 5:7-8 (LSB)
For there are three that bear witness: the Spirit and the water and the blood; and the three are in agreement.

A detailed discussion of the textual variant in 1 John 5:7-8 (the Comma Johanneum) is provided in the appendix.[2]

Three That Bear Witness

John draws us back to the Lord Jesus's words from John 5. Jesus did not rely solely on His own witness as evidence of who He is, because He came in humility, fully submitting Himself to the Father's will (Philippians 2:6-8). The Old Testament establishes a strict standard for testimony: "On the evidence of two or three witnesses a matter shall be confirmed" (Deuteronomy 17:6; 19:15). Jesus explicitly acknowledges this principle: "If I alone bear witness about Myself, My witness is not true" (John 5:31). He is not denying His ability to bear true witness; He is demonstrating obedience to God's law for our benefit. By doing so, He sets the standard for truth in a way that we can recognize and trust. Later, Jesus affirms His authority, saying, "Even if I bear witness about Myself, My witness is true, for I know where I came from and where I am going" (John 8:14). He is not

---

2. Because the Comma Johanneum involves extensive manuscript, historical, and theological discussion, a comprehensive analysis is provided in the Appendix. This preserves the focus on John's primary argument here while addressing the textual evidence fully and responsibly elsewhere.

repudiating His divinity, but showing that He willingly follows the divine standard He Himself established, providing a model for reliable testimony.

After pointing to His own witness as insufficient under the law, Jesus directs attention to three external witnesses. First, John the Baptist: "He has borne witness to the truth" (John 5:33 LSB). Second, the works that Jesus performs: "The very works that I do bear witness about Me" (John 5:36). These works are given by the Father, carried out in perfect unity with the Spirit, and cannot be denied—they are visible, objective evidence of His mission. Third, the Father: "He has borne witness about Me" (John 5:37). This witness is not limited to dramatic moments like His baptism or the transfiguration but is embedded in the Scriptures themselves: "You search the Scriptures because you think that in them you have eternal life; it is these that bear witness about Me" (John 5:39 LSB). Together, these witnesses form a unified, credible standard of truth, demonstrating that God provides reliable evidence for the identity of His Son.

Trustworthy Evidence

When John writes, "There are three that bear witness, the Spirit and the water and the blood" (1 John 5:6), he is highlighting the objective, corroborated testimony of Jesus's life, ministry, and sacrificial work. The Spirit bears witness to the truth of Jesus's identity, present in His baptism, empowering His ministry, and confirming His resurrection. The water—His baptism—reveals Him as the Son of God, obedient and righteous. The blood—His death—confirms Him as the Son of Man, the propitiation for sin. These three witnesses are not in conflict; they harmonize to reveal the full reality of Christ.

John writes against the backdrop of Gnosticism, which denied the true humanity of Christ. He emphasizes that Jesus was fully

God and fully man, born in the flesh, living perfectly under the law, suffering and dying for sin, buried, and raised on the third day. The Spirit, the water, and the blood converge to leave no doubt about this truth. This is why the Comma Johanneum—a later, doctrinally motivated interpolation—is out of place here: John is not defending the Trinity in this moment; he is defending the historical and incarnational reality of Jesus Christ. The witness is empirical, grounded in observable acts and divine testimony, not abstract formulas.

The Spirit's testimony is consistent throughout Scripture. "For no prophecy was ever made by the will of man, but men being moved by the Holy Spirit spoke from God" (2 Peter 1:21). "The witness of Jesus is the spirit of prophecy" (Revelation 19:10). The Spirit was present at baptism: "He who sent me to baptize with water said to me, 'The One upon whom you see the Spirit descending and abiding on Him, this is the One who baptizes with the Holy Spirit'" (John 1:33). Throughout His ministry, Jesus was led and empowered by the Spirit: "Now Jesus, full of the Holy Spirit, returned from the Jordan and was being led around by the Spirit in the wilderness" (Luke 4:1). The Spirit continues to bear witness through the Apostles and believers: "And we are witnesses of these things, and so is the Holy Spirit, whom God gave to those who obey Him" (Acts 5:32). He anointed Jesus for ministry, empowered His works, and confirms His identity in the life of the Church: "You know of Jesus of Nazareth, how God anointed Him with the Holy Spirit and with power, and how He went about doing good and healing all who were oppressed by the devil, for God was with Him" (Acts 10:38).

The testimony of Spirit, water, and blood is comprehensive, objective, and verifiable, leaving no ambiguity. Jesus is who He said He is. The Son of God and the Son of Man came into the world, lived in perfect obedience, died for sinners, and rose again. John emphasizes this truth so that the believer can rest confidently in the reality of Christ, supported by the coordinated testimony of God Himself, historical acts, and the enduring witness of the Spirit.

1 John 5:9 (LSB)
If we receive the witness of men, the witness of God is greater; for the witness of God is this, that He has borne witness about His Son.

Verse 9 elevates the discussion to the ultimate witness: the testimony that comes from God Himself. We do not believe on the testimony of man, but of God. If our faith was found solely in man's testimony, it would not be a secure faith. While human testimony can point us toward the truth, it is never sufficient in itself. People can observe, speak, and even be inspired by what they see, but it is only the testimony of God that establishes certainty in matters of faith. Yes, God can speak through men, and long ago, God spoke through the prophets, but in these last days, he has spoken to us through His Son (Hebrews 1:1).

We see this clearly in the story of the Samaritan woman at the well. She encounters Jesus and is convinced that He is the Messiah. Excited, she goes back to her city to tell others, and John writes, "From that city many of the Samaritans believed in Him because of the word of the woman who bore witness" (John 4:39). Her testimony influenced others to seek Jesus, but it was not the final authority. When the Samaritans finally met Him and heard His words, they declared, "It is no longer because of what you said that we believe, for we have heard for ourselves and know that this One is truly the Savior of the world" (John 4:42). Human testimony can guide, point, and persuade, but it is God's revelation that brings certainty and life.

The Spirit of God is the one who bears true witness. It was not a man who spoke from heaven at Jesus's baptism; it was the

Father. It was not a man who descended on Jesus as the Spirit; it was God. It was not a man who raised Jesus from the grave; it was God. And it is not a man who convicts our hearts and brings us to true faith; it is God. As Jesus declares, "No one can come to Me unless the Father who sent Me draws him" and "It is written in the Prophets, 'And they shall all be taught by God.' Everyone who has heard and learned from the Father comes to Me" (John 6:44-45). Faith in Jesus is ultimately rooted in God's witness, not human observation or persuasion.

Jesus underscores that the validation of His identity and mission comes entirely from the Father, not from human approval or testimony. He explains that His glory is not derived from people: "I do not receive glory from people" (John 5:41). Human praise, even from respected witnesses, cannot establish His truth. Earlier, John the Baptist had borne witness about Him: "You sent to John, and he has borne witness to the truth" (John 5:33). Yet Jesus clarifies, "I do not receive testimony from man; but I say these things so that you may be saved" (John 5:34). Even though John's testimony pointed people toward Him, it was never the ultimate proof of His identity.

Jesus continues, highlighting that the works the Father gave Him to accomplish testify on His behalf: "But the witness I have is greater than the witness of John ..." (John 5:36). Here, the greatest witness is God Himself, revealed through Jesus's works and mission, not human opinion. These works—His miracles, His signs, and ultimately His sacrifice on the cross—serve as the divine signature upon His ministry. They are not merely impressive feats; they are God's own hand-offering proof of the Son's identity. The testimony of men, including John the Baptist, is a part of the broader witness, but the Father's affirmation is the ultimate and decisive validation of who Jesus is.

Thus, John reminds us that the Christian faith rests upon divine testimony—the witness of the Spirit, the water, and the blood—all of which point unerringly to Jesus Christ as fully God and fully man. Human testimony may influence us to seek the Lord, but certainty, conviction, and eternal life are given only through God's own witness.

> *1 John 5:10 (LSB)*
> *The one who believes in the Son of God has this witness in himself. The one who does not believe God has made Him a liar, because he has not believed in the witness which God has borne witness about His Son.*

The One Who Believes

John emphasizes the profound reality that faith in Christ originates within, not from human reasoning or persuasion. "Whoever believes in the Son of God has this witness in himself" (1 John 5:10). This witness is internal, not external, a direct work of the Spirit of God. Paul echoes this truth in Romans 8:16: "The Spirit Himself testifies with our spirit that we are children of God" (LSB). To believe in Jesus is to have the Spirit testify to the truth of His identity and work within your own heart.

Faith is not merely assent to facts or doctrines. It is a living experience, a divine conviction of sin and revelation of Christ, producing repentance and life. God has provided testimony in multiple ways: through the works of Jesus, which bore witness to His divine and human nature; through the prophets, whose words pointed to the Messiah; through the apostles, who proclaimed the gospel under the guidance of the Spirit. As Revelation declares, "the testimony of Jesus is the spirit of prophecy" (Rev 19:10). Hebrews makes clear that Scripture consistently points to Christ and warns that ignoring this witness is a serious and dangerous act (Heb 10:29).

Even human testimony has a role. When Jesus revealed Himself to the Samaritan woman at the well, she shared her witness with her city. "From that city many of the Samaritans believed in Him because of the word of the woman who bore witness" (John 4:39). Yet when they met Jesus themselves, they said, "It is no longer because of what you said that we believe, for we have heard for ourselves and know that this One is truly the Savior of the world" (John 4:42). Human witness may guide a person toward Christ, but it is only God's Spirit that confirms and brings saving belief.

The Liar

John does not mince words regarding the gravity of rejecting God's testimony. To deny the truth of Christ is not merely disbelief—it is to call God a liar. "If we say that we have not sinned, we make Him a liar, and His word is not in us" (1 John 1:10). Likewise, rejecting the witness God has provided about Christ elevates human judgment above divine truth. Jesus made this clear in John 3:18: "Whoever believes in Him is not condemned, but whoever does not believe is condemned already, because he has not believed in the name of the only Son of God."

God's testimony is overwhelming and multifaceted: the works of Jesus, the words of the prophets, the witness of the apostles, and the ongoing testimony of the Spirit. To deny all of this is to embrace the antichrist mindset, trusting personal opinion over divine truth. Paul writes with uncompromising clarity, "Let God be true, and every man a liar" (Romans 3:4).

This is a fearful and sobering truth. Rejecting God's witness is more than skepticism—it is a rejection of reality itself. Believers, however, can rest in certainty: the Spirit within testifies to the Son of God, confirming that Jesus is fully God and fully man, the Savior of the world, and the one who secures eternal life for all who trust in Him. Faith is not of human origin, but the Spirit of God bearing witness within.

1 John 5:11 (LSB)
And the witness is this, that God gave us eternal life, and this life is in His Son.

Jesus Christ is the first and the last, the beginning and the end. All things were made through Him and for Him. This is the witness of Scripture — the testimony of God throughout all history. Moses wrote of Jesus. The Prophets wrote of Jesus. Abraham rejoiced to see His day. David called Him Lord and declared, "The Lord said to my Lord, 'Sit at My right hand, until I make Your enemies Your footstool'" (Matthew 22:44; cf. Psalm 110:1). This consistent witness throughout the ages confirms what John declares here: the life God gives is not a separate gift, but is found exclusively **in His Son**.

In Him is life, and that life is the light of men (John 1:4). There is no life apart from Him. You can possess everything the world provides, yet without Christ, you have nothing. Conversely, you can be broken, impoverished, and pitiful in the eyes of the world, yet in Christ you have everything.

Jesus Himself said, "This is eternal life, that they know You, the one true God, and Jesus Christ whom You have sent" (John 17:3). He was sent to give life — not merely existence, but eternal, abundant life. This is the gospel that forms the foundation of our hope: not just that He came, but that He came so that we may have life. He restores our relationship with God and reconciles us to the Father.

Through Him, we are made sons and daughters of God. This life is given by grace, through faith — not by works, not by our merit, but entirely for the glory of God alone.

1 John 5:12 (LSB)
He who has the Son has the life; he who does not have the Son of God does not have that life.

Honor the Son

You cannot have the Father apart from the Son. You cannot have the Son apart from the Father. John is not speaking in his own words here — he is reiterating the teaching of Jesus throughout the Gospels. Jesus declared, "So that all may honor the Son even as they honor the Father. He who does not honor the Son does not honor the Father who sent Him" (John 5:23). To know the Father is to know the Son; to love the Father is to love the Son. John is hammering this point home with purposeful repetition, mirroring what he wrote earlier in this very letter: "Who is the liar but the one who denies that Jesus is the Christ? This is the antichrist, the one who denies the Father and the Son" (1 John 2:22). This is why the Psalmist warned the world to "Kiss the Son, lest he be angry, and you perish in the way" (Psalm 2:12). To "kiss the Son" is to offer the homage, submission, and love that He is due as the King. To refuse this honor is to remain outside of the life of God.

Those who claim to love God while rejecting the Son, whether Muslims, Jews, or anyone else, fail to truly love God. In fact, as John has already warned in verse 10, to reject the witness of the Son is to make God a liar. There is no middle ground here. Eternal life is not merely a set of beliefs, moral efforts, or religious practices; it is the possession of the Son Himself. Whoever holds Him possesses life, for life in its truest and deepest sense—spiritual, eternal, unbroken—is bound up in relationship with Christ. Without the Son, there is no access to the Father, no fellowship with God, and no participation in His eternal life.

We who are in Christ have been given life. We were dead in our sins, yet through Him we are seated in heavenly places with the Son. This is eternal life. For those who possess the Son, death has no sting; they have life that transcends the grave. But those who do not have the Son do not have life. This life is not simply future; it begins now, in the knowledge of God, in the joy of the Spirit, in the hope and peace that no earthly circumstance can erase.

This final moment in John's letter highlights a theme consistent throughout the entire New Testament: the Triune reality of God. God is one, yet eternally Father, Son, and Spirit. Scripture never collapses this unity into a singular role or identity. In the introductions of every epistle, the authors give glory to the Father through the Son and acknowledge the fellowship of the Holy Spirit. There is an unbroken pattern — an "insulator," if you will — that prevents anyone from claiming God without the Son, or the Son without the Father, or God without the Spirit. Pause for a moment and read the introductions to any letter in the New Testament. You will see the same pattern every time: the Father and the Son are distinct, yet united, and the Spirit brings believers into fellowship with God.

In John's language here, "God" and "the Son" are inseparable in giving life. If the Son were merely a role God assumed for redemption, this language would be redundant. Jesus has completed His mission and returned to the Father. The ongoing differentiation of Father and Son in every New Testament letter affirms the eternal Sonship of Christ. We do not have life apart from the Father — through the Son, by the power of the Holy Spirit. This is salvation. It is a life that begins now, grows in intimacy with God, and continues forever. It is a life rooted in the reality of God's Triune fellowship and sustained by His unchanging power.

As the Apostle Paul concludes in 2 Corinthians, "The grace of the Lord Jesus Christ, and the love of God, and the fellowship of the Holy Spirit be with you all" (2 Corinthians 13:14). This is our reality in Christ: eternal life, grounded in the witness of the Triune God, and sealed by His Spirit within us. Here is the heartbeat of our faith: He who has the Son has life, now and forever, and that life is inseparable from the Triune God who gives it.

1 John 5:13 (LSB)
These things I have written to you who believe in the name of the Son of God, so that you may know that you have eternal life.

That you may Know

These are the words that serve as the foundation of this letter. They were the reason behind my purpose in writing this book, just as they were the heartbeat behind the Apostle's purpose in the first century. John does not leave his readers to wander in the fog of speculation or spiritual ambiguity. He is a writer of definitive conclusions. He writes that they may know. John ends his Gospel similarly by stating its purpose plainly:

"These have been written so that you may believe that Jesus is the Christ, the Son of God; and that believing you may have life in His name" (John 20:31).

There is a divine progression in John's work: The Gospel of John was written so that you might believe unto life, and this letter was written so that you might know you possess that life.

His goal is focused and intentional, and I pray that when you finish reading this book—if you didn't know prior to doing so—that you too can say you know you have eternal life. There are some today who may treat this idea as "arrogance," to think one can know they are saved. There are even Christian groups that would dare to say it is impossible to do so. Yet, John is telling us that this is his very reason for writing the letter.

This is the one thing we can cling to above all things. You may not know every intricate detail of systematic theology. You may not have an answer for every mystery of the infinite. In fact, because our God is infinite, we will spend eternity peering into the depths of His majesty and glory with the wide-eyed awe of a child. But while there is much we have yet to learn, there is one thing John insists we can and should assuredly know: if you believe in His name and are born of God, you possess eternal life.

It reminds me of the word of the Lord spoken through the prophet Jeremiah. He declares not to boast in your wisdom, riches, or might, but rather, "Let him who boasts boast in this, that he understands and knows Me" (Jeremiah 9:23-24). That is the one thing we should seek to proclaim. That is the one thing we shall boast in—not out of arrogance or pride, but in praise and worship. Because the only reason I know Him is by His Spirit. I will boast in the work of the Lord.

Our Hope

This is our hope—a word that must not be confused with the shallow vocabulary of the world. In our modern tongue, "hope" is a fragile thing; it is a wish, a "maybe," or a flickering possibility that things might go our way. But biblical hope is an anchor. It is not found in the shifting sands of our performance or our feeble ability to "do enough."

It is in this hope that we find our rest. Throughout this letter, John has provided a mirror for you to look into—not to see your own perfection, but to see the certainty that you truly know Him. This certainty inevitably leads to peace. Peace is the absence of fear, and as John has already established, perfect love casts out all fear. We no longer live in fear; instead, we have peace in Him.

The Apostle Paul declares the same reality: "Therefore, having been justified by faith, we have peace with God through our Lord Jesus Christ" (Romans 5:1). This is not a mere feeling or a passing emotion; it is a legal standing. While Paul is writing in Greek, he is using the word *eirēnē* (εἰρήνη)—the very word the Septuagint translators used to capture the depth of the Hebrew word *Shalom*. It is a perfect peace; not just a ceasefire, but a state of total wholeness and the absence of imminent danger. It is a peace that is only possible with God because the war between the sinner and the Creator has been brought to an end by the blood of the Cross.

Because of this peace, we do not merely survive our trials; we endure them with purpose. We know we have life in His name, and in Him, we will overcome all things. We can even rejoice in our sufferings, knowing that suffering produces endurance, and endurance produces character, and character produces hope. And this hope—this battle-tested, Spirit-sealed hope—does not put us to shame, because God's love has been poured into our hearts through the Holy Spirit who has been given to us (Romans 5:3-5).

John's bold certainty would be impossible if a "maybe" still lingered in the air. If our hope was a fragile mixture of Christ's work plus our own effort, that hope would not be hope at all—it would be dread. We would be left constantly checking the pulse of our own performance to see if we were still "in." If our security required even a single ounce of our own merit or a single day of perfect consistency, we would inevitably fail. The weight of eternity is far too heavy for the thin shelf of human effort to hold.

Furthermore, if our salvation were that fragile, Paul's claim of having peace with God would be a hollow promise. How could we ever truly experience shalom if we were one mistake away from falling back into condemnation? If at any moment we could revert from being a child of God back into an enemy of God, peace would be an illusion. If the possibility of our failures today or tomorrow could remove us from the safety of His grace, we would not live in rest; we would live in perpetual fear. True peace cannot exist where there is no security.

This is why the foundation is everything. And that foundation must be Christ.

Consider the house built upon the Rock, as described by Jesus in Matthew 7:24-27. The safety of that house does not depend on the impeccable structure of its walls or the beauty of its design; its safety depends entirely on the ground beneath it. A mansion built with the finest materials will still crumble if the foundation is sand. Yet, a simple, weathered structure built upon the Rock will withstand the fiercest hurricane.

If your life is built upon the "sand" of your own self-reliance, the storm of judgment will find the cracks in your foundation. But if your life is built upon the Rock, which is Christ, you can rest. You are safe not because your house is perfect, but because the Rock is immovable.

This assurance is the most vital reality you can possess. Indeed, it is the most important thing you could ever know. For how can we hope for anything from the hand of God if we do not first know that we have life from His Spirit? If we lack the confidence that our sins are forgiven and that we are truly His children, how can we expect Him to answer the miniscule prayers for tomorrow? Before we can exercise trust in the minor issues of our daily lives, we must first trust in the most important aspect of this faith: that we have life in His name. Confidence in the small things is impossible without certainty in the greatest thing.

We can have assurance of our salvation because that assurance is not a feeling we manufacture, but a fact God has declared. We can have confidence for the day of judgment, not because we have a clean record, but because we have a capable Advocate. He is the Capable One, the Anointed One, and He is sufficient to save to the uttermost.

1 John 5:14-15 (LSB)
And this is the confidence which we have before Him, that, if we ask anything according to His will, He hears us. And if we know that He hears us in whatever we ask, we know that we have the requests which we have asked from Him.

According to His Will

If we confidently know that we have eternal life, then we also know that He is with us in all things, and that in all things He provides what we need, according to His will. This is often the portion of the promise that is missed. John is not teaching that whatever we desire, without qualification, will be granted. Rather, he is grounding our confidence in the character and wisdom of our Father. God knows what we need, and He faithfully supplies those needs, but always in perfect alignment with His will.

As we grow in spiritual maturity, our prayers are reshaped. Our requests begin to reflect His purposes rather than merely our preferences. This alignment does not happen by instinct or emotion, but by being formed by His Word. As we come to know His heart through what He has revealed, we learn to ask in ways that accord with His will. This is not a limitation on prayer, but a liberation of it. His will is not an obstacle to our joy; it is the very source of it.

Consider our Lord Jesus Christ. In the moments before His betrayal and crucifixion, He prayed to the Father under the crushing weight of what He was about to endure. Though He knew why He had come and knew that resurrection awaited Him, the flesh He took on for our sake truly felt the anguish of that hour. Luke records that Jesus was in such agony that His sweat became like drops of blood falling to the ground (Luke 22:44). This is not poetic exaggeration. It is a real medical phenomenon known as hematidrosis, a rare condition in which extreme psychological anguish causes the capillaries surrounding the sweat glands to rupture.

This moment reveals something essential. Jesus did not merely appear to be human. He truly bore our flesh. The Spirit was willing, but the flesh was weak (Matthew 26:41). He willingly took on that weakness, not as a defect, but as part of His mission to redeem us. His humanity was not an illusion, nor was it incidental. It was necessary. He assumed our nature fully, with all its instinctual responses to suffering and death.

The human body reacts to overwhelming danger before the mind has time to reason. Even someone who does not fear heights would experience physical distress if seated on the edge of a skyscraper, knowing they were about to be pushed. The response would not be intellectual, but instinctual. Likewise, Jesus, fully aware of what He was about to endure, experienced the natural physical and emotional response of true humanity. Death is not something the flesh welcomes. In that moment, He cried out to the Father, "Father, if You are willing, remove this cup from Me; yet not My will, but Yours be done" (Luke 22:42).

This prayer is not a conflict within the Godhead. It is the obedience of the incarnate Son. Though He existed in the form of God, He did not regard equality with God as something to be grasped, but emptied Himself, taking the form of a slave, being made in the likeness of men. Being found in appearance as a man, He humbled Himself by becoming obedient to the point of death, even death on a cross (Philippians 2:6-8). His submission was not because He lacked authority, but because He had taken our place. His obedience was rendered on our behalf. His perfect righteousness was accomplished for us.

Notice the order of His prayer. The request came first, "let this cup pass." But the greater request followed, "Your will be done." Does the Father remove the cup? No. But neither does He abandon His Son. Luke tells us that an angel from heaven appeared, strengthening Him (Luke 22:43). The Father provided exactly what was needed, according to His will.

Here we learn how to pray. Our Father in heaven knows what we need, and He provides it. Jesus Himself said that the Father knows what you need before you ask Him (Matthew 6:8), and that you are of far more value than the birds He faithfully feeds (Matthew 6:26). Paul reminds us that God will not allow us to be tempted beyond what we are able, but with the temptation will provide the way of escape also (1 Corinthians 10:13). And we are assured that God works all things together for good for those who love Him, for those who are called according to His purpose (Romans 8:28).

How quickly our prayer life changes when we truly believe this. We learn to ask honestly, yet submit fully. We learn to trust that whatever we ask according to His will is heard and answered, even when the answer is not the one our flesh would choose. His will is not always what we want, but it is always what is best. And like our Lord, we learn to say, not my will, but Yours be done.

He Hears Us

John says that *He hears us*. He does not say that God always answers us in the way we expect, or in the timing we prefer.

Hearing is not the same as granting, and silence is not the same as absence. A good parent can listen attentively to a child's need and still remain silent. In fact, sometimes silence is the most loving response.

There have been countless times when I have heard my children's requests and chosen not to step in immediately, not because I lacked love, but because I knew what was best for them. I knew they were capable of handling what they were facing, and that the struggle itself would teach them something they could not learn any other way. If I rushed in to fix everything for them, what would they gain? And what would they expect the next time the difficulty arose? How many children have you seen who have never had to work through a challenge on their own, who grow to expect their parents to solve every problem for them?

I remember once sitting at the living room window, watching my oldest son, Michael Jr., mowing the lawn. It came time to move the large trampoline so he could cut the grass underneath it. Up until that summer, I had always done it myself, and it was easy for me. But now it was his responsibility. I watched as he tugged at it with brute strength, grew frustrated, dropped his head, and walked in circles trying to figure out what to do. All he needed was to use the round shape of the trampoline to his advantage, but he hadn't learned that yet.

I could have walked outside and moved it in a minute. But what would he have learned? And what would he expect next week? He wasn't alone. I was watching the entire time. If it had reached the point where he truly needed me, I would have been there immediately. But the struggle was the lesson. In the struggle, perseverance is formed. In the struggle, resilience is built. Eventually, he figured it out. He moved the trampoline and finished the job.

I remember laughing quietly to myself, because in that moment I realized how often I am the one "outside struggling" while God is "sitting at the window." He is not ignoring me. He is not absent. I cannot see Him, but He can see me. He knows how badly I want Him to step in and remove the obstacle. And He also knows what that struggle is producing in me. And just like any good father, if things ever reached the point of real danger, He would come running.

This is what the writer of Hebrews reminds us when he speaks of the Father's discipline. "For the moment all discipline seems painful rather than pleasant, but later it yields the peaceful fruit of righteousness to those who have been trained by it" (Hebrews 12:11). Difficulty is not evidence of neglect. Pain is not proof of abandonment. Sometimes it is the very means by which the Father is shaping us.

He hears us. That alone is enough for confidence. You could also say that He sees us. How much peace comes from knowing that you are never unheard and never unseen? We do not always need an immediate answer. Sometimes we are not even ready to receive the answer we are asking for. But we can trust that He knows what is best, and we can rest in the assurance that we are never alone.

I no longer fear what tomorrow holds or the directions I must take. Why? Because whether I step in the right direction or stumble along the way, He is there. And the God who hears me will never stop being my Father.

We Have the Requests

When our prayer life is shaped by His will, when we trust that He hears us and never abandons us, we are able to rest in John's bold conclusion: *we know that we have the requests which we have asked from Him.* Prayer is not futile. Prayer is not empty. Prayer works.

Yet there is a quiet assumption that lingers in many hearts, rarely spoken aloud but deeply felt: *prayer doesn't really work.* If it did, why does God so often answer differently than we expect? Why does the door we asked to be opened remain closed? Why does the relief we pleaded for not arrive when we wanted it to?

The issue is not that prayer is ineffective. The issue is often that we approach prayer without submission. Many believers come to God not seeking His will, but presenting Him with a list. We tell Him what we need, what we want, what we think must happen next. We are not aligning ourselves to His purposes; we are asking Him to endorse ours. In doing so, prayer subtly becomes transactional. God is treated like a means to an end, rather than the sovereign Father who knows what is best.

Have you ever thought, *Others have greater needs than mine*? As though God's power were limited, or His attention divided. Did not Jesus say that the Father feeds the birds of the air, and are you not of more value than they? (Matthew 6:26). The problem is never that your request is too small. The problem is when we fail to trust the One to whom we are praying.

Others pray, but only look for the exact answer they have already decided God should give. Jesus prayed that the cup might pass from Him, yet the Father did not remove the cup. Instead, He sent angels to strengthen Him. The prayer was answered, but not in the way the human will desired. How often do you pray for a way out, while overlooking the person God has sent into your life to strengthen you? How often do we miss the answer because it does not look like the one we imagined?

James warns us clearly, "But he must ask in faith without any doubting, for the one who doubts is like the surf of the sea, driven and tossed by the wind. For that person must not expect that he will receive anything from the Lord" (James 1:6-7). Doubt does not mean asking honest questions. It means approaching God without trust, without submission, without confidence in His character.

Some do not doubt God, but they doubt themselves. They wonder whether they are worthy to be heard. If worthiness were the requirement, God would not listen to a single one of us. Others doubt whether their prayers are "good enough," as though the power of prayer lies in eloquence or structure. But the power of prayer does not rest in the words we speak. It rests in the Spirit of God who dwells within us. Even when we do not know what to pray, "the Spirit Himself intercedes for us with groanings too deep for words" (Romans 8:26).

Do not doubt prayer because of your weakness. Trust it because of God's promise.

And if you do not know what to pray, then pray the prayer our Lord Himself taught us (Matthew 6:9-13). Do not let anyone tell you that the Lord's Prayer is insufficient. Yes, it is a perfect blueprint from which all prayer flows, but it is also a perfect prayer in itself. Even if those were the only words you prayed, you could do so with full confidence that the Father hears you.

As Charles Spurgeon wisely said,

"Do not discredit Him by thinking He can teach you to pray a prayer that will not be accepted before God."[3]

This is John's closing confidence. When we ask according to His will, when we trust that He hears us, we may know that we have our requests. Not because we control God, but because we trust Him. Not because prayer bends His will to ours, but because prayer bends our will to His.

And that is where prayer truly works.

---

3. Charles H. Spurgeon, *"Praying and Waiting,"* sermon preached October 23, 1864, Metropolitan Tabernacle Pulpit, vol. 10.

1 John 5:16 (LSB)
If anyone sees his brother committing a sin not leading to death, he shall ask and God will for him give life to those who commit sin not leading to death. There is a sin leading to death; I do not say that he should make request for this.

John moves from the assurance we have in our prayer life to call us to pray for our brothers who we see struggling with sin. Do not just see it and keep moving on with your day. Pray for them, pray for them with such fervancy as you would hope someone would pray for you if they saw you struggling with sin. We are children of God and we pray for the other children, so that they may be restored. We know that life has ups and downs, and not every Christian is the best christian day in and day out. In my experience, the hardest parts of the Christians walk happen when they are furthest from God. They go into seasons where they are not meditating on his word as often, not in prayer as often. In those times, we fill the gap for one another. As James also writes in James 5:15. Let our prayers be always for our brothers and sisters that they may be strengthen and uplifted by our Father in Heaven.

John is not appointing you to be the one to go seeking the sins of your brothers and being the one to rebuke every single person. There is a time for rebuke, but that is not what John is conveying. John is speaking. ofwhen you see your brothers and sisters in times of struggle and times of sin. Include them in your prayers. Take time to pray specifically for them. Sadly, in the 21st century we are quicker to tell others about someone's sins then we are to pray for someone. Gossip is what fuels most social media and so it finds its way into the lips of a Christian. Run to God in prayer for your brethren, not the internet.

Sin Leading to Death

What is sin that leads to death, and why would John say not to pray for the one who commits it? First, let me be clear: John is not forbidding prayer. He is giving guidance for when prayer is no longer fruitful, when someone has hardened their heart so completely that continued pleading is pointless. We do not know the state of a person's heart with certainty. It is always safer to pray for someone than to assume it's hopeless.

All sin is wrong, but not all sin leads to death. Some sins can be forgiven through the blood of Christ. The sin that cannot be forgiven is described in Scripture as blasphemy of the Holy Spirit, trampling underfoot the blood of Christ, or, in some cases, apostasy—but not every act of apostasy qualifies. In chapter 2, John wrote of those who "went out from us because they were never of us" (1 John 2:19). Let me be clear: this is not a Christian losing salvation. This is the person who is not and will never be saved.

Consider the moment in the Gospels when Jesus confronts the Pharisees after casting out a demon. They accuse Him of doing so by Satan's power. Scripture says Jesus perceives their thoughts. He isn't just rebuking their words—He sees the heart. These men are not ignorant; they know exactly what He is doing. Earlier, Nicodemus admitted, "We know that you are from God, for no one can do these signs unless God is with him" (John 3:2). The Pharisees have seen the truth, witnessed miracles, and yet they choose pride and hatred over submission to God.

Jesus responds with a warning: all blasphemy can be forgiven—even blasphemy against Him—but blasphemy of the Spirit will not be forgiven (Mark 3:28-29). Notice two things. First, He is addressing deliberate, knowledgeable rejection of the Spirit's testimony, not ignorance or weakness. Second, this is not the "unforgivable sin" in the sense that God refuses forgiveness. Rather, it is the sin that will not be forgiven because the person will never turn to the cross for mercy. They will never come for forgiveness. They have rejected the very Spirit who draws all men to salvation.

Let's connect this to Hebrews 6. Many use this chapter to argue that believers can lose salvation. But context matters. The audience is primarily Jewish Christians, being warned not to fall away from the truth. Hebrews 6:4-6 describes those who have "tasted the heavenly gift" and "shared in the Holy Spirit," yet remain unrepentant. The imagery is stark: two fields. One receives rain and produces a crop; the other, no matter how much water falls, produces only thorns and is destined for fire. This second field never bore fruit—it was never productive. No matter how much rain fell, no life emerged. John's point is similar: some who appear to experience God's power, even partake of the Spirit, will not respond. They were never truly His.

Look at John 6. Five thousand people walked away from Jesus after hearing Him teach and seeing miracles. They ate the bread He gave. They experienced heavenly wisdom directly from the lips of the Son of God. And yet, they walked away. Jesus said plainly, they were not His sheep (John 6:64-66). If you were there, would you have chased them down to explain one more time? No—you would have been a fool. Their hearts were hardened, and nothing you said or did would have changed that. This is exactly the parallel to Hebrews 6: some are beyond reach.

Hebrews 10 continues this teaching. Jesus, our perfect High Priest, offered Himself once for all. The Temple sacrifices were temporary, shadows pointing to His ultimate work. Hebrews 10:26 warns: if we continue deliberately sinning, there is no longer a sacrifice for sins. Taken in isolation, one could read this as saying that any deliberate sin after hearing the gospel cancels salvation—yet all sin is deliberate in some sense, and if this were the case, we would all lose our salvation daily. Context matters. When we read this passage alongside the chapter prior, which assures us that Jesus intercedes on our behalf, it actually affirms 1 John 2:1: when we, the children of God, sin, we have an Advocate with the Father. The text is not telling Christians that sin can cancel salvation. Rather, it is warning that for those who reject the Spirit and trample Christ's sacrifice underfoot, there is no other means. They insult the perfect, once-for-all sacrifice and cling to their own attempts at righteousness. They reject the Son, and the result is death in sin.

This is the sin that leads to death. It is willful, knowledgeable, and irreversible—not because God refuses forgiveness, but because the individual will never seek it. They have hardened themselves against the Spirit's work. And here is John's practical instruction: for these people, prayer is no longer the tool. You may feel compelled to continue, but the reality is that some are too far gone. They are gone in their sin.

We must always remember our limitations. We cannot see hearts. We do not know who is beyond reach. Better to pray for someone unnecessarily than to assume they are lost. But make no mistake: there are people in this world who have rejected the truth, trampled the blood of Christ, and hardened their hearts. They will die in their sin, and nothing we do can bring them back. This is the weight of John's warning—a solemn, heavy truth for the believer.

1 John 5:17 (LSB)
All unrighteousness is sin, and there is a sin not leading to death.

In the previous verse, John distinguished between sin that leads to death and sin that does not, but here he reminds us clearly: all unrighteousness is sin. There is no minimizing this truth. Sin is a violation of God's character and His commands. As children of God, we ought to hate it, recoil from it, and guard our hearts and lives against it. Even sin that does not lead to death is still a real, serious offense against the holiness of God.

Yet John also offers hope. The sin not leading to death is covered by Christ. As he explained in 1 John 2:1, when we sin, we have an Advocate with the Father—Jesus Christ, the righteous One. Our failures are not ignored, but they are forgiven and atoned for. Grace does not give us a license to sin; it gives us the assurance that even when we fall, we are not abandoned. Grace is permission to fail, not permission to indulge. It reminds us that we serve a God who is both holy and merciful, and that His Son intercedes for us, enabling us to rise again each time we stumble.

1 John 5:18 (LSB)
We know that no one who has been born of God sins; but He who was begotten of God keeps him, and the evil one does not touch him.

At first glance, this verse can seem almost paradoxical. John tells us that no one born of God sins, yet in the previous verses he assures us of an Advocate when we do sin. How can both be true? The answer lies in understanding what it means to be born of God. Sin still resides in our flesh, in our old nature, the "old man," but internally we are made new. The child of God is a new creation, born of the Spirit, with a new nature that sin cannot touch. Our flesh may stumble, but our spirit is guarded, protected from ultimate defeat.

Notice the second part of the verse: "He who was begotten of God keeps him, and the evil one does not touch him." Our protection is not by our own strength, but by the power of Christ. Every sin of yesterday, today, and even tomorrow is covered by His blood and advocacy. All that remains in us is Christ's righteousness, credited to our account. This is how we are shielded from the evil one. The devil cannot claim us, because we belong to God. The Good Shepherd watches over us, restores us when we stray, lifts us when we fall, and keeps us steadfast in His care. Jude sums it up beautifully: "Now to Him who is able to keep you from stumbling, and to make you stand in the presence of His glory blameless with great joy, to the only God our Savior, through Jesus Christ our Lord" (Jude 24-25). It is by His hand that we are kept, by His power that we stand, and by His work that we are considered blameless.

1 John 5:19-20 (LSB)
We know that we are of God, and that the whole world lies in the power of the evil one. And we know that the Son of God has come, and has given us understanding so that we may know Him who is true; and we are in Him who is true, in His Son Jesus Christ. This is the true God and eternal life

When you put this letter down, you step back into a world full of evil. Never forget this truth: you are of God, and the world lies under the power of the evil one (1 John 5:19). The world is blinded, its eyes veiled by the enemy. Its people are consumed with pride, selfish desires, and rebellion against the Creator. There will be days when you feel out of place, isolated, or at odds with those around you. This is natural, because you are not of this world.

Even in those moments, remember this: the Creator of all things abides in you, and you in Him. He is stronger than he who is in the world. That is the anchor for your soul. You will witness the sorrow and brokenness around you, and it may weigh heavily on your heart. Peter expressed this same reality when he spoke of Lot, saying that "his righteous soul was tormented day and night by the lawless deeds he saw and heard" (2 Peter 2:7-8). The Scriptures prepare us for this truth so that we are not surprised or disillusioned by the evil in the world.

But now John brings a truth to counterbalance the darkness: the Son of God has come, and He has given us understanding so that we may know Him who is true (1 John 5:20). Because of Christ, we are no longer blind. We were once lost in darkness, but now we have sight; we were in the shadows of sin, but now we walk in light. There is a blessing in seeing the darkness of the world, for it reminds us that we are no longer consumed by it. The sorrow we feel at injustice, brokenness, and evil is a sign that God has opened our eyes. We are aware of the world, but we are no longer lost in it.

The light of Christ shines in the darkness, and the darkness does not overcome it. Even the smallest flame can illuminate the darkest room; and within us, the light of the Son of God shines, guiding our steps. Consider how fitting this is: two of humanity's greatest fears are death and darkness. In Christ, both are overcome. John declares in his introduction that Christ is the Light of the world, and this light is Life itself. Not mere breath or heartbeat, but the source of eternal life. When we abide in Him, we are united to that life, part of His body with Him as the Head. As long as the Head lives, the body lives—and He is eternal.

Take this truth to heart: though you will face the darkness of the world, you walk in the light of God, and nothing can separate you from Him. Your hope is unshakable, your life secure, your path guided by the One who is true. The Creator has opened your eyes, and with every step, He illuminates your way. The world may lie in the power of the evil one, but you are of God—and in His Son Jesus Christ, you possess the light, the truth, and eternal life.

1 John 5:21 (LSB)
Little Children, guard yourselves from idols.

John closes his letter with a statement that, at first glance, feels almost out of place. After assurance, light, truth, and eternal life, he ends with this simple but weighty charge: *Little children, guard yourselves from idols.* Why end here? Why close a letter filled with theological depth and pastoral comfort with a warning about something never explicitly mentioned?

Let me be clear. I do not believe John is suddenly concerned about statues of gold or stone. The children of God know better than that. We know the Lord detests such things. John is not speaking to the world here, he is speaking to believers, and he addresses them tenderly as *little children*, the same way he does throughout this letter when offering pastoral instruction. What he is warning us about is far more subtle, and far more dangerous: the idols of the heart. The desires of the flesh, the desires of the eyes, and the pride of life. These are not merely ancient problems. They are present realities, and they take hold quietly.

John tells us to *guard yourselves*. This is not a casual suggestion. It is a call to vigilance. Do not grow complacent. Complacent Christians tempt Satan to tempt them. We are called to guard ourselves from idols, and in doing so, we are guarding ourselves from deception.

But there is an even greater danger here, one that often goes unnoticed. A false Jesus is an idol.

John was already dealing with a counterfeit Christ in his own day through docetism, and false versions of Jesus have existed in every generation since the apostolic age. Many today construct a version of Jesus shaped by preference rather than Scripture. They keep the parts they like and dismiss the parts that confront them. This is not devotion, it is idolatry. It is a Jesus shaped idol.

Cultural Christianity wants the benefits of Christ without submission to His authority. They want the Jesus who is gentle and affirming, but they reject the Jesus who condemns sin, calls for repentance, and demands transformation. Job could say, "The Lord gives, and the Lord takes away; blessed be the name of the Lord," but many today only want a God who gives, never a God who takes. They want a God whose authority never overrules their own, a Savior who exists to serve their desires rather than reign over their lives.

And what does this counterfeit Jesus always serve? The same thing every idol serves: self.

As I approached the end of this letter, I initially thought this would be a difficult place to end a commentary, on what seemed like a random verse about idols. Now I am convinced it is the only place to end. This is not random. It is essential. We live in a world fueled by instant gratification. Comfort is idolized. Entertainment is constant. Self is exalted.

A few years ago, I walked the streets of ancient Ephesus and saw the remains of statues once dedicated to Hercules, Athena, and Artemis. Idols filled the city. They were visible, obvious, and openly worshiped. But the truth is this: there are more idols in our cities today than there were then. They simply are not carved from stone. They are hidden in habits, desires, and unchecked affections.

So hear John's final words as they were meant to be heard. Not as an afterthought. Not as a footnote. But as a charge to carry with you. My brothers and sisters, guard yourselves. Guard your hearts. Guard your affections. Guard yourself from the idol of self, the idol of pride, the idol of comfort, the idol of money, and every other rival hiding in plain view. Set your eyes on Him alone. He is the only one worthy of your devotion, the only one who gives true joy in this life, and the only one who gives eternal life in the life to come.

Do not let the fleeting pleasures of this world deceive you. Every idol, no matter how small it seems, competes with the fullness of Christ in your life. Watch over your desires, examine your motives, and remember daily who you belong to. Place your affection, your time, your energy, and your hope in Jesus. He is faithful. He is true. He is constant. And as you walk forward, let this truth guide you, sustain you, and guard your soul: in Him alone you have everything, and apart from Him, you have nothing. Live in that reality, and walk free.

God Bless and Go in Peace

Epilogue

Over the course of these pages, we have walked through the truths of light and darkness, explored the depths of love and the reality of sin, and peered into the hidden chambers of the human heart. We have wrestled with the tension between our weakness and His strength, examined the assurance of eternal life, and stood in awe of the glory and faithfulness of God revealed in His Son. Though this book is centered on 1 John, we have journeyed throughout Scripture to explore the fullness of the Christian faith, connecting the words of the Apostle to the broader story of God's redemption. My hope is that the young believer reading these pages has found a firm foundation on which to build their faith, and that the older believer has been stirred anew to love God's Word in all its depth and richness.

John did not write this letter to give you a checklist of religious duties or a ladder of moral achievement. He wrote it so that you would know. Throughout this book, we have discussed the "skyscraper" of God's sovereignty—that He stands at the top, seeing the end from the beginning, while we navigate the ground floor. We have talked about the "trampoline" of His grace—that when we fall, we do not fall away from Him, but into the safety of

His finished work. We have explored the Advocate—the One who stands before the Father on our behalf, not because we are innocent, but because He is righteous.

As you close this book, my prayer is that you are no longer looking at your own reflection to find assurance. If you look at yourself, you will see both weakness and grace, moments of failure and moments of faith. If you look at your performance, you will find inconsistency. But if you look at the Son, you will find the Truth. Your questions may not all be answered here, and your curiosity will always lead to more. That is as it should be. In our culture, we seek comfort in understanding, hoping that knowledge alone will settle our hearts. But true comfort is not found in more answers—it is found in Christ. And in Him, we can know with certainty: we know Him, and we know that we know Him.

Do not let the "magic genie" of cultural Christianity deceive you. Do not settle for a Jesus who exists only to serve your desires or grant your manifestos. That is an idol, and as we have seen, idols cannot give life. Instead, cling to the Christ of Scripture—the One who was from the beginning, who stepped into our darkness, and who will stand at the end of all things. The world will try to pull you back into the shadows. It will offer you the pride of life and the fleeting pleasures of the flesh. But you are a child of God. You have been born of the Spirit. You have an inheritance that cannot be defiled. You have been given eyes to see the light, ears to hear the Advocate, and a heart to love as He loves.

So walk in the light. Love the brethren. Guard your heart from the idols of this age. Trust in Him when the silence of God feels heavy, and keep moving forward when the path ahead seems dark. The Advocate is still speaking. The blood is still sufficient. The Light is still shining. The victory is already won, and it is yours in Christ.

Jesus is the Alpha and the Omega. He was there at the start of your faith, and He will be there when you cross the finish line. Live in that reality. Walk in that peace. Let it shape your every thought, action, and devotion. Let it anchor your soul in the truth that nothing in this world—not sin, not suffering, not uncertainty—can separate you from the love of God that is in Christ Jesus.

God Bless and Go in Peace.

Chapter Six
Appendix: The Comma Johanneum

Whether you are familiar with it or not, 1 John 5 is the location of one of the most well-known textual variants in the entire Bible. A textual variant occurs whenever a word, phrase, or clause appears differently in one manuscript or translation compared to others. Because this variant has a long and complex history, it cannot be ignored in a careful study of the passage. The textual variant in question is known as the Comma Johanneum. The name comes from Latin: *comma* means "a short clause or phrase," and *Johanneum* means "pertaining to John." Put together, it literally means "the short clause in John." Specifically, it refers to a phrase that appears in 1 John 5:7-8 in traditional translations such as the King James Version:

> *"For there are three that bear record in heaven, the Father, the Word, and the Holy Ghost: and these three are one. And there are three that bear witness in earth..."*
> *(1 John 5:7-8 KJV)*

The variant is the addition of the clause "the Father, the Word, and the Holy Ghost: and these three are one." This portion is not found in the earliest Greek manuscripts and does not appear in the vast majority of modern translations.

For those reading from a Bible that includes the clause, this section will explain why it is not present in the translations used in this book. For those who do not have it, you will gain an understanding of why some may claim that your Bible is "missing" something or has been "corrupted." My goal is not to provide a technical masterclass in manuscripts—as I am not a manuscript scholar—but to equip the serious student of Scripture with the truth regarding this particular textual issue.

Sadly, I have met many Christians who are completely unaware of where this textual variant comes from or why it is absent in modern Bibles. Too often, people jump straight to the conclusion that their Bible has been "corrupted" without examining the evidence. That kind of thinking is not only intellectually dishonest—it is also lazy. With thousands of years of the Bible passing through countless hands, we should want to be sure that we have the words that John, and the other apostles, actually wrote. We fear so much what might have been taken from Scripture, but we must also ensure that nothing is added, regardless of intention.

If the Comma Johanneum were truly part of the original writings of John, we would have to explain how it disappears from history for so long without leaving a single trace. Dr. James White observes that if the Comma Johanneum were truly part of the original text, it would force the conclusion that entire passages can disappear from the Greek manuscript tradition without leaving any trace—an idea that, in his assessment, *"destroys the very basis upon which we can have confidence that we still have the original words of Paul or John."*[1]

To understand the weight of this statement, one must realize that we possess thousands of ancient Greek manuscripts of the New Testament. This "embarrassment of riches" is what allows us to have such high confidence in the text; by comparing these

---

1. James R. White, *The King James Only Controversy*, "Erasmus and the Comma Johanneum," 104.

thousands of copies, we can easily identify where a scribe might have made a slip of the pen or added a marginal note. If a verse as significant as the Comma Johanneum were original, it would have to appear in the earliest and most reliable of these thousands of copies. Yet, it is absent from every single one of them for the first several centuries. To claim it is original is to claim that the entire manuscript record—the very evidence we use to prove the Bible is reliable—somehow failed us in this one specific spot. We cannot have it both ways; we cannot trust the manuscript tradition to give us the Gospel but then ignore that same tradition when it reveals a later addition.

While it appears in the KJV, the New King James Version, and the Douay-Rheims Bible, along with a few other less common translations that rely on the same underlying Greek and Latin sources, it is absent from most modern editions. Understanding this history equips us to defend the integrity of Scripture, rather than blindly questioning it or accepting it at face value. Handling the Word of Truth requires both integrity and clarity.

Textual Variants

Before diving further into the Comma Johanneum, I want to take a moment to discuss textual variants in general. Understanding why these differences exist will give you the proper context for what we are about to examine. The Comma Johanneum is not the only textual variant in Scripture. In fact, the specific variant we are addressing here is not even a full verse—it is only part of a verse. There are other instances where a variant involves an entire verse. You may have noticed this in your own Bible: for example, John 5:4 is absent in many modern translations, as is Matthew 17:21. As I mentioned in the introduction, there are a handful of these variants scattered throughout the New Testament, and they arise for reasons that are both historical and practical.

For some readers, especially those unfamiliar with how translations are produced or how verse numbers were later assigned, encountering a "missing" verse immediately raises suspicion. The first assumption is often, "Why would there be a missing verse?" and from there it is easy to jump to the conclusion that something nefarious must have taken place. Yet this assumption quickly collapses under even minimal scrutiny. It assumes that an enemy intent on corrupting Scripture would selectively remove non-essential verses while leaving untouched the central truths of the gospel and the content necessary for salvation. If that were the case, it would be a remarkably ineffective strategy.

In reality, most modern translations that omit these verses do not hide them at all. They are typically preserved in the footnotes, along with an explanation of why they are absent from the main text. In other words, the verses are not missing, they are documented. If someone were attempting something nefarious, they are doing a terrible job.

The real issue is accuracy. As important as it is not to remove anything from Scripture, it is equally critical not to add to it. When a reading can be identified as a later addition, faithfulness demands that we prioritize the earliest and best manuscript evidence. This is precisely why modern translations omit the Comma Johanneum from the main text.

It is also worth noting that the decision to omit a verse rather than renumber surrounding verses is intentional. Renumbering would create confusion and break uniformity across translations. Leaving the verse number in place, while explaining the omission in a footnote, is actually the more transparent and honest approach. If anything were to appear suspicious, it would be the quiet shifting of verse numbers, not the open acknowledgment of why a disputed reading is excluded.

Before the modern age and the advancement of communication, Bible translations were created using only the manuscripts available at the time. Scholars could not pick up a phone, access a database, or instantly compare manuscripts from Africa with those from Turkey, Italy, or Germany. With fewer manuscripts to compare, the likelihood of textual variants naturally increased. Many of these variants are the result of what is known as scribal error.

It is important to understand how we even have the Bible if we want to make sense of why textual variants exist. The earliest manuscripts were not created by professional scribes, and they were certainly not set aside with the intention that someone centuries later would compile them into a single, perfect volume. The Apostles wrote letters and accounts to specific churches, conveying their testimony and teaching in writing. These letters were hand-delivered, read publicly, and then copied so that other believers could benefit from them.

The manuscripts that survive today come from these early handwritten copies, produced by ordinary Christians—people who were faithful, but not always highly educated or trained in copying texts. While the Apostles and their writings are inspired by God and therefore inerrant, those who copied their letters were human and fallible. When someone reproduced a Gospel account or an apostolic letter, it was easy for them to insert a word, phrase, or detail they remembered hearing or believed should be included. That addition would then appear in that particular manuscript and be passed on to subsequent copies.

Consider how many Christians today write in their own Bibles, adding personal notes, cross-references, or reminders in the margins. Now imagine living before the printing press, when every copy had to be hand-copied from an existing manuscript. How many of those copies might unintentionally include a note, a memory of a phrase, or a small addition? Five hundred years later, someone examining that manuscript might see these additions as part of the text itself. This helps us understand why variants appear in manuscripts without any intentional attempt to corrupt Scripture.

However, this is precisely why manuscript comparison matters. When one manuscript differs from two hundred others, and those two hundred agree with one another, textual scholars can reasonably identify the outlier as a variant. These decisions are not made by random individuals, but by experts who work collectively, examining the evidence with rigor and care. When all known manuscripts are compared, the overwhelming majority of these variants are minor and entirely nonessential to Christian doctrine.

Even in cases where an entire verse is involved, such as Matthew 17:21, the omission does not alter Christian teaching. The same event—Jesus casting out a demon from a boy—is recorded in Mark 9:29, which includes the detail about fasting and prayer. It is plausible that a copyist of Matthew, familiar with the account in Mark, could have inserted this detail to harmonize the two accounts or to clarify the story for readers. Beyond that, fasting and prayer are consistently taught and encouraged throughout the New Testament. No core doctrine is lost, weakened, or altered. There is no textual variant that affects the substance of the Christian faith.

Our ability to identify these variants has improved dramatically thanks to advances in technology. Modern translators can now access digital databases containing thousands of manuscripts from around the world, comparing variations with ease.[2] By contrast, Erasmus, working in the early sixteenth century,

---

2. You can access high-resolution images of thousands of New Testament manuscripts online at the Center for the Study of New Testament Manuscripts: https://www.csntm.org/

had access to only a handful of Greek manuscripts—often cited as between 6 and 9 for his first edition of the New Testament. The translators of the King James Version similarly worked from roughly 12 to 20 Greek manuscripts available at the time, along with the Latin Vulgate and other sources. These men did the best they could with extremely limited resources. Today, however, the vast wealth of manuscripts and the ability to cross-reference them allows scholars to determine textual variants with a precision and confidence that was simply impossible in the past.

Origins of the Comma Johanneum

Where does the Comma Johanneum come from, and why is it not present in modern Bibles? The Comma is a reading associated with 1 John 5:7-8 that ultimately originates from the Latin textual tradition, specifically the Latin Vulgate. For the majority of church history in the West, the Latin Vulgate functioned as the most widely used and authoritative Bible. For roughly a thousand years, it was the primary Scriptures read, copied, preached, and taught throughout much of Christianity.

The Latin Vulgate was produced in the late fourth century by Jerome, who translated the Scriptures from Hebrew and Greek into Latin at the request of the church. Importantly, the Comma Johanneum was not part of Jerome's original translation and does not appear in the earliest Vulgate manuscripts. It enters the Latin tradition later through marginal notes and secondary copies, gradually finding its way into the text itself over time. This means the Comma did not originate with John, nor with Jerome, but developed within the Latin manuscript tradition centuries after the New Testament was written.

In the sixteenth century, Desiderius Erasmus, a Catholic scholar, set out to produce a printed Greek New Testament using the Greek manuscripts available to him at the time. This was a groundbreaking endeavor. For centuries, the Western church had relied almost exclusively on the Latin Vulgate, but Erasmus sought to return to the Greek text itself. His successive editions of the Greek New Testament would later come to be known as the Textus Receptus, a collection of printed Greek texts that eventually served as the primary source for the translators of the King James Bible and several other early English translations.

Erasmus's first edition did not include the Comma Johanneum because it was entirely absent from the Greek manuscripts he consulted. This omission immediately caused controversy among his Catholic peers, not because the phrase was known to exist in Greek, but because it was familiar from the Latin Vulgate. Erasmus's position was simple and principled: if the Comma could be demonstrated from Greek manuscript evidence, he would include it. Only later, under intense pressure, and after a late Greek manuscript containing the Comma was produced, did Erasmus include it in subsequent editions, even though the authenticity of that Greek evidence was highly questionable.

Erasmus's work, while monumental, was not without other issues. One notable example is the end of the book of Revelation. He did not have access to any Greek manuscripts containing the final verses in time for his first edition, and rather than delay publication, he back-translated the ending from the Latin Vulgate into Greek. This means that certain phrases, such as "the book of life" in Revelation 22:19 (KJV), reflect the Latin wording (*liber vitae*) rather than the wording found in the earliest Greek manuscripts. Modern translations based on the earliest Greek often render this phrase as "the tree of life," highlighting the difference.

When Erasmus attempted to revise this section in later editions, he relied in part on a contemporary's work, unaware that this work itself had been based on his own earlier translation. The result is that certain words and phrasing at the end of Revelation in the Textus Receptus—and carried over into the King James Version—do not have a clear basis in the earliest Greek manuscript tradition. It is important to note, however, that these textual issues are minor and do not affect doctrine or the core teaching of Scripture; the meaning and theological truths of the passage remain intact.

While Erasmus's work was foundational for the King James translation, it is important to understand what the Textus Receptus actually was and what it was not. It was not a pristine recovery of the original text, nor was it based on the wealth of manuscript evidence available today. It was a limited compilation produced at a specific moment in history, using a relatively small number of late Greek manuscripts, some of which reflected readings influenced by the Latin tradition.

Many modern "King James Only" Christians argue that contemporary translations are corrupt simply because they differ from the KJV. What is often missed in these arguments is that the KJV translators themselves were working from a Greek text already shaped by historical limitations, editorial decisions, and, in the case of the Comma Johanneum, documented controversy. In fact, the translators acknowledged in their preface that their work was not perfect, but a faithful rendering based on the manuscripts and knowledge available to them.

Many "KJV Only" Christians hold views contrary to the translators themselves. Because of this, they often treat the KJV as the ultimate standard, assuming that any deviation from it must be wrong. Yet this approach reflects faithfulness to a particular tradition or preference rather than faithfulness to Scripture itself. Elevating the Textus Receptus—or the KJV translation based on it—to an untouchable standard is not a defense of Scripture; it misunderstands how the KJV was created, the sources the translators used, and the historical context in which they worked.

To be clear, this is not an attack on the King James Version itself. I am not anti-KJV. I deeply appreciate its history, its influence on the English-speaking church, and its enduring beauty. Some of the verses I still quote from memory come from the KJV. The issue is not the translation, but the claim that the KJV is the final, perfect, or exclusive standard by which all other translations must be judged. Honesty about textual history does not undermine Scripture, it honors it. Recognizing that translations are the product of real manuscripts, real editors, and real historical limitations is not a threat to faith, but a refusal to confuse reverence for God's Word with reverence for one particular English rendering of it.

Why the Comma Johanneum likely exists

Many scholars hold that the Comma Johanneum is a later addition *made by scribes out of devotion and reverence for God and eventually incorporated into tradition. Even those who defend its inclusion do so primarily from a position of tradition, appealing to its presence in the Latin Vulgate and later Church usage, rather than to early Greek m*anuscript evidence, which does not support it.

In the history of manuscript transmission, it was not uncommon for scribes to insert small clarifying or devotional phrases. For example, a scribe might add "Lord" before the name "Jesus," or adjust a verb tense, in order to make the text more explicit or honorific. These changes were made with good intentions, but they were not part of the original writings. The manuscript evidence shows that the Comma Johanneum was absent from the earliest Greek texts, making its later insertion a well-documented historical fact. This raises the question: did it originate in oral tradition, or was it added by later scribes?

The Comma Johanneum appears to follow this same pattern. It first emerges centuries after John wrote his letters and is absent from the vast majority of early Greek manuscripts, as well as the writings of the Church Fathers. Its presence in later copies reflects a desire to make explicit what the Church already believed about the Trinity, not a revelation from John himself. For translators seeking fidelity to God's Word, the goal is to follow the earliest and most reliable manuscripts, rather than later devotional expansions. Understanding this helps us distinguish between the inspired text and pious additions that, while well-meaning, were never part of the original letter of John.

There is a natural desire to hold onto the Comma Johanneum because, on the surface, it seems to provide a very strong proof text for the Trinity. It would be foolish to deny that this verse is easy to quote in a debate about the Trinity—its language appears to provide a clear, concise argument. That temptation, however, can lead people to lower their standards and cling to a textual tradition that has no support in the earliest manuscripts or the writings of the church fathers.

The reality is that we do not need this verse to defend the doctrine of the Trinity. The Trinity is evident throughout every book of the New Testament. To cling to something that lacks historical support is to diminish the credibility and strength of Scripture as a whole. Both Catholics who rely on the Douay-Rheims and Protestants who are KJV-only often find it difficult to let go of this verse because it reads so persuasively. Someone might hear it and think: "Show me in Scripture where the Trinity is! Here it is: the Father, the Word, and the Holy Spirit."

But if this verse were truly central to defending the doctrine, why did the early defenders of the Trinity—the men who wrote tirelessly against heresies like Arianism—never reference it?

Athanasius composed *On the Incarnation*, Augustine wrote *De Trinitate*, and countless others labored to defend the truth. Yet none of them quote the Comma Johanneum. The truth is simple: If the Comma Johanneum had existed in the original letters of John, it would have been central to the early defenders' arguments.

Textual evidence confirms this. Regarding 1 John 5:7, Robert A. Sungenis, in Commentary on the Catholic Douay-Rheims New Testament, Exegeted from the Original Greek and Latin, Volume IV, notes that:

> "Textual evidence is sparse for this reading. Most Greek texts omit most of verse 7. All patristic usage also omits it: Irenaeus, Clement, Tertullian, Hippolytus, Origen, Cyprian, Dionysius, Hilary, Lucifer of Cagliari, Athanasius, Basil, Faustinus, Nazianzen, Ambrose, Didymus, Epiphanius, Chrysostom, Jerome, Augustine, Cyril."

Even if these names are unfamiliar, understand who these men were: leaders and theologians from the first 400 years of church history, fierce defenders of the Trinity. They wrote tirelessly, debated heretics, and risked personal safety to combat heresies like Arianism, which denied the full divinity of Christ. If the Comma had been in the earliest texts, it would have been an obvious verse to cite—but it is completely absent from their writings.

If we are willing to overlook historical records and manuscript evidence simply to preserve this verse, we undermine our ability to defend the reliability of the New Testament. How can we claim the Scriptures are trustworthy while simultaneously ignoring the textual evidence that this verse was absent in the earliest manuscripts? This is the kind of question every serious reader must answer for themselves.

Why the Comma Johanneum doesn't work contextually

On top of the manuscript evidence, the Comma Johanneum also fails when we examine the context of John's argument. John is not suddenly inserting a formal Trinitarian statement in the middle of his flow. His purpose throughout 1 John is to present careful, cumulative evidence for who Jesus is—fully God and fully man, the Christ, the Savior. To drop in the Comma Johanneum is to interrupt that flow and impose a doctrinal proof text where John himself never intended one.

Many defenders of the Comma Johanneum point to this verse as a convenient proof for the Trinity. On the surface, it reads like a tidy formula: "See! Three in heaven—the Father, the Word, and the Holy Spirit—are one!" Yet this kind of reasoning ignores the broader witness of Scripture. The doctrine of the Trinity is not reliant on a single, isolated clause in 1 John 5:7-8; it is woven throughout the New Testament in the life, teaching, and work of the Father, Son, and Spirit.

When we read John's letters carefully, it becomes clear that he is focused on authenticating Christ's identity, warning against false teachers, and calling believers into fellowship with God and one another. Inserting the Comma Johanneum shifts the reader's attention away from this central purpose, turning a carefully constructed argument into a doctrinal aside that John never intended. Contextually, it does not belong, and the integrity of the text is stronger when we rely on what the earliest manuscripts preserve.

Bibliography

Baucham, Voddie. *Walk in the Light.* Sermon, Grace Family Baptist Church, October 9, 2022.

Barry, John D., et al., eds. "Pelagianism." In *The Lexham Bible Dictionary.* Bellingham, WA: Lexham Press, 2016.

Birdsall, J. N. "Logos." In *New Bible Dictionary,* edited by D. R. W. Wood et al., 693.

Brannan, Rick, ed. *Lexham Research Lexicon of the Greek New Testament.* Lexham Research Lexicons. Bellingham, WA: Lexham Press, 2020.

Danker, Frederick W., ed. *BDAG: A Greek-English Lexicon of the New Testament and Other Early Christian Literature.* 3rd ed.

Easton, M. G. *Illustrated Bible Dictionary and Treasury of Biblical History, Biography, Geography, Doctrine, and Literature,* 146.

Goble, Philip E., Jr. "The Roman Context of Adoption." *The American Journal of Biblical Theology* 22, no. 23 (June 6, 2021).

Geaves, Ron. "Apologetics." In *Continuum Glossary of Religious Terms,* 29. London; New York: Continuum, 2002.

Heiser, Michael S. "Which Bible Translation? A Few Thoughts." DrMSh.com, February 11, 2011. https://drmsh.com/which-bible-translation-a-few-thoughts/ (accessed December 9, 2025).

Mangum, Douglas. *The Lexham Glossary of Theology.* Bellingham, WA: Lexham Press, 2014.

Merriam-Webster. "Begotten." Merriam-Webster.com Dictionary. https://www.merriam-webster.com/dictionary/begotten (accessed January 1, 2026).

Merriam-Webster. s.v. "love." Accessed December 29, 2025. https://www.merriam-webster.com/dictionary/love.

Osborne, Grant R. *Baker Encyclopedia of the Bible,* 1025.

Pliny the Younger. *Letters* 10.96–97. Written c. AD 112 to Emperor Trajan. Translated by Betty Radice. Loeb Classical Library. Cambridge, MA: Harvard University Press, 1969.

Sines, Taylor. *Deconstructing Atheism: The Son of David Who Gave His Years to Skepticism, a Study on Ecclesiastes.* Self-published.

Spurgeon, Charles H. "Praying and Waiting." Sermon preached October 23, 1864. *Metropolitan Tabernacle Pulpit,* vol. 10. Accessed January 4, 2026. https://www.spurgeon.org/resource-library/sermons/praying-and-waiting.

Souter, Alexander. *A Pocket Lexicon to the Greek New Testament.* Oxford: Clarendon Press, 1917.

Taylor, G. D. "Testimony." In *Lexham Theological Wordbook,* edited by Douglas Mangum et al. Lexham Bible Reference Series. Bellingham, WA: Lexham Press, 2014.

Washer, Paul. *Narrow Gate Narrow Way.* Greenville, SC: HeartCry Missionary Society, 2010.

White, James R. *The Forgotten Trinity: Recovering the Heart of Christian Belief.* Minneapolis: Bethany House Publishers, 1998; revised edition, Baker Publishing Group, 2019. Chapter 4, "A Masterpiece: The Prologue of John."

White, James R. *The King James Only Controversy.*

Watson, Richard. *A Biblical and Theological Dictionary.* s.v. "Hypostatical Union."

www.ingramcontent.com/pod-product-compliance
Lightning Source LLC
LaVergne TN
LVHW091711070526
838199LV00050B/2353